100 PURSES
TO KNIT & CROCHET

by Jean Leinhauser and Rita Weiss

Sterling Publishing Co., Inc.
New York

Senior Technical Editors
Ellen W. Liberles
Susan Lowman

Technical Editors
Janet Bates
Karen J. Hay

Photography
James Jaeger
Carol Wilson Mansfield

Book Design
Graphic Solutions, inc-chgo

Produced by
The Creative Partners, LLC™

Library of Congress Cataloging-in-Publication Data Available

10 9 8 7 6 5 4 3 2 1

Published by Sterling Publishing Co., Inc.
387 Park Avenue South, New York, NY 10016
© 2006 by The Creative Partners™ LLC
Distributed in Canada by Sterling Publishing
c/o Canadian Manda Group, 165 Dufferin Street,
Toronto, Ontario, Canada M6K 3H6
Distributed in the United Kingdom by GMC Distribution Services
Castle Place, 166 High Street, Lewes, East Sussex
England BN7 1XU
Distributed in Australia by Capricorn Link (Australia) Pty. Ltd.
P.O. Box 704, Windsor, NSW 2756, Australia

Sterling ISBN-13: 978-1-4027-3348-2
ISBN-10: 1-4027-3348-8

For information about custom editions, special sales, premium
and corporate purchases, please contact Sterling Special Sales
Department at 800-805-5489 or specialsales@sterlingpub.com.

INTRODUCTION

You can never have too many bags to carry all your stuff!

Purses, handbags, totes, backpacks, duffles, carry-alls—whatever you call them, these essential items of a woman's wardrobe have suddenly become a hot fashion accessory. Because they are among the easiest and most fun to make in either knitting or crochet, no knitter or crocheter can ever have too many purse patterns.

In this book you'll find 100 of the very best, in a variety of sizes, styles, and colors. They range from a tiny amulet bag worn as a necklace to a giant felted tote, and include backpacks, beach bags, and elegant evening clutches. There's a jeweled iPod case, a special carry-all for a yoga mat, and a traditional string bag for a bottle of wine. And for that special child: a purse shaped as a toy elephant or one that's a teddy bear.

Whether you choose to make a traditional envelope bag or a purse shaped like a Chinese lantern, you'll find a pattern here. Wouldn't you like to make a backpack for your favorite school girl, or a prom purse for that special day? Looking for the tiniest bag to hang on milady's finger at the formal dance, or a tote for your beach attire? You'll find those patterns here.

If you're intrigued with felting, try making one of the felted bags. If you've always wanted to try some new techniques such as tapestry crochet or overlay crochet, a purse is a great project for testing the waters.

We had great fun collecting these patterns. We hope you'll have as much fun making any of them.

Jean Leinhauser   *Rita Weiss*

CONTENTS

CONTENTS

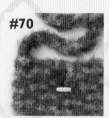

#1 FELTED TOTE OF MANY COLORS

Designed by Barbara Goldhamer

SIZE BEFORE FELTING
21" x 22"

SIZE AFTER FELTING
16" x 15"

MATERIALS
Worsted weight wool yarn
40 oz various colors

Note: Photographed model made with Noro Kureyon, 11 skeins of various colors

One round shank button, 2 3/4" diameter

5 stitch holders

4 stitch markers

24" Size 10 1/2 (6.5 mm) circular knitting needle (or size required for gauge)

Two Size 10 1/2 double-point knitting needles

GAUGE
Before felting 7 sts and 9 rows = 4" in Garter St (knit every row)

INSTRUCTIONS

Bag Bottom

With circular needle, CO 60 sts. Do not join; work back and forth in rows.

Row 1: Sl first st as to purl, knit across.

Rep Row 1, fifty-nine times more (30 ridges). This completes the bottom piece.

Body

Row 1: Place marker after last st; the 60 sts on needle form the Back of bag; do not turn.

Pick up and knit 30 sts down side of piece (for side), place marker; pick up and knit 60 sts across cast-on row (these 60 sts form Front of bag), place marker; pick up and knit 30 sts on opposite side (for side), place marker: 180 sts; join. Move markers up as you work.

Join and knit in rnds for 22", changing colors as desired.

Shape Top

Note: On next rnd you will be placing sts on holders to be picked up later and used for handles and for button lp.

Rnd 1: For Back section, K19, place last 9 sts worked onto a holder; K14, place last 6 sts worked onto a holder; K17, place last 9 sts worked onto a holder; knit to next marker. For Side, knit to next marker. For Front, K19, place last 9 sts worked onto a holder; K31, place last 9 sts worked onto a holder; knit to next marker. For Side, knit to next marker

Rnd 2: Knit to first set of sts on holder, CO 9 sts behind holder; knit to next set of sts on holder, CO 6 sts behind holder; (knit to next set of sts on holder, CO 9 sts behind holder) 3 times; knit to end of round.

Rnd 3: Knit.

Rnds 4 and 5: Purl; these 2 purl rows form fold for hem.

Rnds 6 through 13: Knit.

BO.

Handles

With Front of bag facing, pick up 9 sts from holder at right and work a 36" I-Cord (see page 253); graft or sew end of cord to the other 9 sts on holder on bag Front.

With Back of bag facing, work handle same as for Front.

Button Loop

Pick up the 6 sts on holder in center of bag Back. Make a 10" I-Cord and tack it down behind the picked up sts to make a lp.

Finishing

Sew closed the holes formed between bases of I-Cords and CO sts behind them.

Fold the hem to inside and sew down loosely.

Bottom Lining

Work same as Bottom for 30 ridges. Sew lining loosely inside bag at bottom.

Felting

Follow general Felting Instructions on page 252.

The photographed bag was washed three times. Pull and tug the bag to the shape you want and put towels inside to hold it in shape until it dries. Because of its size, bag may take several days to dry completely.

Button

When bag is completely dry, sew on button on Front, centered and placed about 2 1/2" down from top edge.

#2 WHITE IS RIGHT

SIZE
15" high x 13" wide

MATERIALS
Worsted weight cotton yarn
  15 oz natural

*Note: Photographed model made
with Lion Brand® Lion Cotton
#098 Natural*

Size G (4 mm) crochet hook
  (or size required for gauge)

GAUGE
14 sc = 4"

INSTRUCTIONS

Strap/Handle
Ch 7.

Row 1 (right side): Sc in 2nd ch from hook and in each ch across: 6 sc; ch 1, turn.

Row 2: Sc in each st across: 6 sc; ch 1, turn.

Row 3: Sc in first sc, FPdc, sc in next sc, FPdc, sc in each of last 2 sc: 2 FPdc and 4 sc; ch 1, turn.

Rep Rows 2 and 3 until strap/handle measures 46" or to desired length.

Rep Row 2 two times more. At end of last row, do not ch 1. Finish off; weave in ends.

Base
Ch 5, sl st to form a ring.

Rnd 1: Ch 1, 8 sc in ring: 8 sc; join with sl st in beg ch-1.

Rnd 2: Ch 1, 2 sc in each sc around: 16 sc; join as before.

Rnd 3: Ch 1; *2 sc in next sc, sc in next sc; rep from * around: 24 sc; join.

Rnd 4: Ch 1; *2 sc in next sc, sc in next 2 sc; rep from * around: 32 sc; join.

Rnd 5: Ch 1; *sc in next 3 sc, 2 sc in next sc; rep from * around: 40 sc; join.

Rnd 6: Ch 1; *2 sc in next sc, sc in next 4 sc; rep from * around: 48 sc; join.

Rnd 7: Ch 1; *sc in next 5 sc, 2 sc in next sc; rep from * around: 56 sc; join.

Rnd 8: Ch 1; *2 sc in next sc, sc in next 6 sc; rep from * around: 64 sc; join.

Rnd 9: Ch 1; *sc in next 7 sc, 2 sc in next sc; rep from * around: 72 sc; join.

Rnd 10: Ch 1; *2 sc in next sc, sc in next 8 sc; rep from * around: 80 sc; join.

Rnd 11: Ch 1; *sc in next 9 sc, 2 sc in next sc; rep from * around: 88 sc; join.

Rnd 12: Ch 1; *2 sc in next sc, sc in next 10 sc; rep from * around: 96 sc; join.

Rnd 13: Ch 1; *sc in next 11 sc, 2 sc in next sc; rep from * around: 104 sc; join.

Rnd 14: Ch 1, sc in each sc around: 104 sc; join.

Rep Rnd 14 until circle measures 9 1/4" in diameter. Finish off; weave in ends.

Body
Ch 104.

Row 1 (right side): Sc in 2nd ch from hook and in each ch across: 103 sc; ch 1, turn.

Row 2: Sc in each st across: 103 sc; ch 1, turn.

Rows 3 through 6: Rep Row 2 four times more.

Row 7: Sc in first 2 sc, FPdc, sc in next sc, FPdc; *sc in next 4 sc, puff st in next sc, sc in next 4 sc, FPdc, sc in next sc, FPdc; rep from * across to last 2 sc; sc in last 2 sc: 18 FPdc, 8 puff sts and 77 sc; ch 1, turn.

Row 8: Rep Row 2.

Row 9: Sc in first 2 sc, FPdc, sc in next sc, FPdc; *sc in next 2 sc, puff st in next sc, sc in next 3 sc, puff st in next sc, sc in next 2 sc, FPdc, sc in next sc, FPdc; rep from * across to last 2 sc; sc in last 2 sc: 18 FPdc, 16 puff sts and 69 sc; ch 1, turn.

Row 10: Rep Row 2.

Row 11: Rep Row 7.

Row 12: Rep Row 2.

Row 13: Sc in first 2 sc, FPdc, sc in next sc, FPdc; *sc in next 9 sc, FPdc, sc in next sc, FPdc; rep from * to last 2 sc; sc in last 2 sc: 18 FPdc and 85 sc; ch 1, turn.

Row 14: Rep Row 2.

Row 15: Rep Row 13.

Row 16: Rep Row 2.

Rep Rows 7 through 16 three times more, then rep Rows 7 through 14 once. Do not finish off.

Finishing

With right sides tog, sc side seam of tote body from top to bottom, then sc bottom edge of tote body to edge of tote base. Finish off; weave in ends. Turn tote right side out. Sew one end of strap to tote body from bottom edge to top edge of tote body along both sides and bottom of strap, covering side seam. Sew other end of strap to other side of tote body directly across from side seam in same manner.

#3 QUEST FOR BLING

Designed by Vashti Braha

SIZE
9" wide x 7" high

MATERIALS
Worsted weight brushed
   metallic yarn
   5 ¼ oz pink

Note: *Photographed model made
with Berroco® Quest™ #9831
Marilyn Pink*

Size I (5.5 mm) crochet hook
   (or size required for gauge)

1 pair circular clear acrylic bag
   handles, 5" diameter

11" x 19" piece of luxurious
   lining fabric (optional)

10" x 18" piece of fusible
   fleece (optional)

Sewing needle (optional)

Matching thread (optional)

2 or 3 assorted packages of
   flat-backed white, iridescent,
   and/or pastel rhinestones

Fabric glue

Old pair of tweezers (recommended)

GAUGE
4 WSS and 4 sc = 6"

Instructions continue on next page. →

SPECIAL STITCHES

Foundation Woven Shell Stitch (FWSS): 3 dc in specified ch, ch 3; working over 3 dc just made, work 3 Ldc in 2nd skipped ch before base of FWSS: FWSS made.

Long dc (Ldc): YO, insert hook in specified st and draw up a 1" long lp, (YO and draw through 2 lps on hook) twice: Ldc made.

Woven Shell Stitch (WSS): Skip next (3 dc, sc, dc), 3 dc in next dc (middle Ldc of 3 Ldc), ch 3, working over 3 dc just made, work 3 Ldc in 2nd skipped dc (middle dc of 3 dc): WSS made.

Front Post dc (FPdc): YO, insert hook from front to back to front around post of next st and draw up a lp, (YO and draw through 2 lps on hook) twice: FPdc made.

Front Post tr (FPtr): YO twice, insert hook from front to back to front around post of next st and draw up a lp, (YO and draw through 2 lps on hook) 3 times: FPtr made.

INSTRUCTIONS

Bag

Starting at top, ch 39.

Row 1 (right side): Work FWSS in 7th ch from hook; *skip next ch after 3 dc of FWSS, sc in next ch, skip next 3 chs, FWSS in next ch; rep from * across to last 2 chs; skip next ch after 3 dc of FWSS, sc in last ch: 6 FWSS; ch 3, turn.

Row 2: 3 dc in first sc, sc in next ch-3 sp; *work WSS, sc in next ch-3 sp; rep from * across; 4 dc in first skipped ch at beg of Row 1: 5 WSS; ch 1, turn.

Row 3: Sc in first dc; *work WSS, sc in next ch-3 sp; rep from * across, working last sc in 3rd ch of turning ch-3: 6 WSS; ch 3, turn.

Row 4: 3 dc in first sc, sc in next ch-3 sp; *work WSS, sc in next ch-3 sp; rep from * across; 4 dc in last sc: 5 WSS; ch 1, turn.

Rows 5 through 16: Rep Rows 3 and 4 six times more.

Row 17: Rep Row 3.

Row 18: Dc in first sc; *sc in next ch-3 sp, 2 dc in next sc; rep from * across: 19 sts not including turning ch; ch 1, turn.

Row 19: Sl st in each st across somewhat loosely: 19 sl sts; ch 1, turn.

Row 20: Sc in next st and in each st across: 19 sc; ch 1, turn.

Rows 21 and 22: Rep Row 20 two times more.

Row 23: FPtr in first 2 sc of Row 20 (2 rows below); *sc in next 2 sc of Row 22, FPtr in next 2 sc of Row 20; rep from * across to last sc; sc in last sc of Row 22: 10 FPtr and 9 sc; ch 1, turn.

Row 24: Rep Row 20.

Row 25: FPdc in first 2 post sts one row below; *sc in next 2 sc, FPdc in next 2 post sts one row below; rep from * across to last sc; sc in last sc: 10 FPdc and 9 sc; ch 1, turn.

Rows 26 through 31: Rep Rows 20 and 25 three times more. At end of Row 31, do not ch 1. Finish off; weave in ends.

With wrong side facing and working in opposite side of foundation ch, join yarn with sl st in 3rd skipped ch at beg of foundation ch, ch 3, dc in same ch; *sc in ch between 3 dc and 3 Ldc at base of next FWSS, 2 dc in ch at base of next sc; rep from * across: 19 sts not including beg ch-3; ch 1, turn. Rep Rows 19 through 31.

Stabilize Stitches (optional)

Note: *Practice fusing on a swatch first. Never let yarn come in direct contact with iron. Read instructions on packaging before fusing.*

With wrong side facing, stretch bag slightly to 18" long x 10" wide at center; allow sc rows to draw in to width of 5" - 6". Trim fusible fleece to match width of sc rows. Following package instructions for fusing, use lowest amount of heat and steam to fuse. Note: Yarn used in this model is nylon, which is usually not very heat-tolerant. A high temperature with steam was used carefully with no change in yarn after practicing on swatches. It is all right if stabilizer is not completely bonded at edges. It is better to avoid overheating yarn.

Add Rhinestones

Practice on a swatch first to learn how much glue to apply neatly. Holding smaller gems with tweezers is recommended. Apply glue liberally to entire back of rhinestone, which will also help prevent metallic backing from rubbing off. Then press gently onto right side of crochet piece, anywhere in a random pattern. Note: Avoid placing rhinestones on woven shells and beg and end 1 1/2" at edges of center row of bag (to facilitate shaping gusset seams). After 10 minutes, apply more pressure to stones so glue adheres to stabilizer under sts as well. This gives gems an embedded or quilted look and helps woven shells puff up. Leave flat for 8 hours to dry completely.

Prepare Lining (optional)

Fold fabric in half crosswise with right sides together. Cut off 1 1/2" diagonally at folded corners. Using 1/2" seam allowance, seam each side from diagonally cut bottom fold to 4 1/2" up from bottom. Turn remaining unseamed side edges to wrong side and hem. Do not hem handle ends of fabric.

Seam Bag and Attach Handles

When glue is dry, fold right sides of bag together crosswise, inserting layer of paper or scrap fabric between sides to protect gems. Starting 1 1/2" in from fold with needle and thread, seaming through all layers, sew diagonal seam from bottom fold to side edge and up side edge to 4 1/2" up from bottom. Note: Sew seam tightly to pucker seam slightly. Rep for other side edge of bag. Turn bag right side out. Insert lining into bag with wrong side out and seam lining to bag around entire opening.

Attach Handle

Wrap top sc rows of bag around handles to inside of bag. Seam last sc row to first sc row with needle and thread. Reinforce seam with discreet line of fabric glue and let dry 8 hours.

#4 LITTLE TREASURE BAGS

Designed by Marty Miller

SIZE

5 ¹/₂" wide x 4 ¹/₂" high plus
  24" handle

MATERIALS

Worsted weight cotton yarn
  2 ¹/₂ oz Soft Violet (for little
  sister's purse)
  2 ¹/₂ oz Grape (for big
  sister's purse)

Novelty fur yarn
  1 ¹/₂ oz Violet (for little
  sister's purse)
  1 ¹/₂ oz Lavender (for big
  sister's purse)

Note: *Photographed models
made with Lily® Sugar 'n
Cream® #93 Soft Violet and #71
Grape and Lion Brand® Fun Fur
#9155 Violet and #144
Lavender*

Size H (5 mm) crochet hook
  (or size required for gauge)

GAUGE

Rnds 1 through 10 = 5 ¹/₂"
  diameter

INSTRUCTIONS

With worsted yarn, ch 2.

Rnd 1 (right side): 6 sc in 2nd ch from hook: 6 sc; join with sl st in first sc.

Rnd 2: Ch 1, 2 sc in first sc and in each sc around: 12 sc; join as before.

Rnd 3: Ch 1, 2 sc in first sc, sc in next sc; *2 sc in next sc, sc in next sc; rep from * 4 times more: 18 sc; join.

Rnd 4: Ch 1, 2 sc in first sc, sc in next 2 sc; *2 sc in next sc, sc in next 2 sc; rep from * 4 times more: 24 sc; join.

Rnd 5: Ch 1, 2 sc in first sc, sc in next 3 sc; *2 sc in next sc, sc in next 3 sc; rep from * 4 times more: 30 sc; join.

Rnd 6: Ch 1, 2 sc in first sc, sc in next 4 sc; *2 sc in next sc, sc in next 4 sc; rep from * 4 times more: 36 sc; join.

Rnd 7: Ch 1, 2 sc in first sc, sc in next 5 sc; *2 sc in next sc, sc in next 5 sc; rep from * 4 times more: 42 sc; join.

Rnd 8: Ch 1, 2 sc in first sc, sc in next 6 sc; *2 sc in next sc, sc in next 6 sc; rep from * 4 times more: 48 sc; join.

Rnd 9: Ch 1, 2 sc in first sc, sc in next 7 sc; *2 sc in next sc, sc in next 7 sc; rep from * 4 times more: 54 sc; join.

Rnd 10: Ch 1, 2 sc in first sc, sc in next 8 sc; *2 sc in next sc, sc in next 8 sc; rep from * 4 times more: 60 sc; join. TURN.

Rnd 11 (wrong side): With one strand worsted yarn and one strand fur yarn held tog, ch 1, sc in first sc and in each sc around: 60 sc; join.

Rnds 12 through 24: Rep Rnd 11 thirteen times more. At end of Rnd 24, drop fur yarn, TURN.

Rnd 25 (wrong side): With worsted yarn only, ch 1, sc in first sc and in each sc around: 60 sc; join.

Rnds 26 through 28: Rep Rnd 25 three times more. At end of Rnd 28, do not finish off.

Handle

With worsted yarn, ch 80 (about 24", or to desired length), skip 30 sc on Rnd 28, taking care not to twist ch, sc in next sc, sl st in next sc, turn. Working back along chain, sl st in each ch across to beg of ch, sc in next sc on Rnd 28, sl st in next sc. Finish off; weave in ends.

#5 FELTED HOUNDSTOOTH

Designed by Patons Design Staff

SIZE AFTER FELTING
8" x 11" after felting

MATERIALS
Worsted weight wool yarn
- 7 oz black (MC)
- 3 ½ oz white (A)
- 3 ½ oz red (B)

Note: Photographed model made with Patons® Classic Merino Wool #226 Black (MC), #201 Winter White (A) and #230 Bright Red (B)

1 yd ½" thick black cable cord

Size 7 (4.5 mm) straight knitting needles (or size required for gauge)

Set of four Size 7 (4.5 mm) double-point knitting needles

GAUGE
20 sts and 26 rows = 4" in stock st (knit 1 row, purl 1 row)

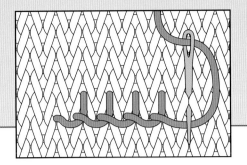

Blanket stitch

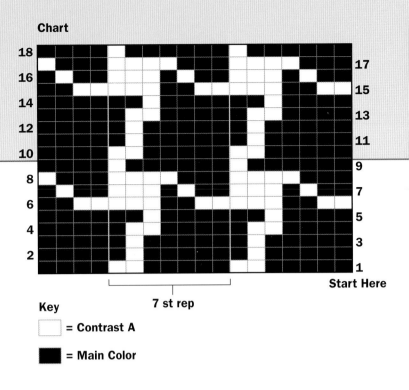

Chart

18
17
16
15
14
13
12
11
10
9
8
7
6
5
4
3
2
1

Start Here

7 st rep

Key

☐ = Contrast A

■ = Main Color

INSTRUCTIONS

Note: When working from chart, carry yarn not in use loosely across wrong side of work, but never over more than 5 sts. When yarn must pass over more than 5 sts, weave it over and under color in use on next st or at center point of sts it passes over.

Front and Back Section

With MC and straight needles, cast on 88 sts.

Work Rows 1 through 18 of the Chart in stock st to end of chart, reading knit rows from right to left and purl rows from left to right.

Rep Rows 1 through 18 until piece measures 35 ½", ending by working a knit side row. BO with MC.

Side Section (make 2)

With MC and straight needles, CO 38 sts. Work 16" in stock st, ending by working a purl row. BO.

Handle

With MC, CO 9 sts on one double-point needle. Divide sts evenly on 3 needles and place a marker to indicate beg of rnds. Knit in rnds until piece measures 28". BO.

Finishing

Felt all pieces following instructions on page 252.

Using the cutting diagram, cut front and back section and sides to measurements shown on Cutting Diagram. Pin sides in position, noting narrow end is at top of bag. Using 2 strands of B, work blanket st embroidery to join sides to front and back. Continue embroidery around front of flap as illustrated. Trim strap to measure 23" and insert cable cord through center of strap. Tack ends of cord to strap. Sew ends of strap to tops of side sections.

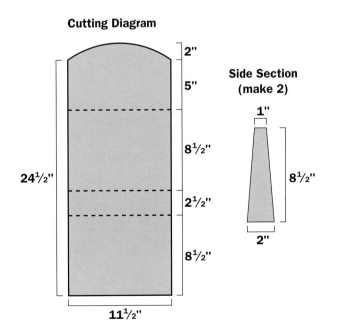

Cutting Diagram

2"
5"
8½"
2½"
8½"

24½"

11½"

Side Section (make 2)

1"
8½"
2"

#6 CHINESE LANTERN

Designed by Shelby Allaho

SIZE

8" high (not included curly tassels) x 22" diameter

MATERIALS

Light worsted weight yarn
200 yds variegated pinks.

FOR TRIM

Tapestry wool
50 yds fuchsia (CC 1)
25 yds turquoise (CC 2)
20 yds dark purple (CC 3)

Note: *Photographed model made with Artyarns "Supermerino" #110 and DMC tapestry wool #7157 Fuchsia, #7927 Turquoise, #7257 Aubergine.*

4 stitch markers

Size F (3.5 mm) crochet hook (or size required for gauge)

GAUGE

22 sts = 4"

INSTRUCTIONS

Bottom Circle

With worsted weight yarn, ch 4; join with sl st to form a ring.

Rnd 1: Ch 1, 6 sc in ring; join in beg sc.

Rnd 2: Ch 4 (counts as hdc and ch-2 sp); *hdc in next st, ch 2; rep from * around, join with sl st in 2nd ch of beg ch-4: 6 ch-2 sps.

Rnd 3: Sl st in next ch-2 sp, ch 1, 3 sc in same sp; *3 sc in next ch-2 sp; rep from * around to first sc, do not join: 18 sc.

Note: *From here on, do not join rnds unless specified. Place a marker to indicate beg of rnds. Move marker up as you work.*

Rnd 4: Working in back lps only, *2 sc in next sc, sc in next sc; rep from * around: 27 sc.

Note: *Rnds 5 through 9 are worked in both lps.*

Rnd 5: *2 sc in next st, sc in next 2 sts; rep from * around: 36 sc.

Rnd 6: *2 sc in next st, sc in next 3 sts; rep from * around: 45 sc.

Rnd 7: *2 sc in next st, sc in next 4 sts; rep from * around: 54 sts.

Rnd 8: *2 sc in next st, sc in next 5 sts; rep from * around: 63 sts.

Rnd 9: *2 sc in next st, sc in next 6 sts; rep from * around: 72 sts.

Rnd 10: Working in back lps only, *2 sc in next st, sc in next 7 sts; rep from * around: 81 sts. Place a marker in front lp of last sc of rnd.

Sides

Note: *Rnds 11 through 18 are worked in both lps.*

Rnd 11: *Hdc in next 3 sts, 2 hdc in next st; rep from * around to last st, hdc in last st: 101 sts.

Rnd 12: Hdc in each st around.

Rnds 13 through 18: Rep Rnd 12.

Rnd 19: Working in back lps only, hdc in each st around. Place a marker in front lp of last hdc of rnd.

Rnd 20: Working in both lps, hdc in each st around.

Rnd 21: Rep Rnd 20.

Rnd 22: Rep Rnd 19. Place a marker in front lp of last hdc of rnd.

Rnd 23: *Working in both lps, hdc2tog, hdc in next 3 sts; rep from * around to last st, hdc in last st: 81 sts.

Rnd 24: Working in both lps, hdc in each st around.

Rnd 25: Rep Rnd 23: 65 sts.

Rnd 26: Rep Rnd 24.

Instructions continue on next page. →

Rnd 27: Hdc2tog, hdc in next 3 sts; rep from * around: 52 sts.

Rnd 28: Rep Rnd 24.

Rnd 29: Sc in each st around.

Rnd 30: Sc in each st around to last 2 sts, sc2tog: 51 sts.

Rnd 31: Sl st in first sc, ch 5; *skip 2 sc, hdc in next sc, ch 3; rep from * around to last 2 sc, sk next 2 sc, changing to CC 1, join with sl st in 4th ch of beg ch-5: 17 hdc, 17 ch-3 sps.

Rnd 32: Ch 3, 6 dc in ch-3 lp; *7 dc in next ch-3 lp; rep from * around, join: 119 dc.

Rnd 33: Ch 3, dc in each st around, changing to CC 2, join.

Rnd 34: Ch 3, sl st in next dc;* hdc, ch 1, sl st in next st; rep from * around, join in 2nd ch of beg ch-3: Finish off; weave in all ends.

Trimming

Top Ruffle Trim

With top of purse facing and with CC 1, sl st through first front lp and last front lp of Rnd 22; *ch 4, sc in next front lp, sl st in next front lp; rep from * around to last front lp of round, sl st in first ch of beg ch-4. Finish off; weave in ends.

Ruffle Trim Insert

Using CC 3, make a chain 21 ½" long, cut yarn leaving a 2" tail. Do not finish off.

Weave insert through ch spaces in the ruffle. Put last st of trim insert back on hook, then sl st in other end of trim insert to join. Finish off; weave in ends.

Middle Band Trim

Rnd 1: With bottom of purse facing and with CC2, sl st in first front lp, then last front lp of Rnd 19, ch 2; hdc in same lp, sl st in first front lp;* 2 hdc in next front lp, sl st in next front lp; rep from * around to ch-2; changing to CC 1, join in top of beg ch-2

Rnd 2: *Ch 2; sc around sl st lps from prev rnd; rep from * around, join in beg ch-2.

Bottom Ruffle Trim

Rnd 1: With bottom of purse facing and with CC 1, sl st through first front lp and last front lp of Rnd 10, ch 3; dc in same lp; *2 dc in next lp; rep from * around to beg ch-3, join, ch 1; turn.

Rnd 2: Sc in top of ch-3; sc around to first sc, join. Finish off; weave in ends.

Curly Tassels

Note: *The first 6 tassels are worked in the 6 hdc from Rnd 2.*

Tassel

With CC 3, join in any hdc in Rnd 2, ch 35; working in back bumps of ch, sl st in 2nd ch from hook, sc in each rem ch. Finish off; weave in ends.

Rep for each rem hdc.

Note: *Seventh tassel is worked separately and sewn in center of the six previously worked coils.*

Seventh Tassel

With CC3, ch 35; working in back bumps of ch, sl st in 2nd ch from hook, sc in each rem ch. Finish off; weave in ends.

Tassel Top

Rnd 1: With bottom of purse facing and with CC 2, insert hook in last front lp and first front lp of Rnd 4, draw yarn through both lps, ch 1; *sc in next lp; rep from * around to first sc, join with sl st.

Rnd 2: Sl st in next 2 sc; *ch 15, sl st in same st and in next 2 sc*; rep from * to * 6 times; ch 15, sl st in same st. Finish off; weave in ends.

Drawstring (make 2)

With worsted weight yarn, make a chain 30" long. Sl st in back lp of 2nd ch from hook, sl st in each rem ch. Cut yarn, leaving 2" tail.

Beginning from the inside of the purse, weave first drawstring through spaces under ruffle at top of purse around to beginning. Beginning from the inside of the purse, on the opposite side from the first drawstring, weave 2nd drawstring in the same manner as the first. Put last st of first drawstring on hook, sl st in other end to join. Finish off; weave in ends. Rep for 2nd drawstring.

#7 BEADED TAPESTRY CROCHET

Designed by Carol Ventura for Coats & Clark

SIZE

8" wide x 6 $\frac{1}{2}$" high plus 10 $\frac{1}{2}$" handles

MATERIALS

Size 3 Cotton crochet thread
   150 yds green
   150 yds white

Note: *Photographed model made with Aunt Lydia's® Fashion Crochet Thread, Size 3, #625 Sage and #926 Bridal White*

#8 seed beads, 120 gm Emerald Green, Fire Mountain Gems & Beads #12-4451SB

#8 seed beads, 110 gm Clear, Fire Mountain Gems & Beads #12-4436SB

Heavy beading needle, Fire Mountain Gems & Beads #1570 TL

$\frac{5}{8}$" x 6" piece white hook & loop fastener

Transparent thread

Sewing needle

Stitch marker

Size 1 (2.75 mm) steel crochet hook (or size required for gauge)

GAUGE

33 sc and 32 sc rows = 4"

To carry tail: Lay tail over top of sts being worked into, then sc across as usual, encasing carried tail within sts (see diagram). If done correctly, carried tail will not be visible from front or back of work.

Back bead sc (BBsc): Insert hook in specified st, slide bead up to hook, draw up a lp, YO and draw through both lps on hook: BBsc made. Note: Bead will be on the back side (right side) of work.

Tapestry crochet st: While carrying non-working thread over top of sts in rnd below, insert hook in next st and draw up a lp with working thread, YO and draw through 2 lps on hook, encasing carried (non-working) thread within sts (see diagram): tapestry crochet st made.

To change color in tapestry crochet: Work st until 2 lps rem on hook, drop working thread, pick up non-working (carried) thread and draw through both lps on hook. Non-working thread now becomes working thread. Working thread now becomes non-working thread and is carried over top of sts in rnd below.

INSTRUCTIONS

With beading needle, string all clear beads onto white thread and all green beads onto green thread. Push beads down thread, leaving 1 yard at beg without beads.

Starting at bottom, ch 54 with green, leaving 8" tail at beg of ch.

Rnd 1 (wrong side): BBsc in 2nd ch from hook, BBsc in next 51 chs, 3 BBsc in last ch; working in free lps on other side of foundation ch and carrying green tail, BBsc in next 51 chs, 2 BBsc in last ch: 108 BBsc. Do not join. Insert stitch marker in last st and move up to last st of each rnd.

Note: Work rest of purse in tapestry crochet sts, changing colors as necessary and carrying non-working thread on top of sts in rnd below (see diagram).

Rnd 2: Cut green thread tail close to work and start to carry white thread under sts being worked. Tapestry crochet with green, while carrying white as follows: *2 BBsc in each of next 2 sts, 1 BBsc in each of next 50 sts, 2 BBsc in each of next 2 sts; rep from * once: 116 BBsc.

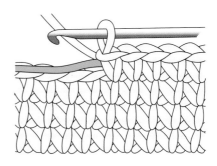

Tapestry crochet

Rnd 3: Tapestry crochet with green while carrying white as follows: *2 BBsc in next st, 1 BBsc in next st, 2 BBsc in next st, 1 BBsc in each of next 52 sts, 2 BBsc in next st, 1 BBsc in next st, 2 BBsc in next st; rep from * once: 124 BBsc.

Rnd 4: Tapestry crochet with green while carrying white as follows: *(1 BBsc in next st, 2 BBsc in next st) twice, 1 BBsc in each of next 54 sts, (2 BBsc in next st, 1 BBsc in next st) twice; rep from * once: 132 BBsc.

Rnd 5: *Tapestry crochet 6 white BBsc, 5 green BBsc; rep from * 11 times more.

Rnd 6: *Tapestry crochet 7 white BBsc, 4 green BBsc; rep from * around.

Rnd 7: *Tapestry crochet 8 white BBsc, 3 green BBsc; rep from * around.

Instructions continue on next page. →

Rnd 8: *Tapestry crochet 3 white BBsc, 3 green BBsc, 3 white BBsc, 2 green BBsc; rep from * around.

Rnd 9: *Tapestry crochet 3 white BBsc, 4 green BBsc, 3 white BBsc, 1 green BBsc; rep from * around.

Rnd 10: *Tapestry crochet 3 white BBsc, 5 green BBsc, 3 white BBsc; rep from * around.

Rnd 11: *Tapestry crochet 1 green BBsc, 3 white BBsc, 4 green BBsc, 3 white BBsc; rep from * around.

Rnd 12: *Tapestry crochet 2 green BBsc, 3 white BBsc, 3 green BBsc, 3 white BBsc; rep from * around.

Rnd 13: *Tapestry crochet 3 green BBsc, 8 white BBsc; rep from * around.

Rnd 14: *Tapestry crochet 4 green BBsc, 7 white BBsc; rep from * around.

Rnd 15: *Tapestry crochet 5 green BBsc, 6 white BBsc; rep from * around.

Rnds 16 through 48: Rep Rnds 5 through 15 three times more. At end of Rnd 48, tapestry crochet 33 green BBsc, ending on other side where handle will start. Cut carried white thread close to work. Do not cut green thread.

Top Edge and Handles

Rnd 1 (wrong side): *With green, ch 80 without beads, or to desired length for handle, skip 38 sts on Rnd 48, making sure ch is not twisted, beg carrying white thread, BBsc in next st, BBsc in next 27 sts*. Cut carried white thread close to work. Rep from * to * once. Do not cut white thread.

Rnd 2: Tapestry crochet in green while carrying white as follows: *1 BBsc in each of next 80 chs on handle, 1 BBsc in each of next 28 sts on purse; rep from * once.

Rnd 3: Tapestry crochet in green while carrying white as follows: 1 BBsc in each of next 80 sts on handle, 1 BBsc in each of next 28 sts on purse, 1 BBsc in each of next 80 sts on handle. Cut carried white thread close to work. Sl st in next st with green. Finish off green; weave in ends.

Rnd 4: With wrong side facing, join green with sl st in first free lp on other side of ch on either handle, leaving a 2" tail, ch 1; tapestry crochet in green while carrying white thread and green tail as follows: 1 BBsc in same ch, 1 BBsc in free lp of each of next 79 chs on handle, 1 BBsc in each of next 38 sts on top rim of purse between handles.

Rnd 5: Tapestry crochet in green while carrying white as follows: 1 BBsc in each of next 80 sts on handle, 1 BBsc in each of next 38 sts on top rim of purse between handles. Cut carried white thread close to work. Sl st in next st with green. Finish off green; weave in ends.

Rep Rnds 4 and 5 on other handle.

Finishing

Center and sew hook & loop fastener on inside of each side of purse ⅜" below top edge of purse with transparent thread. Block purse with steam iron set on cotton from cloth side (wrong side). DO NOT place iron on beaded side. Turn purse right side out.

#8 LACE EDGE CLUTCH

Designed by Jodi Lewanda

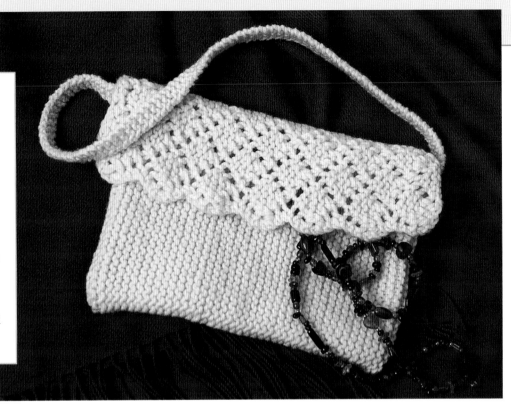

SIZE
5 ¹/₂" x 7 ¹/₂"

MATERIALS
Worsted weight yarn
  3 oz off white

Note: *Photographed model made with Cascade 220 Superwash #817 Off White*

Size 6 (4 mm) knitting needles, or size required for gauge

GAUGE
20 sts = 4" in garter stitch (knit every row)

INSTRUCTIONS

Note: *Purse is worked sideways in one piece.*

CO 71 sts.

Row 1: K60, K2tog, YO, K4, K2tog, YO, K3tog: 69 sts.

Row 2: YO, K69.

Row 3: K59, K2tog, YO, K1, YO, K2tog, K1, K2tog, YO, K1, YO, K2tog: 70 sts.

Row 4: YO, K70.

Row 5: K58, K2tog, YO, K3, YO, K3tog, YO, K3, YO, K2tog: 71 sts.

Row 6: YO, K71.

Row 7: K57, K2tog, YO, K4, K2tog, YO, K5, YO, K2tog: 72 sts.

Row 8: YO, K72.

Row 9: K59, YO, K2tog, K1, K2tog, YO, K1, YO, K2tog, K1, K2tog, YO, K3tog: 71 sts.

Row 10: YO, K71.

Row 11: K60, YO, K3tog, YO, K3, YO, K3tog, YO, K3tog: 70 sts.

Row 12: YO, K70.

Repeat Rows 1 through 12, six times more, then repeat Row 1 once more.

BO. Weave in ends.

Strap
CO 3 sts. Knit until piece measures 25" slightly stretched. BO.

Assembly
Fold straight side edge up 5" and sew side seams. Sew strap to inside of clutch, at the top edge of each side seam.

#9 BASKETWEAVE

Designed by Judi & Co.

SIZE
8" x 9" plus 22" strap

MATERIALS
Rayon cord
  288 yds red

Note: Photographed model made with Judi & Co. Rayon Cordé red

2 magnetic snap sets

Size G (4 mm) crochet hook
  (or size required for gauge)

GAUGE
16 dc = 4"

INSTRUCTIONS

Front

Starting at bottom, ch 29.

Row 1: Dc in 4th ch from hook and in each rem ch: 27 dc (counting beg skipped chs as a dc); ch 3 (counts as first dc of following row throughout), turn.

Row 1: BPdc around each of next 2 sts; *FPdc around each of next 3 sts, BPdc around each of next 3 sts; rep from * across, ending last rep with BPdc around each of last 3 sts; ch 3, turn.

Rows 2 and 3: FPdc around each BPdc; BPdc around each FPdc; ch 3, turn.

Row 4: FPdc around each of next 2 sts; *BPdc around each of next 3 sts, FPdc around each of next 3 sts; rep from * across, ending last rep with FPdc around each of last 3 sts; ch 3, turn.

Rows 5 and 6: Rep Rows 2 and 3.

Rep Rows 2 through 6 until piece measures 7". At end of last row, turn piece and work one row sc around all four edges, working 3 sc in each corner. Join in beg sc. Finish off; weave in ends.

Back

Work same as front.

Gusset

Ch 9.

Row 1: Sc in 2nd ch from hook and in each rem ch: 8 sc; ch 1, turn.

Row 2: Sc in each sc, ch 1, turn.

Rep Row 2 until gusset measures 23". Finish off.

Handle

Ch 5.

Row 1: Sc in 2nd ch from hook and in each rem ch: 4 sc; ch 1, turn.

Row 2: Sc in each sc, ch 1, turn.

Rep Row 2 until piece measures 22"; finish off, leaving a long yarn end.

Fold piece in half lengthwise to form a tube and sew long edges tog.

Assembly

Sew gusset to front and back along 2 sides and bottom, adjusting gusset as needed to fit. Leave top open.

Finishing

Work one rnd of sc around top opening of bag, then work one rnd of reverse sc. Finish off.

Instructions continue on next page. →

To stablize magnetic snaps, work as follows:

Stabilizer (make 4)
Ch 5.

Row 1: Sc in 2nd ch from hook and in each rem ch: 4 sc; ch 1, turn.

Row 2: Sc in each sc, ch 1, turn.

Rep Row 2 until piece measures 1". Finish off.

Attach each piece of each closure to a stabilizer. Insert prongs through stabilizer and bend prongs in. Sew stablizers inside bag at top, 1" down from top edge and 2" in from side seams.

Flower

Ch 6; join with a sl st to form a ring.

Rnd 1: Ch 1, 10 sc in ring; join in first sc.

Rnd 2: Ch 1, sc in joining, ch 3; *skip next sc, sc in next sc; ch 3; rep from *3 times, skip last sc, join in beg sc: 5 ch-3 lps.

Rnd 3: In each ch-3 lp work (sc, hdc, dc, tr, dc, hdc, sc); at end, join in beg sc: 5 petals made.

Rnd 4: Working behind petals of Rnd 3, sc in first skipped st of Rnd 2, ch 4; *sc in next skipped st of Rnd 2, ch 4; rep from * 3 times more, join in beg sc.

Rnd 5: In each ch-4 lp work (sc, hdc, dc, 3 tr, dc, hdc, sc); at end, join in beg sc; finish off, leaving a long yarn end for sewing to purse.

Sew flower on upper right corner of purse as shown in photo.

#10 LITTLE FAUX FUR TOTE

SIZE
7" x 7"

MATERIALS
Bulky weight faux fur yarn
  1 3/4 oz turquoise

Sport weight yarn
  2 1/2 oz turquoise

Note: *Photographed model made with Lion Brand® Fun Fur #148 Turquoise and Microspun #148 Turquoise.*

Size 11 (8 mm) knitting needles (or size required for gauge)

Size 8 (5 mm) knitting needles

GAUGE
13 sts and 26 rows = 4" with faux fur on larger needles in garter st (knit all rows)

17 sts and 24 rows = 4" with sport weight on smaller needles in stock st (knit 1 row, purl 1 row)

INSTRUCTIONS

Bag
With larger needles and faux fur, CO 24 sts. Work in garter st until piece measures 14". BO all sts.

Lining
With smaller needles and sport weight, CO 30 sts. Work in stock st until piece measures 13". BO all sts.

Handle (make 2)
With larger needles and two strands of sport weight held tog, CO 9 sts. Work in stock st until piece measures 12". BO all sts.

Finishing
Fold bag in half and sew side seams. Rep for lining. Insert lining into bag, tack down at bottom corners and sew around top edge. Sew side seam of handles to form tubes. Sew handles to inside of bag at top of lining.

Ties
Cut three 24" pieces of sport weight and thread through center top on one side of bag. Match ends and tie an overhand knot at bag. Separate strands into three groups of 2 and braid for 8". Tie an overhand knot and trim ends. Rep for other side.

#11 BEADED CANISTER

Designed by Tammy Hildebrand

SIZE
11" long x 5 ¹/2" high plus 29" strap

MATERIALS
Worsted weight yarn
   6 ¹/2 oz red

Note: Photographed model made with Lion Brand® Glitterspun, #113 Ruby

412 metallic pony beads, 4 mm x
   7 mm, in various colors

2 sheets 10 ¹/2" x 7 ¹/2" red plastic
   canvas

Large rubber band

Five 2" metal craft rings

Small metal closure hook

Sewing needle and thread

Tapestry needle

Size G (4 mm) crochet hook (or size
   required for gauge)

GAUGE
6 FPdc plus 6 BPdc = 3"

8 FPdc or 8BPdc rows = 3"

SPECIAL STITCHES

Front post dc (FPdc): YO, insert hook from front to back to front around post of specified st on previous row and draw up a lp, (YO and draw through 2 lps on hook) 2 times: FPdc made.

Back post dc (BPdc): YO, insert hook from back to front to back around post of specified st on previous row and draw up a lp, (YO and draw through 2 lps on hook) 2 times: BPdc made.

INSTRUCTIONS

Purse End (make 2)

Using tapestry needle, string 50 beads onto yarn, ch 3; join with sl st to form ring.

Rnd 1 (wrong side): Ch 3 (counts as dc now and throughout), pull up bead; *dc in ring, pull up bead; rep from * 8 times more: 10 dc; join with sl st in 3rd ch of beg ch-3. Turn.

Rnd 2 (right side): Ch 1, 2 sc in same ch as joining, 2 sc in next st and in each st around: 20 sc; join with sl st in beg sc. Do not turn.

Rnd 3: Ch 3, dc in same sc as joining, dc in next st; *2 dc in next st, dc in next st; rep from * around: 30 dc; join with sl st in 3rd ch of beg ch-3.

Rnd 4: Ch 3, dc in same ch as joining, dc in next 2 sts; *2 dc in next st, dc in next 2 sts; rep from * around: 40 dc; join with sl st in 3rd ch of beg ch-3. Turn.

Rnd 5 (wrong side): Ch 1, sc in same ch as joining, pull up bead, ch 1; *sc in next st, pull up bead, ch 1; rep from * around: 40 sc and 40 ch-1 sps; join with sl st in beg sc. Turn.

Rnd 6 (right side): Ch 3, dc in same sc as joining, (skip next ch-1 sp, dc in next st)

3 times; *skip next ch-1 sp, 2 dc in next st, (skip next ch-1 sp, dc in next st) 3 times; rep from * around: 50 dc; join with sl st in 3rd ch of beg ch-3. Finish off.

Purse Body

Using tapestry needle, string 72 beads onto one ball of yarn. String 72 beads onto second ball of yarn to use when first ball runs out. Ch 38.

Row 1 (right side): Sc in 2nd ch from hook and in each ch across: 37 sc; ch 1, turn.

Row 2 (wrong side): Sc in first st; *pull up bead, sc in next st; rep from * across; ch 1, turn.

Row 3: Sc in first st and in each st across; ch 1, turn.

Row 4: Sc in first st; *pull up bead, sc in next st; rep from * across; ch 3 (counts as dc on next row now and throughout), turn.

Row 5: Dc in next st and in each st across: 37 dc; ch 3, turn.

Row 6: FPdc in next st; *BPdc in next st, FPdc in next st; rep from * 16 times more; dc in 3rd ch of turning ch-3: 2 dc, 18 FPdc and 17 BPdc; ch 3, turn.

Row 7: BPdc in next st; *FPdc in next st, BPdc in next st; rep from * 16 times more; dc in 3rd ch of turning ch-3: 2 dc, 18 BPdc and 17 FPdc; ch 3, turn.

Rows 8 through 39: Rep Rows 6 and 7 sixteen times more.

Instructions continue on next page. →

Rows 40 through 42: Rep Rows 2 through 4.

Row 43: Rep Row 3. At end of row, do not ch 1. Finish off; weave in ends.

Purse Body Edging

Using tapestry needle, string 84 beads onto yarn.

Row 1: With right side facing, join with sc in edge of first sc on Row 1 of Purse Body, sc in edge of each row across side: 43 sc; ch 1, turn.

Row 2: Sc in first st; *pull up bead, sc in next st; rep from * across; ch 1, turn.

Row 3: Sc in first st and in each st across; ch 1, turn.

Row 4: Rep Row 2. At end of row, do not ch 1. Finish off; weave in ends.

Using tapestry needle, string 84 beads onto yarn. Rep Rows 1 through 4 on other edge of Purse Body, joining with sc in edge of last sc on Row 43 of Purse Body.

Purse Top

Ch 34.

Row 1: Sc in 2nd ch from hook and in each ch across: 33 sc; ch 1, turn.

Rows 2 through 14: Sc in first st and in each st across; ch 1, turn. At end of Row 14, do not ch 1. Finish off; weave in ends.

Strap

Rings 1 and 5

First Side

Row 1: Join with sc in craft ring, work 4 more sc in craft ring: 5 sc; ch 1, turn.

Rows 2 through 5: Sc in first st and in each st across; ch 1, turn. At end of Row 5, do not ch 1. Finish off, leaving 8" end for joining.

Second Side

Row 1: Join with sc on opposite side of same ring, work 4 more sc in ring: 5 sc; ch 1, turn.

Rows 2 through 10: Sc in first st and in each st across; ch 1, turn. At end of Row 10, do not ch 1. Finish off, leaving 8" end for joining.

Rings 2, 3 and 4

First Side

Rows 1 through 5: Using another ring, rep Ring 1, First Side, Rows 1 through 5.

Second Side

Rows 1 through 5: Working on opposite side of same ring, rep Ring 1, First Side, Rows 1 through 5.

Strap Assembly

Using tapestry needle, lining up sts on Row 5 on Ring 1, First Side and Row 5 on either side of Ring 2, whipstitch together. Rep for rem rings, lining up sts on Row 5 on each ring with sts on Row 5 on next ring, ending with Ring 5. Note: Second Side of Rings 1 and 5 with 10 rows should be at ends of Strap. Each ring should have a total of 10 rows between them for a total strap length of about 29".

Purse Assembly

Cut out 2 ³/₄" x 10 ¹/₄" piece from one sheet of plastic canvas. Using tapestry needle, stitch edges of Purse Top to edges of plastic canvas piece.

Using same sheet of plastic canvas, cut out 2 circles by using coffee can or bowl with 5" diameter to trace around. Using tapestry needle, stitch edge of one Purse End to edge of each plastic canvas circle.

Using tapesty needle, stitch edges of Purse Body to edges of full sheet of plastic canvas.

Curl Purse Body lengthwise into canister shape, leaving 3" opening. Hold curl in place with rubber band. Using tapestry needle, sew Purse Ends to curled edges of Purse Body. Sew one long edge of Purse Top to one long end of Purse Body at opening. With sewing needle and thread, center and stitch hook to unjoined long edge of Purse Top. With tapestry needle, whipstitch Row 10 at end of Strap to top center of Purse End. Rep for other end of Strap.

#12 AMERICAN BEAUTY CLUTCH

Designed by Margaret Hubert

SIZE
6" x 8"

MATERIALS
Super bulky weight chenille
  100 yds scarlet

Note: Photographed model made with Lion Brand® Chenille Thick & Quick® #113 Scarlet

1/2" rhinestone shank button
  for center of rose

1" shank button for purse
  closure

1/2 yd red satin fabric for lining (optional)

Needle and sewing thread
  to match lining fabric
  (optional)

Size L (8 mm) crochet hook
  (or size required for gauge)

GAUGE
9 1/2 sts = 4"

INSTRUCTIONS

Note: Bag is made in one piece

Ch 20

Row 1: Sc in 2nd ch from hook and in each ch across; ch 1, turn: 19 sc.

Row 2: Sc in each sc; ch 1, turn.

Rep Row 2 until piece measures 15".

Last row: Sc in next first 9 sc, ch 3 (button lp made); skip 1 sc, sc in rem 9 sc: 18 sc. Finish off; weave in ends.

Rose

Ch 4, join with sl st to form a ring.

Rnd 1 (right side): (Sc in ring, ch 3) 6 times; join with sl st in beg sc: 6 ch-3 lps.

Rnd 2: * In next ch-3 lp work [sc, ch 1, (dc, ch 1) twice, sc]; rep from * 5 times more, join in beg sc: 6 petals. Turn so wrong side faces you.

Rnd 3: Ch 1, FPsc around next sc on Rnd 1; * ch 5, FPsc around first sc of next petal of Rnd 1; rep from * 4 times more, ch 5; join in first sc: 6 ch-5 lps. Turn so right side faces you.

Rnd 4: * In next ch-5 lp work [sc, (ch 1, 1 dc) 3 times, ch 1, sc]; rep from * 5 times more, join. Turn so wrong side faces you.

Rnd 5: Ch 1, FPsc in next sc of Rnd 3, *ch 5, FPsc in next sc of Rnd 3; rep from * 4 times more, ch 5; join in first sc: 6 ch-5 lps; do not turn to right side.

Rnd 6: Still working on wrong side, sc in first ch-5 sp, ch 5; *sc in next ch-5 sp, ch 5; rep from * 4 times more, join. Turn back to right side.

Rnd 7: Sl st in each of first 2 chs of next ch-5 sp, sc in same ch-5 sp; * ch 1; in next sc work (dc, ch 1) 4 times, sc in next ch-5 sp; rep from * 4 times more, ch 1; in last sc work (dc, ch 1) 4 times, join. Finish off, leaving a long yarn end for attaching rose. Weave in other end.

Finishing
Lining (optional)

Cut lining fabric about ½" larger than outside edges of purse. Pin lining to inside, turning raw edges under about ¼". Sew lining in place.

Assembly

Fold bag 5" up from bottom edge; sew side seams. Sew rose to top flap, sew rhinestone button to center of rose. Align closure button on front of bag to button loop on top flap, sew in place.

#13 MP3 PLAYER NECKLACE

Designed by Donna Druchunas

SIZE

1 ¹/₂" wide x 4" high plus 30" strap

MATERIALS

Worsted weight cord yarn,
  50 yds black/blue/green
  variegated

Note: Photographed model made with Noro Daria Multi #4 Black/Blue/Green

160 size E seed beads

Black sewing thread

Sewing needle with small eye

Fabric glue (optional)

Size H (5 mm) crochet hook
  (or size required for gauge)

GAUGE

8 sc = 1 ³/₄"

INSTRUCTIONS

Pouch

Ch 4; sl st in first ch to form a ring.

Rnd 1: 8 sc in ring: 8 sc.

Rnd 2: *2 sc in back lp of next sc; rep from * 7 times more: 16 sc.

Rnd 3: Sc in back lp of next sc and in back lp of each sc around.

Rnds 4 through 6: Rep Rnd 3 three times more.

Rnd 7: *Sc in back lp of next 4 sc, ch 4 (opening for controls made), skip 4 sc; rep from * once.

Rnd 8: *Sc in back lp of next 4 sc, 4 sc in ch-4 sp; rep from * once.

Rnds 9 through 16: Rep Rnd 3 eight times more, or to desired height to fit player inside Pouch. Do not finish off.

Beaded Flap

Row 1 (right side): Sc in back lp of first 4 sc on last rnd of Pouch (or to area directly above solid area between control openings); ch 1, turn.

Row 2: Sc in front lp of first 8 sc: 8 sc; ch 1, turn.

Row 3: Sc in back lp of first sc and in back lp of each sc across; ch 1, turn.

Row 4: Sc in front lp of first sc and in front lp of each sc across; ch 1, turn.

Row 5 and 6: Rep Rows 3 and 4 once. At end of Row 6, do not ch 1. Finish off; weave in ends.

Beaded Fringe

With right side facing, attach 32" long double strand of sewing thread to back lp of first st on Flap edge. String 20 beads onto thread and push beads up to Flap. Knot thread around back lp of same st on Flap edge. *Knot thread around back lp of next st on Flap edge. String 20 more beads onto thread and push beads up to Flap. Knot thread around back lp of same st on Flap edge. Rep from * in back lp of each rem st on Flap edge to make 8 beaded fringe. Knot thread around back lp of last st to secure. Cut off excess thread; weave in ends. If desired, use fabric glue to secure thread in place.

Strap

Join yarn by inserting hook in st next to Flap on last rnd of Pouch and pulling lp through. Ch about 120 or until strap is long enough to fit Pouch over head comfortably; sl st in st next to other end of Flap on last rnd of Pouch. Finish off; weave in ends. Knot ends of yarn or apply dab of fabric glue to prevent yarn from unraveling.

#14 16 TRILLIUM BAGS

Designed by Noreen Crone-Findlay

CASUAL BAG

SIZE
7" high x 6" along each edge of base

MATERIALS
Bulky weight yarn
   3 1/2 oz off-white with speckles
   3 1/2 oz dk. gray

Note: *Photographed model made with Bernat® Country Wool #45008 Country Club and #44040 Midnight Shadow*

6" square cardboard

Ruler, protractor or triangle

Pencil and scissors

Size L (8 mm) crochet hook (or size required for gauge)

GAUGE
8 sc and 8 sc rows = 3"

INSTRUCTIONS

Triangle Base
With off-white, ch 16.

Row 1 (wrong side): Sc in 2nd ch from hook and in each rem ch: 15 sc; ch 1, turn.

Rows 2 through 15: Skip first sc, sc in each rem sc across: 1 fewer sc in each row than in previous row; ch 1, turn. At end of Row 15: 1 sc.

First Side

Row 1 (right side): Sc in edge of each row on side of base: 15 sc; ch 1, turn.

Rows 2 through 14: Sc in first sc and in each sc across; ch 1, turn.

Row 15: Sc in first sc and in each sc across; ch 5, turn.

Row 16: Skip first 2 sc, sc in next sc; *ch 5, skip next 2 sc, sc in next sc; rep from * 3 times more: 5 sc and 5 ch-5 sps; ch 3, turn.

Row 17: 2 sc in first ch-5 sp and in each ch-5 sp across: 10 sc; ch 1, turn.

Rows 18 through 25: Skip first sc, sc in each rem sc across: 1 fewer sc in each row than in previous row; ch 1, turn. At end of Row 25: 2 sc. Finish off; weave in ends.

Second Side

With right side facing, join off-white with sc in free lp of foundation ch at next corner of base.

Row 1: Sc in free lp of next ch and in free lp of each ch across base: 15 sc; ch 1, turn.

Rows 2 through 25: Rep Rows 2 through 25 on first side.

Third Side

With right side facing, join off-white with sc in edge of Row 1 at next corner of base.

Row 1: Sc in edge of next row and in edge of each row on side of base: 15 sc; ch 1, turn.

Rows 2 through 25: Rep Rows 2 through 25 on first side.

Finishing

With right side facing, join dk gray with sl st in last sc in Row 25 on second side, ch 1, sc in edge of each row from Row 25 down to Row 17. Fold bag so second and third side edges line up. *Working through both sides together, work 3 sc in edge of ch-5 sps on Row 16, sc in edge of each row from Row 15 down to Row 1, ch 3*. Fold bag so second side is folded at Row 1. **Working through both layers together (side and base), work 15 sc along edge of base, ch 3**. Fold bag so first and second side edges line up. Working through both sides together, sc in edge of each row from Row 1 up to Row 15, work 3 sc in edge of ch-5 sps on Row 16. On second side only, sc in edge of each row from Row 17 up to Row 25, ch 3, sl st in joining sl st and in each of first 9 sc from Row 25 down to Row 17. On third side only, ***sc in edge of each row from Row 17 up to Row 25, ch 3, sc in last sc in Row 25, sc in edge of each row from Row 25 down to Row 17***. Fold bag so third and first side edges line up. Rep from * to * once. Fold bag so third side is folded at Row 1. Rep from ** to ** once. Sl st in each of 15 sc across edge of base and second side, ch 3. Fold bag so first side is folded at Row 1. Rep from ** to ** once. Sl st in each of first 18 sc from Row 1 up to Row 16 on first and third sides. On first side only, rep from *** to *** once. Sl st in next sc. Finish off; weave in ends.

Draw Strings (make 2)

With one strand dk gray (or 2 strands for a heavier handle), ch 100. Finish off, leaving 3" end. Thread end of one draw string through ch-5 sps on Row 16, beginning and ending at edge of joined first and third sides. Thread ends of second draw string through ch-5 sps on Row 16, beginning and ending at center of second side. With ends of each draw string together, tie knot in ends and pull up to close bag. Fray ends of draw strings, if desired.

Cardboard Base

Draw triangle onto cardboard with all 3 sides 6" long. Cut out triangle and trim 1/8" off each corner. Place cardboard triangle inside bag.

EVENING BAG

SIZE
3 1/2" high x 4" along each edge of base

MATERIAL
Novelty ladder yarn
  1 3/4 oz purple

Note: Photographed model made with Bernat® Matrix #02315 Graphic Grape

4" square cardboard

Ruler, protractor or triangle

Pencil and scissors

Size G (4 mm) crochet hook
  (or size required for gauge)

GAUGE
10 sc and 10 sc rows = 2"

INSTRUCTIONS

With purple ladder yarn, work as for Casual Bag. Make draw strings with ladder yarn.

Cardboard Base

Draw triangle onto cardboard with all 3 sides 4" long. Cut out triangle and trim 1/8" off each corner. Place cardboard triangle inside bag.

AMULET BAG

SIZE
2 ¹/₂" high

MATERIALS
Sock yarn
   1 ³/₄ oz blue/purple variegated

Note: Photographed model made with Patons® Kroy Socks #54561 Winter Eclipse.

2 ¹/₂" square cardboard

Ruler, protractor or triangle

Pencil and scissors

Size D (3.25 mm) crochet hook
   (or size required for gauge)

GAUGE
12 sc and 12 sc rows = 2"

INSTRUCTIONS

With sock yarn, work as for Casual Bag. Make draw strings with sock yarn.

Cardboard Base

Draw triangle onto cardboard with all 3 sides 2 ¹/₂" long. Cut out triangle and trim ¹/₈" off each corner. Place cardboard triangle inside bag.

#17 CASUAL DAYS

Designed by Glenda Winkleman for Coats and Clark

SIZE

8 1/2" wide x 8 1/4" high without handles (14 1/2" high with handles)

MATERIALS

Super bulky weight novelty yarn
3 1/2 oz brown multicolor

Bulky weight yarn
4 oz tan multicolor

Note: Photographed model made with Moda Dea™ Orbit #3936 Milky Way and Red Heart® Casual Cot'n #3463 Mushroom

Size K (6.5 mm) crochet hook (or size required for gauge)

1 Pair Purse Handles by Dritz #9801 Mangos

2" x 1" black hook and loop fastener

9 1/2" x 19" brown fabric for lining (optional)

Needle and sewing thread to match lining fabric (optional)

GAUGE

11 sts and 10 rows = 4"

INSTRUCTIONS

Starting at bottom with brown multicolor, ch 24.

Rnd 1: (Sc, dc, sc) in 2nd ch from hook; *(dc in next ch, sc in next ch) 10 times, dc in next ch*, (sc, dc, sc) in last ch; working in free lps on other side of foundation ch; rep from * to * once, changing to tan multicolor in last st: 24 sc and 24 dc; do not join.

Rnd 2: With tan multicolor; *dc in next sc, sc in next dc; rep from * around, changing to brown multicolor in last st; do not join.

Rnd 3: With brown multi-color; *sc in next dc, dc in next sc; rep from * around, changing to tan multi-color in last st; do not join.

Rnds 4 through 21: Rep Rnds 2 and 3 nine times more. At end of Rnd 21, join with sl st in next st. Finish off; weave in ends.

Handle Assembly

With brown multicolor, center and whip-stitch handles to top edge of front and back of Handbag.

Lining (optional)

Fold short ends 1/2" to wrong side twice, press. Sew folded ends. Fold lining in half with right sides together and folded ends aligned at top, sew along raw edges with 1/4" seam allowance, leaving top folded edges open. Insert lining into handbag, hand sew in place along top edge.

Finishing

Sew hook & loop fastener to inside top center of front and back of Handbag, aligning to fit properly.

#18 SEEING RED

Designed by Patons Design Staff

SIZE AFTER FELTING
11" x 15"

MATERIALS
Worsted weight 100% wool yarn
   14 oz red

*Note: Photographed model made
with Patons® Classic Merino Wool
#207 Rich Red*

1 set of snap fasteners

Red sewing thread

Sewing needle

Size 7 (4.5 mm) straight knitting
   needles (or size required for
   gauge

Set of four Size 7 (4.5 mm) double-
   point knitting needles

GAUGE BEFORE FELTING
20 sts and 26 rows = 4" in stock st
   (knit 1 row, purl 1 row)

INSTRUCTIONS

Body

With straight needles, CO 100 sts.

Row 1 (right side): Knit.

Row 2: Purl.

Rep Rows 1 and 2 until piece measures 31" from CO edge, ending by working a wrong-side row. BO.

Handle (make 2)

CO 11 sts on one double-point needle. Divide sts evenly on 3 needles and place a marker to indicate beg of rnds. Knit in rnds until work from beg measures 33". BO.

I-Cord for Motif

CO 4 sts on one double-point needle. Following I-Cord instructions on page 253, make 45" of I-Cord. BO.

Finishing

Felt all pieces following felting instructions on page 252.

Felted piece for body should measure approx 17" wide x 23" long. Felted pieces for handles should measure about 1 3/4" wide x 24 3/4" long.

From main piece, cut body of Bag 15" wide by 23" long. With right sides facing tog, fold bag crosswise and sew side seams with blanket st (Diagram 1).

Fold bottom corners flat. Sew diagonally straight across corners. Trim corners, leaving 1/2" seam allowance. Turn bag right side out.

Trim Handles to measure 24" and sew to top of bag.

Trim cord for Motif to 33" long. Form Cord into shape and use small hand stitches to tack each successive loop as it is formed and tiny invisible stitches to attached the finished Motif to Bag (Diagram 2).

Sew snap fastener on inside, centered at top.

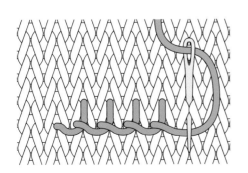

Diagram 1
Blanket stitch

Diagram 2

#19 EVENING PEARLS

Designed by Cynthia Grosch

SIZE

7" wide x 5" high plus 14" strap

MATERIALS

Light worsted weight cotton yarn
 3 ¹/₂ oz green

Note: Photographed model made with Patons® Grace #60027 Ginger

700 pearl beads, 4 mm diameter
 (with adequate size hole to fit
 onto yarn)

Pearl shank button, ¹/₂" diameter

Floss threader or bead threader

Tapestry needle

Size 2 (2.25 mm) steel crochet
 hook (or size required for
 gauge)

GAUGE

25 sc in bead pattern = 4"

INSTRUCTIONS

Bag

String 500 beads onto yarn using floss threader or bead threader. Ch 46.

Row 1 (wrong side): Sc in 2nd ch from hook and in each rem ch: 45 sc; ch 1, turn.

Row 2 (right side): Sc in first 3 sts; *FBsc in next st, sc in next 3 sts; rep from * across to last 2 sts; FBsc in next st, sc in last st: 34 sc and 11 FBsc; ch 1, turn.

Row 3: Sc in first st and in each st across: 45 sc; ch 1, turn.

Row 4: Sc in first 2 sts; *FBsc in next st, sc in next 3 sts; rep from * across to last 3 sts; FBsc in next st, sc in last 2 sts: 34 sc and 11 FBsc; ch 1, turn.

Row 5: Rep Row 3.

Row 6: Sc in first st; *FBsc in next st, sc in next 3 sts; rep from * across: 34 sc and 11 FBsc; ch 1, turn.

Row 7: Rep Row 3.

Row 8: FBsc in first st; *sc in next 3 sts, FBsc in next st; rep from * across: 33 sc and 12 FBsc; ch 1, turn.

Row 9: Rep Row 3.

Rep Rows 2 through 9 ten times more, or until piece measures about 13". At end of last row, do not ch 1. Finish off; weave in ends.

Joining

With wrong sides together, fold bottom up 5". Sew side seams. Fold top down 3" for front flap.

Flap Scallop Edging

Starting at one end of flap and working across last row toward other end of flap, sew yarn to first sc with tapestry needle; *string 6 beads onto yarn, skip next 4 sc, sew yarn to next sc*; rep from * to * 3 times more; string 3 beads onto yarn, skip next sc, sew yarn to next sc; string 12 beads onto yarn, sew yarn to same sc; string 3 beads onto yarn, skip next sc, sew yarn to next sc; rep from * to * 4 times more. Finish off; weave in ends.

Strap

String 90 beads onto yarn.

Row 1 (wrong side): With wrong side facing, join with sl st to top of left side seam; ch 1, sc in same st as joining and in next 3 sts: 4 sc; ch 1, turn.

Row 2 (right side): FBsc in first st, sc in next 2 sts, FBsc in last st: 2 sc and 2 FBsc; ch 1, turn.

Row 3: Sc in first st and in each st across: 4 sc; ch 1, turn.

Rep Rows 2 and 3 until strap measures about 14". At end of last row, do not ch 1. Finish off. Sew last row to 4 sts next to top of right side seam.

Finishing

With flap folded over front of bag, sew button in position on front of bag behind 12-bead lp.

#20 SAND DOLLAR

Designed by Judith Solomon

SIZE

11 1/2" wide x 10 3/4" high
   before adding hem

MATERIALS

Worsted weight cotton yarn
   4 oz natural

Linen warp
   8 1/2 oz natural

Medium cotton string
   200 yds natural

Size 10 crochet cotton
   225 yds ecru

Note: *Photographed model made with Lily® Sugar 'n Cream® #00004 Ecru, Halcyon Yarn 3-ply Linen Warp Natural, medium cotton string and J&P Coats® Knit-Cro-Sheen #61 New Ecru*

Size G (4 mm) crochet hook
   (or size required for gauge)

Bamboo or wood purse handle
   with bar or space 7" wide

GAUGE

Rnds 1 through 3 = 2 7/8" at
   widest point

SPECIAL STITCHES

Popcorn stitch (popcorn st): 5 dc in both lps of specified st, slip lp off hook, insert hook in top of first dc, replace lp on hook, pull lp through dc, ch 1: popcorn st made.

Beginning popcorn stitch (beg popcorn st): Ch 3, 4 dc in both lps of same st, slip lp off hook, insert hook in 3rd ch of beg ch-3, replace lp on hook, pull lp through dc, ch 1: beg popcorn st made.

Sc decrease (sc dec): (Insert hook in next st and draw up a lp) 2 times, YO and draw through all 3 lps on hook: sc dec made.

2 dc and 1 sc cluster decrease (2 dc and 1 sc cluster dec): (YO, insert hook in next st and draw up a lp, YO and draw through 2 lps on hook) 2 times, insert hook in next st and draw up a lp, YO and draw through all 4 lps on hook: 2 dc and 1 sc cluster dec made.

1 sc and 2 dc cluster decrease (1 sc and 2 dc cluster dec): Insert hook in next st and draw up a lp, (YO, insert hook in next st and draw up a lp, YO and draw through 2 lps on hook) 2 times, YO and draw through all 4 lps on hook: 1 sc and 2 dc cluster dec made.

Note: Work in back lps unless instructed to work in both lps. Work all rnds on right side.

INSTRUCTIONS

With worsted cotton yarn, ch 3; join with sl st to form a ring.

Rnd 1 (right side): Ch 1, work 7 sc in ring: 7 sc.

Rnd 2: Working in both lps around; work beg popcorn st in next sc, ch 1; *popcorn st in next sc, ch 1; rep from * 5 times more: 7 popcorn sts and 7 ch sps; join with sl st in beg popcorn st. Finish off; weave in ends.

Rnd 3: Join linen warp with sl st in any ch sp between popcorn sts, ch 3 (counts as dc), 4 dc in same ch sp; *5 dc in next ch sp; rep from * 5 times more: 35 dc; join with sl st in 3rd ch of beg ch-3. Finish off; weave in ends.

Rnd 4: Working in both lps around; join worsted cotton yarn with sc in center st of any 5-dc cluster on Rnd 3; *sc in next 5 dc, ch 5, sc in back bar of 2nd ch from hook and in back bar of each rem ch (short point made); sc in same dc as last sc before ch-5; rep from * 3 times more; **sc in next 5 dc, ch 8, sc in back bar of 2nd ch from hook and in back bar of each rem ch (long point made)***; sc in same dc as last sc before ch-8; rep from ** once; rep from ** to *** once, ending in same st as first sc: 79 sc; join with sl st in first sc. Finish off; weave in ends.

Rnd 5: Join cotton string with sc in 2nd sc worked on Rnd 4; sc in next 3 sts; *sc dec in next 2 sts, sc in next 3 sts on short points (or in next 6 sts on long points), 3 sc in tip of point (5th ch of ch-5 or 8th ch of ch-8), sc in next 3 sts on short points (or in next 6 sts on long points), sc dec in next 2 sts**; sc in next 4 sts; rep from * 5 times more; rep from * to ** once: 123 sc; join as before. Finish off; weave in ends.

Rnd 6: Join 3 strands of crochet cotton with sc in 2nd sc of 3 sc in any tip; 2 sc in same st; *sc in next 4 sts on short points (or in next 7 sts on long points), skip next 2 sts, popcorn st in next st, ch 1, popcorn st in next st, skip next 2 sts, sc in next 4 sts on short points (or in next 7 sts on long points) to tip**; 3 sc in 2nd sc of 3 sc in tip; rep from * 5 times more; rep from * to ** once: 14 popcorn sts, 95 sc and 7 ch-1 sps; join. Finish off; weave in ends.

Rnd 7: Join linen warp with sc in 2nd sc of 3 sc in any tip; 2 sc in same st; *sc in next 4 sts on short points (or in next 7 sts on

Instructions continue on next page. →

long points), skip next sc and next popcorn st, 3 dc in ch-1 sp between popcorn sts, skip next popcorn st and next sc, sc in next 4 sts on short points (or in next 7 sts on long points)**; 3 sc in 2nd sc of 3 sc in tip; rep from * 5 times more; rep from * to ** once: 95 sc and 21 dc; join. Finish off; weave in ends.

Rnd 8: Join worsted cotton yarn with sc in 2nd sc of 3 sc in any tip; 2 sc in same st; *sc in next 2 sts on short points (or in next 5 sts on long points), hdc in next st; work 2 dc and 1 sc cluster dec in next 3 sts, sc in next st; work 1 sc and 2 dc cluster dec in next 3 sts, hdc in next st, sc in next 2 sts on short points (or in next 5 sts on long points)**; 3 sc in 2nd sc of 3 sc in tip; rep from * 5 times more; rep from * to ** once: 74 sc, 14 hdc and 14 cluster dec; join. Finish off; weave in ends.

Rnd 9: Join 3 strands of crochet cotton with sl st in sc between any 2 cluster dec of Rnd 8, work beg popcorn st in same st; *skip cluster dec, hdc in next st, sc in next 2 sts on short points (or in next 5 sts on long points), 2 sc in next st, sc in next st at tip, 2 sc in next st, sc in next 2 sts on short points (or in next 5 sts on long points), hdc in next st, skip next cluster dec**; popcorn st in next st; rep from * 5 times more; rep from * to ** once: 7 popcorn sts, 81 sc and 14 hdc; join with sl st in beg popcorn st. Finish off; weave in ends.

Rnd 10: With long points at top, join linen warp with sl st in popcorn st between last short point and first long point; ch 3 (counts as dc), 2 dc in same st; *ch 4, sc in back bar of 2nd ch from hook and in back bar of next 2 chs (point made); 3 dc in same st as last dc made**; skip next 2 sts, sc in next 5 sts; 2 sc in next st, sc in next st at tip, 2 sc in next st, sc in next 5 sts; skip next 2 sts; 3 dc in next popcorn st; rep from * 2 times more; rep from * to ** once; ***skip next 2 sts, sc in next 2 sts, 2 sc in next st, sc in next st at tip, 2 sc in next st, sc in next 2 sts, skip next 2 sts****; 5 dc in next popcorn st; rep from *** 2 times more; rep from *** to **** once: 93 sc and 39 dc; join with sl st in 3rd ch of beg ch-3. Finish off; weave in ends.

Rnd 11: Join cotton string with sc dec in last sc on Rnd 10 and 3rd ch of beg ch-3 on Rnd 10; *sc in next 2 dc, sc in next 3 sc, 3 sc in tip of next point (4th ch of ch-4); sc in next 3 sc, sc in next 2 dc, sc dec in next dc and sc**, sc in next 6 sts, 2 sc in next st, sc in next 6 sts, sc dec in next sc and dc; rep from * 2 times more; rep from * to ** once; sc in each rem st around to beg: 151 sc; join with sl st in first sc dec. Finish off; weave in ends.

Rnd 12: Join worsted cotton with sc in tip of first point, 2 sc in same tip; *sc in next 3 sts, skip next st, popcorn st in next st, skip next st, dc in next 2 sts, hdc in next st**; sc in next 10 sts, hdc in next st, dc in next 2 sts, skip next st, popcorn st in next st, skip next st, sc in next 3 sts, 3 sc in tip of next point; rep from * 2 times more; rep from * to ** once; sc in next 6 sts, popcorn st in next st, sc in next 3 sts, popcorn st in next st; ***sc in next 9 sts, popcorn st in next st, sc in next 3 sts, popcorn st in next st; rep from *** once; sc in next 6 sts, hdc in next st, dc in next 2 sts; skip next st, popcorn st in next st, skip next st, sc in next 3 sts: 105 sc, 16 dc, 8 hdc and 14 popcorn sts; join with sl st in first sc. Finish off; weave in ends.

Note: *Bottom edge will begin to cup.*

Rnd 13: Join linen warp with sc in 2nd sc of 3 sc at tip of 2nd point; 2 sc in same st; *sc in next 2 sts, hdc in next st, skip next st, 3 dc in popcorn st, skip next st*; sc in next 2 sts, hdc in next 10 sts, sc in next 2 sts, skip next st, 3 dc in popcorn st, skip next st, hdc in next st, sc in next 2 sts, 3 sc in tip of next point; rep from * to * once; sc in next 2 sts, hdc in next 2 sts, dc in next 6 sts, hdc in next 2 sts, sc in next 2 sts, skip next st, 3 dc in popcorn st; skip next st, hdc in next st, sc in next 2 sts, 3 sc in tip of next point; rep from * to * once; sc in next 2 sts, hdc in next st, dc in next 5 sts; **3 dc in next popcorn st, skip next st, sc in next st, skip next st, 3 dc in next popcorn st***; dc in next 9 sts; rep from ** once; rep from ** to *** once; dc in next 5 sts, hdc in next st, sc in next 2 sts, skip next st, 3 dc in next popcorn st, skip next st, hdc in next st, sc in next 2 sts, 3 sc in tip of point; rep from * to * once; sc in next 2 sts, hdc in next 10 sts, sc in next 2 sts, skip next st, 3 dc in next popcorn st, skip next st, hdc in next st, sc in next 2 sts: 47 sc, 76 dc and 34 hdc; join as before. Do not finish off.

Rnd 14: Ch 1, 3 sc in 2nd sc of 3 sc at tip, sc in next st, hdc in next st; *skip next st, popcorn st in next st, skip next st, sc in next st, skip next st, popcorn st in next st, skip next st*; hdc in next 3 sts, sc in next 4 sts, hdc in next 3 sts; rep from * to * once; **hdc in next st, sc in next st, 3 sc in 2nd sc of 3 sc at tip, sc in next st, hdc in next st**; rep from * to * once; hdc in next 10 sts; rep from * to * once; rep from ** to ** once; rep from * to * once; sc in next st, hdc in next 6 sts, sc in next st; (***skip next st, popcorn st in next st, skip next st***; sc in next 2 sts, hdc in next 9 sts, sc in next 2 sts) two times; rep from *** to *** once; sc in next st, hdc in next 6 sts, sc in next st; rep from * to * once; rep from ** to ** once; rep from * to * once; hdc in next 10 sts; rep from * to * once; hdc in next st, sc in next st: 19 popcorn sts, 44 sc and 64 hdc; join. Do not finish off.

Top Hem

Row 1: Working in both lps, ch 1, sc in 2nd sc of 3 sc at tip, sc in each sc across to 2nd sc of 3 sc at next tip: 24 sc; ch 1, turn.

Row 2: Sc in first sc and in each sc across; ch 1, turn.

Rep Row 2 until hem covers handle (about 7 rows). At end of last row, do not ch 1. Finish off, leaving 20" end for sewing.

***Note:** If handles are too large for purse, sc around entire front and back pieces with linen warp, increasing 2 sc at each top corner.*

Assembly

With wrong sides together, pin front to back, aligning pattern. Working through both layers, join linen warp with sl st in back lp of st below 3rd pair of popcorn sts in Rnd 14 on front and in back lp of st below last pair of popcorn sts in Rnd 14 on back; matching sts, sl st in back lp of each st on Rnd 14. Fold wrong side of hems over handles and sew last row of hem on inside with 20" end. *With right side facing, working in one layer only; join linen warp with sl st in first st on Rnd 14 of front below hem at left side of handle, sl st in each st down to joining, turn purse and work in each st on Rnd 14 of back up to hem. Finish off; weave in ends. Rep from * on other side of purse, working on back first, then on front.

#21 GOING SHOPPING

Designed by Judi & Co.

SIZE
8" x 9"

MATERIALS
Rayon cord
   288 yds black

Rayon ribbon yarn
   200 yds black and white
   blend

*Note: Photographed model
made with Judi & Co's Cordé
black and Judi & Co's Ribbon*

Two 6" diameter plastic ring
   purse handles

Stitch holder

20" Size 5 (3.75 mm) circular
   knitting needles (or size
   required for gauge)

Size F (3.75 mm) crochet
   hook

GAUGE
16 sts = 4" in garter st (knit
   each row)

INSTRUCTIONS

Front

With crochet hook and rayon cord, make a sl knot on hook.

Row 1: Work 36 sc around a handle ring; ch 1, turn.

Rows 2 and 3: Sc in each sc, ch 1, turn.

Row 4: Sc in each sc; draw up long loop on hook and pass yarn ball through loop to secure sts. Do not cut yarn.

With knitting needle and ribbon yarn, pick up one st in each sc: 36 sts; do not join, work back and forth in rows.

Rows 1 through 8: With ribbon yarn, knit.

Rows 9 through 15: With rayon cord, knit.

Rep Rows 1 through 16 three times more. BO; weave in ends.

Back

Work same as Front.

Gusset

With rayon cord, CO 7 sts.

Row 1: Knit.

Rep Row 1 until strip measures 26". Do not BO, place rem sts on a holder.

Begin sewing one long edge of gusset (starting with CO edge) to one side of purse Front, starting at beg of first ribbon section under handle and ending at beg of same section on opposite side. Adjust length of gusset if needed and BO gusset. Sew opposite long edge of gusset to Back in same manner.

#22 SWINGY RUFFLES

Designed by Vashti Braha

SIZE

5" high x 11" wide at base

MATERIALS

Medium weight fluffy chenille yarn
  7 oz periwinkle blue

Note: Photographed model made with Moda Dea™ Dream #3502 Lavender

4 stitch markers

Lining fabric (optional)

Low-heat iron-on adhesive

Iron

Stabilizer

Hot glue gun or fabric glue

Sewing needle and matching thread

1 Magnetic snap

Decorative silver metal chain, 3 to 4 feet long

2 big silver clasps

2 eyelet pairs, 1/4" size "large"

Eyelet tools

1" diameter jump ring

48 glass E beads, 6/0 silver

4 yds Metallic silver embroidery floss

Size K (6.5 mm) crochet hook

Size I (5.5 mm) crochet hook (or size required for gauge)

GAUGE

11 hdc = 4" with I hook

SPECIAL STITCHES

Front Post hdc (FP hdc): YO, insert hook from front to back to front around post of next st and draw up a lp, YO and draw through all 3 lps on hook: FP hdc made.

Front Post hdc decrease (FP hdc dec): *YO, insert hook from front to back to front around post of next st and draw up a lp; rep from * once more; YO and draw through all 5 lps on hook: FP hdc dec made.

Hdc decrease (hdc dec): *YO, insert hook in next st and draw up a lp; rep from * once more; YO and draw through all 5 lps on hook: hdc dec made.

INSTRUCTIONS

Note: Work in top 2 lps of sts unless directed otherwise. Turning chs do not count as sts. Avoid placing increases or decreases directly above increases or decreases in previous rows.

Front, Bottom and Back

Starting at top front with I hook, ch 19 loosely.

Row 1 (right side): Hdc in back bar of 3rd ch from hook and in back bar of each rem ch: 17 hdc; ch 2, turn.

Row 2: Dc in lp below top 2 lps of first hdc (lp created by first YO on hdc) and in lp below top 2 lps of each hdc across: 17 dc; ch 2, turn. Note: Working in lp below top 2 lps creates free lps on right side of previous row for adding ruffles later.

Row 3: Hdc in first st and in each st across, increasing 4 sts evenly spaced across: 21 hdc; ch 2, turn.

Row 4: Hdc in first st and in each st across; ch 2, turn.

Row 5: Rep Row 3: 25 hdc; ch 2, turn.

Rows 6 through 13: Rep Rows 2 through 5 two times more. At end of Row 13: 41 hdc. Place stitch marker in each edge of Row 13.

Rows 14 and 15: Rep Row 4 two times more.

Row 16: Hdc in first st and in each st across, decreasing 4 sts evenly spaced across: 37 hdc; ch 2, turn. Place stitch marker in each edge of row.

Row 17: Rep Row 4.

Row 18: Rep Row 16: 33 hdc.

Row 19: Rep Row 4.

Row 20: FP hdc in first st and in each st across to last st, decreasing 4 sts evenly across; hdc in lp below top 2 lps of last st: 29 hdc; ch 2, turn.

Rows 21 through 24: Rep Rows 17 through 20. At end of Row 24: 21 hdc.

Rows 25 through 27: Rep Rows 17 through 19. At end of Row 26: 17 hdc.

Row 28: FP hdc in first st and in each st across to last st; hdc in lp below top 2 lps of last st. Finish off; weave in ends.

Gussets

Row 1: With right side facing, join with sl st in edge of marked row on right; ch 2, work 8 hdc evenly across to next marker: 8 hdc; ch 2, turn.

Row 2: Hdc in first hdc and in each hdc across; ch 2, turn.

Row 3: Rep Row 2.

Row 4: Rep Row 2, decreasing one st: 7 hdc; ch 2, turn.

Rows 5 through 13: Rep Rows 2 through 4 three times more. At end of Row 13: 4 hdc.

Instructions continue on next page. →

Rows 14 and 15: Rep Row 2 two times more. At end of Row 15, do not ch 1. Finish off; weave in ends. Rep for other gusset on other edge of bag.

Assembly

Lay crochet piece with gussets flat on table. Cut stabilizer same size as bag and gussets except 1/8" smaller on gusset side seams, and 1/2" shorter than length from Row 1 to Row 28. Iron creases into stabilizer where bottom edges will fold (base of Rows 13 and 17 of front and back and base of Row 1 of Gussets). Inward-folding side of stabilizer is right side of stabilizer.

Optional: Cut lining fabric 1/2" larger than stabilizer on all sides. Place right side of stabilizer against wrong side of fabric. Wrap excess fabric around stabilizer edges to wrong side of stabilizer and fuse edges with iron-on adhesive.

Center magnetic snap on right side of lining at top front and back of bag. Secure through stabilizer and fabric layers according to package instructions. Fuse a scrap of fabric over backs of snaps to avoid yarn abrasion. Cut snug holes for eyelets on gussets through stabilizer and fabric layers, centered 1/2" at most from top of each gusset. Set eyelets aside.

Fuse iron-on adhesive to wrong side of stabilizer, let cool. Remove paper backing and fuse to wrong side of crochet, starting with rectangular bottom of bag. While hot, fold stabilizer and crochet along 4 creases, coaxing crochet to remain in a shape 1/4" larger on all sides than stabilizer. Fuse one side at a time; let side cool for about 3 minutes while folded into bag shape before fusing next side.

Hammer eyelet through all thicknesses of gusset. Rep for other gusset.

Ruffles

With right side facing and top of bag closest to you, with K hook, join yarn with sl st to both free lps of first st in Row 1.

Row 1: Ch 4, tr in same st as joining, 2 tr in both free lps of next st and in both free lps of each st across: 33 tr on top ruffle (49 tr on middle ruffle, 65 tr on bottom ruffle); ch 3, turn.

Row 2: Work 2 dc in first tr; *dc in next tr, 2 dc in next tr; rep from * across: 50 dc on top ruffle (74 dc on middle ruffle, 98 dc on bottom ruffle); ch 3, turn.

Row 3: Dc in first dc and in each dc across. Finish off; weave in ends.

Rep for all free lps in Rows 5, 9, 19, 23 and 27, making sure top front or back of bag is closest to you when working ruffles. Note: Top ruffles are on Rows 1 and 27, middle ruffles are on rows 5 and 23, bottom ruffles are on Rows 9 and 19.

Finishing

With needle and thread, sew side edges of stabilizer gussets to side edges of stabilizer front and back from outside of bag, then reinforce with glue. Sew side edges of crochet gussets to side edges of crochet front and back, including side edges of each ruffle in seam. Fold top edge of crochet bag over top edge of stabilizer and glue discreetly on inside of bag for a finished edge.

Attach silver clasps to eyelets. Thread metal chain through clasps. Link ends of metal chain into jump ring.

Divide embroidery floss into 2 strands. String beads onto divided embroidery floss. With I hook and embroidery floss held together with yarn, join with sl st in center of jump ring, ch 1, work (3 sc, ch 5) 6 times in ring, pulling up a bead in each st: 18 sc with beads and 30 chs with beads; join with sl st in first sc. Finish off; weave in ends.

#23 SCHOOL DAYS

SIZE
24" diameter x 11" high

MATERIALS
Bulky weight yarn
  5 oz multi-color (burgundy, denim,
  sage, green, gold)

Note: *Photographed model made with
Lion Brand® Jiffy® #325 El Paso*

1" button

One bead with ¹/₂" hole for drawstring

Size 10 (6 mm) circular knitting needles (or size required for gauge)

Size 10 double-point knitting needles

GAUGE
12 sts and 24 rows (12 ridges) = 4" in
  garter st (knit every row)

INSTRUCTIONS

Base

CO 15 sts. Work 30 rows of garter st, forming 15 ridges. BO all sts.

Body

CO 25 sts.

Rows 1 through 9: Knit.

Row 10 (right side): K2, YO, K2tog, knit to end of row.

Rep Rows 1 through 10 until piece measures 24", ending by working a Row 10. Knit 4 more rows. BO.

Finishing

Sew backpack body into a tube by joining the CO edge to the BO edge. Line up center ridge of base (8th ridge) with back seam of body. Sew base to tube, ridge to ridge, 2 times, 1 base ridge to 2 body ridges; * ridge to ridge 5 times, 1 base ridge to 2 body ridges, rep from * around until last 2 ridges; sew ridge to ridge.

Note: *This gives the bag a bit of fullness.*

Backpack Flap

With right side facing, pick up 18 sts (9 ridges each side of back center seam).

Rows 1 through 10: Knit.

Begin Shaping

Row 11: K1, SSK; knit to last 3 sts, K2tog, K1: 16 sts.

Rows 12 through 14: Rep Row 11: 10 sts.

Row 15 (buttonhole row): K3, K2tog, YO, SSK, K3: 9 sts.

Rows 16 and 17: Knit.

BO all sts.

Drawstring

Following basic I-Cord instructions on page 253, work a 55" I-Cord on double-point needles.

Thread cord, beginning at back center, in and out through each drawstring hole. Thread both ends of drawstring through large bead. Tack each end of drawstring to each back corner of base. Pull drawstring to close, fold flap over opening. Mark where buttonhole falls and sew on button. Weave in loose ends.

#24 BLUE COTILLION

Designed by Elizabeth Ann White for Coats & Clark

SIZE
5 ½" x 6 ½"

MATERIALS
Size 3 crochet cotton thread
450 yds blue

Note: *Photographed model made with J&P Coats® Royale Fashion Crochet, Size 3 #0175 Warm Blue*

Size F (3.75 mm) crochet hook (or size required for gauge)

Size G (4 mm) crochet hook

5 ³/8" diameter plastic canvas circle

GAUGE
Rnds 1 through 8 = 5 ½" diameter

STITCH GUIDE
Shell: Work 5 dc in specified st: shell made.

INSTRUCTIONS

Ch 5, join with sl st to form a ring.

Rnd 1 (right side): Ch 3 (counts as a dc throughout), 11 dc in ring: 12 dc; join with sl st in 3rd ch of beg ch-3.

Rnd 2: Ch 3, dc in same ch as joining, 2 dc in next dc and in each dc around: 24 dc; join as before.

Rnd 3: Ch 3, dc in same ch as joining, dc in next dc; *2 dc in next dc, dc in next dc; rep from * around: 36 dc; join.

Rnd 4: Ch 3, dc in same ch as joining, dc in next 2 dc; *2 dc in next dc, dc in next 2 dc; rep from * around: 48 dc; join.

Rnd 5: Ch 3, dc in same ch as joining, dc in next 3 dc; *2 dc in next dc, dc in next 3 dc; rep from * around: 60 dc; join.

Rnd 6: Ch 3, dc in same ch as joining, dc in next 4 dc; *2 dc in next dc, dc in next 4 dc; rep from * around: 72 dc; join.

Rnd 7: Ch 3, dc in same ch as joining, dc in next 5 dc; *2 dc in next dc, dc in next 5 dc; rep from * around: 84 dc; join.

Rnd 8: Ch 3, dc in same ch as joining, dc in next 6 dc; *2 dc in next dc, dc in next 6 dc; rep from * around: 96 dc; join.

Rnd 9: Working in back lps only, ch 1, sc in same ch as joining, skip next 2 dc, shell in next dc, skip next 2 dc; *sc in next dc, skip next 2 dc, shell in next dc, skip next 2 dc; rep from * around: 16 shells and 16 sc; join with sl st in first sc.

Rnd 10: Sl st in first 3 dc, ch 1, sc in same dc as last sl st, shell in next sc; *sc in center dc of next shell, shell in next sc; rep from * around, working last shell in joining sl st on last rnd: 16 shells and 16 sc, join as before.

Rnds 11 through 25: Rep Rnd 10 fifteen times more.

Rnd 26: Ch 6 (counts as dc and ch-3 sp), sc in center dc of next shell, ch 3; *dc in next sc, ch 3, sc in center dc of next shell, ch 3; rep from * around: 16 dc, 16 sc and 32 ch-3 sps; join with sl st in 3rd ch of beg ch-6.

Rnd 27: Ch 6 (counts as dc and ch-3 sp), dc in next sc, ch 3; *dc in next dc, ch 3, dc in next sc, ch 3; rep from * around: 32 dc and 32 ch-3 sps; join as before.

Rnd 28: Ch 1, sc in same ch as joining, shell in next dc; *sc in next dc, shell in next dc; rep from * around: 16 shells and 16 sc; join with sl st in first sc.

Rnds 29 through 31: Rep Rnd 10 three times more. At end of Rnd 31, finish off; weave in ends.

Bottom Lining

Work same as Rnds 1 through 8 of purse. Finish off; weave in ends.

Ties (make 2)

With larger hook and 2 strands held tog, ch 2, sc in 2nd ch from hook; *insert hook into 4 strands at left of last sc made; YO and draw up a lp, YO and draw through both lps on hook. Rep from * until tie is 45" long. Finish off; do not weave in ends.

Finishing

Insert plastic canvas circle in bottom of purse. With right side facing, insert lining on top of plastic canvas and sew to bottom of purse through plastic canvas. Starting at opposite sides of purse, weave ties through spaces on Rnds 26 and 27. Alternate weaving pattern on rows (if cording goes under a dc on Rnd 26, weave cording over dc directly above on Rnd 27). Sew ends of ties together on inside of purse and weave in ends.

#25 STRIPED PATCHES

Designed by Jodi Lewanda

SIZE

12" X 12"

MATERIALS

Worsted weight cotton yarn
 3 ¹/₂ oz Pale Blue (A)
 3 ¹/₂ oz Orange (B)
 3 ¹/₂ oz Purple (C)
 3 ¹/₂ oz Off-white (D)

Note: Photographed model made with JCA Reynolds Saucy #869 Chambray (A), #125 Persimmon (B), #408 Grape (C) and #820 Parchment (D)

One 1 ³/₄" long Button

Size 6 (4 mm) straight needles (or size required for gauge)

24" Size 6 circular knitting needles

Size F (3.75 mm) crochet hook

Tapestry needle

GAUGE

20 sts = 4" in garter stitch (knit every row)

INSTRUCTIONS

Square (make 8)

With A, CO 32 sts.

Rows 1 and 2: With A, knit.

Rows 3 and 4: With B, knit.

Rows 5 and 6: With C, knit.

Rows 7 and 8: With D, knit.

Rep Rows 1 through 8, six times more (or until piece is square).

BO with last color. Weave in ends.

Assembly

Sew 4 pairs of 2 squares tog, CO edge to side edge; then sew 2 of the sets tog, again turning squares so that CO edges attach to the side edges. You now have two 4-square pieces. Sew these pieces tog on 3 sides to form tote.

Trim

With circular needle and B, pick up and knit 120 sts around top open edge of tote; join. Place marker and purl one row. BO as to knit.

Button Loop

With crochet hook, join B to inside of center back seam. Ch 24; sc in 2nd chain from hook and each rem ch; finish off, leaving a 4" yarn end. Thread end into a tapestry needle and sew to beg ch to form a lp.

Strap

Measure and cut 10 yards of each of the 4 colors. Fold in half to 5-yard length. Tie one end of all of the pieces into one knot. Twist strands until cord twists back onto itself (see Twisted Cord instructions on page 253) Fasten with knot at opposite end.

Whipstitch cord to sides of tote, placing knots at bottom edges of each side as shown in photo. Sew button to center front of tote at top.

#26 A LITTLE BIT RETRO

Designed by Marty Miller

SIZE
13" wide x 6" high plus 25" handle

MATERIALS
Bulky weight ribbon yarn 320 yds black with white Stripes

Note: *Photographed model made with Crystal Palace Deco-Ribbon Yarn #102 White on Black*

One $1/2$" magnetic snap

Four $7/8$" shank buttons

Black sewing thread

Sewing needle

Stitch markers

Safety pins

Size H (5 mm) crochet hook (or size required for gauge)

GAUGE
Rnds 1 through 8 = 4" diameter

INSTRUCTIONS

Note: Work first st(s) in Rnds 2 through 26 in same sc as joining.

Body

Ch 2.

Rnd 1 (right side): 8 sc in 2nd ch from hook, place marker in last sc made and move up to last sc in each rnd: 8 sc; join with sl st in first sc.

Rnd 2: Ch 1; *2 sc in each of next 3 sc, sc in next sc; rep from * once: 14 sc; join as before.

Rnd 3: Ch 1; *(2 sc in next sc, sc in next sc) 3 times, sc in next sc; rep from * once: 20 sc; join.

Rnd 4: Ch 1; *(sc in next sc, 2 sc in next sc, sc in next sc) 3 times, sc in next sc; rep from * once: 26 sc; join.

Rnd 5: Ch 1; *(sc in next 3 sc, 2 sc in next sc) 3 times, sc in next sc; rep from * once: 32 sc; join.

Rnd 6: Ch 1; *(sc in next 2 sc, 2 sc in next sc, sc in next 2 sc) 3 times, sc in next sc; rep from * once: 38 sc; join.

Rnd 7: Ch 1; *(2 sc in next sc, sc in next 5 sc) 3 times, sc in next sc; rep from * once: 44 sc; join.

Rnd 8: Ch 1; *(sc in next 3 sc, 2 sc in next sc, sc in next 3 sc) 3 times, sc in next sc; rep from * once: 50 sc; join.

Rnd 9: Ch 1; *(sc in next 7 sc, 2 sc in next sc) 3 times, sc in next sc; rep from * once: 56 sc; join.

Rnd 10: Ch 1; *(sc in next 4 sc, 2 sc in next sc, sc in next 4 sc) 3 times, sc in next sc; rep from * once: 62 sc; join.

Rnd 11: Ch 1; *(2 sc in next sc, sc in next 9 sc) 3 times, sc in next sc; rep from * once: 68 sc; join.

Rnd 12: Ch 1; *(sc in next 5 sc, 2 sc in next sc, sc in next 5 sc) 3 times, sc in next sc; rep from * once: 74 sc; join.

Rnd 13: Ch 1; *(sc in next 11 sc, 2 sc in next sc) 3 times, sc in next sc; rep from * once: 80 sc; join.

Rnd 14: Ch 1; *(sc in next 6 sc, 2 sc in next sc, sc in next 6 sc) 3 times, sc in next sc; rep from * once: 86 sc; join.

Rnd 15: Ch 1; *(2 sc in next sc, sc in next 13 sc) 3 times, sc in next sc; rep from * once: 92 sc; join.

Rnd 16: Ch 1; *(sc in next 7 sc, 2 sc in next sc, sc in next 7 sc) 3 times, sc in next sc; rep from * once: 98 sc; join.

Rnd 17: Ch 1; *(sc in next 15 sc, 2 sc in next sc) 3 times, sc in next sc; rep from * once: 104 sc; join.

Rnd 18: Ch 1; *(sc in next 8 sc, 2 sc in next sc, sc in next 8 sc) 3 times, sc in next sc; rep from * once: 110 sc; join.

Instructions continue on next page. →

Rnd 19: Ch 1; *(2 sc in next sc, sc in next 17 sc) 3 times, sc in next sc; rep from * once: 116 sc; join.

Rnd 20: Ch 1; *(sc in next 9 sc, 2 sc in next sc, sc in next 9 sc) 3 times, sc in next sc; rep from * once: 122 sc; join.

Rnd 21: Ch 1; *(sc in next 19 sc, 2 sc in next sc) 3 times, sc in next sc; rep from * once: 128 sc; join.

Rnd 22: Ch 1; *(sc in next 10 sc, 2 sc in next sc, sc in next 10 sc) 3 times, sc in next sc; rep from * once: 134 sc; join.

Rnd 23: Ch 1; *(2 sc in next sc, sc in next 21 sc) 3 times, sc in next sc; rep from * once: 140 sc; join.

Rnd 24: Ch 1; *(sc in next 11 sc, 2 sc in next sc, sc in next 11 sc) 3 times, sc in next sc; rep from * once: 146 sc; join.

Rnd 25: Ch 1; *(sc in next 23 sc, 2 sc in next sc) 3 times, sc in next sc; rep from * once: 152 sc; join.

Rnd 26: Ch 1; *(sc in next 12 sc, 2 sc in next sc, sc in next 12 sc) 3 times, sc in next sc, place marker in last sc made; rep from * once: 158 sc; join. Finish off; weave in ends.

Note: There should be 2 markers in Rnd 26 spaced 79 sc apart. Do not remove these markers until bag is finished.

Gusset (make 2)

Note: Work first st(s) in Rnds 2 through 4 in same sc as joining.

Ch 21.

Rnd 1 (right side): 3 sc in 2nd ch from hook, sc in next 18 sc, 3 sc in last ch, working in free lps along other side of foundation ch, sc in next 18 chs, place marker in last sc made and move up to last sc in each rnd: 42 sc; join with sl st in first sc.

Rnd 2: Ch 1; *2 sc in each of next 3 sc, sc in next 18 sc; rep from * once: 48 sc; join as before.

Rnd 3: Ch 1; *(2 sc in next sc, sc in next sc) 3 times, sc in next 18 sc; rep from * once: 54 sc; join.

Rnd 4: Ch 1; *(sc in next 2 sc, 2 sc in next sc) 3 times, sc in next 18 sc; rep from * once: 60 sc; join. Finish off; weave in ends.

Handle

Note: Work first st(s) in Rnds 2 through 4 in same sc as joining.

Ch 103.

Rnd 1 (right side): 3 sc in 2nd ch from hook, sc in next 100 sc, 3 sc in last ch, working in free lps along other side of foundation ch, sc in next 100 chs, place marker in last sc made and move up to last sc in each rnd: 206 sc; join with sl st in first sc.

Rnd 2: Ch 1; *2 sc in each of next 3 sc, sc in next 100 sc; rep from * once: 212 sc; join as before.

Rnd 3: Ch 1; *(2 sc in next sc, sc in next sc) 3 times, sc in next 100 sc; rep from * once: 218 sc; join.

Rnd 4: Ch 1; *(sc in next 2 sc, 2 sc in next sc) 3 times, sc in next 100 sc; rep from * once: 224 sc; join. Finish off; weave in ends.

Flap (make 2)
Ch 9.

Row 1 (wrong side): Sc in 2nd ch from hook and in each ch across: 8 sc; ch 1, turn.

Row 2 (right side): Sc in first sc and in each sc across; ch 1, turn.

Rows 3 through 6: Rep Row 2 four times more. At end of Row 6, do not ch 1. Finish off, leaving long end for sewing.

Attach one part of snap to center of right side of each Flap.

Finishing
With sewing thread, sew button to Rnd 24 below marked sts on right side of Body. Place wrong side of each Flap on wrong side of Body below marked sts. Whipstitch Flaps to Body through both lps of sts on Row 6 of Flap and through inside lp of sc sts on Rnd 25 of Body. Finish off; weave in ends.

Attaching Gussets
Count 39 sts on each side of both marked sts on Rnd 26 of Body. Place markers in these four sts. Count 6 sts along curved end after marked st on Rnd 4 of each Gusset. Place markers in 6th and 7th st on this curved end. Count 23 sts on each side of newly marked sts on Body and Gusset. Place markers in these four sts. With wrong sides together, pin these four newly marked sts on Gussets to four newly marked sts on Body. With right side of Body facing, sc through both thicknesses, matching sts, beg at top pinned st on straight edge of Gusset, working down and around bottom curved end of Gusset and end at top pinned st on other straight edge of Gusset, leaving twelve sts at top curved end of Gusset unworked. Attach other Gusset in same manner. Finish off; weave in ends.

Attaching Handle
With right side facing, center end of Handle on outside of one Gusset, overlapping top end of Gusset by about 2". Sew Gusset and Handle together from inside of bag. With sewing thread, sew button on Handle near bottom of Handle. Attach other Handle in same manner.

#27 REALLY RED

Designed by Joyce Bragg

SIZE
14 1/2" wide x 7" high plus 5" handles

MATERIALS
Sport weight yarn
  560 yds red

Note: Photographed model made with Katia Granada #11

Size G (4 mm) crochet hook (or size required for gauge)

Size F (3.75 mm) crochet hook

18 gauge wire

GAUGE
20 sc = 4" with G hook

19 sc rows plus 3 Blk St rows = 4"

INSTRUCTIONS

Sides (make 2)

Starting at bottom, with G hook, ch 41.

Row 1 (wrong side): Sc in 2nd ch from hook and in each ch across: 40 sc; ch 1, turn.

Row 2 (right side): Sc in first sc and in each sc across, sc in turning ch-1: 41 sc; ch 1, turn.

Rows 3 through 5: Rep Row 2 three times more: 1 more sc in each row than in previous row. At end of Row 5: 44 sc.

Row 6: 2 sc in first sc, sc in next sc and in each sc across, sc in turning ch-1: 46 sc; ch 3 (counts as dc on next row now and throughout), turn.

Row 7: With F hook, skip first sc, work Blk St in next sc; *dc in next sc, work Blk St in next sc; rep from * across; dc in turning ch-1: 23 Blk Sts and 24 dc; ch 1, turn.

Row 8: With G hook, sc in first dc, work 2 sc in each Blk St (working 1 sc in beg dc on Blk St and 1 sc in first YO on Blk St) and 1 sc in each dc between Blk Sts across; sc in 3rd ch of turning ch-3: 70 sc; ch 1, turn.

Rows 9 through 11: Rep Row 2 three times more: 1 more sc in each row than in previous row. At end of Row 11: 73 sc.

Row 12: Sc in first sc and in each sc across, sc in turning ch-1: 74 sc; ch 3, turn.

Row 13: Rep Row 7: 37 Blk Sts and 38 dc.

Row 14: With G hook, sc in first dc, work 1 sc in beg dc on each Blk St and 1 sc in each dc between Blk Sts across: 74 sc; ch 1, turn. Note: Do not work sc in 3rd ch of turning ch-3.

Rows 15 through 18: Sc in first sc and in each sc across: 74 sc; ch 1, turn. At end of Row 18, ch 3, turn (instead of ch 1, turn).

Row 19: Rep Row 7: 37 Blk Sts and 38 dc.

Row 20: Rep Row 14: 74 sc.

Rows 21 and 22: Skip first sc, sc in next sc and in each sc across; ch 1, turn: 1 sc fewer in each row than in previous row. At end of Row 22: 72 sc.

Rows 23 and 24: Skip first sc, sc in next sc and in each sc across to last sc; ch 1, turn, leaving last sc unworked: 2 sc fewer in each row than in previous row. At end of Row 24: 68 sc; ch 3, turn (instead of ch 1, turn).

Row 25: Rep Row 7: 34 Blk Sts and 35 dc.

Rows 26: Rep Row 14: 68 sc.

Row 27: Sc dec in first 2 sc; *sc dec in next 2 sc; rep from * across: 34 sc; ch 1, turn.

Instructions continue on next page. →

Rows 28 through 30: Sc dec in first 2 sc, sc in next sc and in each sc across to last 2 sc, sc dec in last 2 sc; ch 1, turn: 2 less sc in each row than in previous row. At end of Row 30: 28 sc; ch 3, turn (instead of ch 1, turn).

Row 31: Rep Row 7: 14 Blk Sts and 15 dc.

Row 32: Rep Row 14: 28 sc.

Rows 33 through 38: Sc in first sc and in each sc across; ch 1, turn. At end of Row 38, do not ch 1. Do not finish off.

Edging

With F hook, sc in edge of each row down left side to foundation ch, sc around each foundation ch across (between sc sts on Row 1), sc in edge of each row up right side, working 2 sc in bottom corners. Finish off; weave in ends.

Handle (make 2)

Cut a piece of wire 22 1/2" long. Bend wire into an oval shape. Overlap 5" at each end and twist overlapped ends. With F hook, sc around single wire section of oval. Fold Row 38 of side piece over twisted section of wire and pin to wrong side of Row 30. Sl st edges of fold together down to Row 38. On wrong side, sc Row 38 to Row 30. Sl st edges of fold together up to top. Sc over wire and sc of previous rnd. Finish off; weave in ends.

Assembly

With wrong sides together and F hook, join with sc through both layers in left edge of Row 29, sc through both layers in each sc along left edge, bottom and right edge, ch 1, do not turn. Work rev sc in each sc around. Finish off; weave in ends.

Curlicue

With F hook, ch 42, 3 hdc in 3rd ch from hook; *4 hdc in next ch*; rep from * to * 9 times more; sl st in next 19 chs; rep from * to * 10 times more. Finish off; weave in ends. Tie around one purse handle as desired.

Leaves
First Leaf

With F hook, ch 10, sl st in 2nd ch from hook, sl st in next 5 chs, ch 3; join with sl st in first ch.

Rnd 1: Work (sc, hdc, 3 dc) in first ch-3 sp, dc in next ch, hdc in next 2 chs, sc in next 3 chs, ch 1, working on other side of ch: sc in next 3 chs, hdc in next 2 chs, dc in next ch, work (3 dc, hdc sc) in next ch-3 sp; join with sl st in first sc. Finish off; weave in ends.

Second Leaf

Work same as first leaf. Do not finish off. With F hook and wrong sides of leaves together, working through both layers: join with sc in first st, sc in next 10 sts, 3 sc in ch-1 sp, sc in next 11 sts; join with sl st in first sc; ch 12. Finish off. Attach end of ch to purse handle as desired.

#28 TINY EVENING BAG

Designed by Laura Gebhardt

INSTRUCTIONS

Note: Work with one strand of each color held tog throughout.

Ch 6; join with a sl st to form a ring.

Rnd 1: Ch 1, 8 sc in ring; do not join; place marker to indicate beg of rnds.

Rnd 2: 2 sc in each sc: 16 sc.

Rnds 3, 5, 7 and 9: Sc in each sc.

Rnd 4: *Sc in next sc, 2 sc in next sc; rep from * around: 24 sc.

Rnd 6: *Sc in next 2 sc, 2 sc in next sc; rep from * around: 32 sc.

Rnd 8: *Sc in next 3 sc, 2 sc in next sc; rep from * around: 40 sc.

Rnd 10: *Sc in next 4 sc, 2 sc in next sc; rep from * around: 48 sc.

Rnds 11 through 30: Sc in each sc.

Rnd 31 (eyelet round): Ch 4 (counts as a dc and ch-1 sp); *skip next sc, dc in next sc, ch 1; rep from * around, join with sl st in 3rd ch of beg ch-4: 24 dc and 24 ch-1 sps.

Rnd 32: Ch 4; *skip next dc, (3 dc, ch 3, 3 dc) in next dc; ch 1, skip next dc, dc in next dc, ch 1; rep from * around, join in 3rd ch of beg ch-4. Finish off; weave in yarn ends.

SIZE
4" x 5" (without tassel)

MATERIALS
Size 10 bedspread weight cotton thread
100 yds blue
100 yds silver

Note: Photographed model made with J&P Coats® South Maid #480 Delft Blue and Metallic Knit-Cro-Sheen® #410S Silver/Silver

Stitch marker

Size C (2.75 mm) crochet hook (or size required for gauge)

GAUGE
24 sc and 24 sc rows = 4" with one strand of each color held tog

Drawstring (make 2)
With one strand of each color held together, ch 90; sl st in each ch. Finish off; weave in yarn ends. Thread drawstrings through eyelets, starting at opposite sides and working in opposite directions; and knot ends.

Tassel
Cut strands of each color 10" long. Following Tassel instructions on page 253, make tassel and sew to bottom of bag.

#29 BLACK AND WHITE

Designed by Anne Rubin for Judi & Co.

SIZE
5" diameter by 6 ¹/₂"

MATERIALS
Rayon cord
  144 yds black

Ribbon yarn
  100 yds black and white mix

Note: *Photographed model made with Judi & Co. Cordé black and Charmeuse black and white blend*

4" black tassel

60" black twisted cord for handle

Size 5 (3.75 mm) knitting needles
  (or size required for gauge)

GAUGE
18 sts = 4"

INSTRUCTIONS

Starting at top, with rayon cord, CO 72 sts.

Rows 1 and 2: Knit.

Row 3 (eyelet row): K1; *YO, K2tog; rep from * across, ending K1.

Row 4: Purl.

Row 5: Knit.

Row 6: Purl.

At end of Row 6, finish off rayon cord; change to ribbon yarn.

Rows 7 through 12: With ribbon yarn, knit.

At end of Row 12, finish off ribbon yarn, change to rayon cord.

Rows 13 and 14: With rayon cord, knit.

Rep Rows 7 through 14, five more times.

Bottom

Row 1: Continuing with rayon cord, *K6, K2tog; rep from * across.

Row 2 (and all even rows): Purl.

Row 3: *K5, K2tog; rep from * across.

Row 5: *K4, K2tog; rep from * across.

Row 7: *K3, K2tog; rep from * across.

Row 9: *K2, K2tog; rep from * across.

Row 11: *K1, K2tog; rep from * across

Row 13: *K2tog across. Finish off, leaving an 18" cord end for sewing.

Finishing

With right sides tog, sew side seam. Turn right side out. Cut twisted cord into 2 pieces. Thread one piece through every other hole of eyelets, thread other piece through unused holes. Knot ends to secure. Sew tassel in place as shown in photograph.

#30 TRAVEL BAG

Designed by Nancy Nehring

SIZE
10" long x 6" diameter

MATERIALS
Nylon crochet thread, size 2
  1200 yds mint green
  300 yds white

Note: *Photographed model made with Omega Nylon #2 Mint Green and White*

Size 7 (1.65 mm) steel crochet hook (or size required for gauge)

14" white sport zipper

Sharp sewing needle

Mint green sewing thread

Tapestry needle

Clear nail polish

Straight pins

Stitch marker

GAUGE
40 sc = 4"

17 sc and 17 dc = 4"

INSTRUCTIONS

Ends (make 2)

With mint green, ch 4; join with sl st to form a ring.

Note: *Work in a spiral without joining rem rnds.*

Rnd 1: Ch 1, 8 sc in ring: 8 sts. Do not join. Place stitch marker in last st and move to last st in each rnd.

Rnd 2: 2 sc in first st and in each st around: 16 sc.

Rnd 3: Sc in first st, 2 sc in next st; *sc in next st, 2 sc in next st; rep from * around: 24 sc.

Rnd 4: Sc in first 2 sts, 2 sc in next st; *sc in next 2 sts, 2 sc in next st; rep from * around: 32 sc.

Rnds 5 through 26: Rep Rnd 4 twenty two times more, increasing between increases numbers by one more in each rnd: 8 more sc in each rnd than in previous rnd. At end of Rnd 5: 40 sc. At end of Rnd 10: 80 sc. At end of Rnd 26: 208 sc. At end of Rnd 26, sl st in next 2 sts; finish off; weave in ends.

Body

With mint green, ch 86.

Row 1: Sc in 2nd ch from hook; *dc in next ch, sc in next ch; rep from * across: 85 sts; ch 3 (counts as dc on next row now and throughout), turn.

Row 2: Sc in first dc, dc in next sc; *sc in next dc, dc in next sc; rep from * across: 85 sts; ch 1, turn.

Row 3: Sc in first dc; *dc in next sc, sc in next dc; rep from * across: 85 sts; ch 3, turn.

Rep Rows 2 and 3 until piece measures 18 1/4" long. At end of last row, do not ch 3. Finish off; weave in ends.

Handle

Starting at center of handle, with mint green, ch 480.

Rnd 1 (right side): Sl st in back bar of 2nd ch from hook and in back bar of each ch across; making sure ch is not twisted, join with sl st in first sl st to form a ring.

Note: *Work remainder of handle in a spiral; do not join rnds.*

Rnds 2 and 3: Sc in next st and in each st around. At end of Rnd 3, finish off; weave in ends.

Rnd 4: Join white with sc in last sc made; sc in next st and in each st around.

Rnds 5 and 6: Sc in next st and in each st around. At end of Rnd 6, sl st in next 2 sts. Finish off; weave in ends.

Rnd 7: With right side facing, join mint green with sc in other side of any sl st on Rnd 1 (other side of handle center), sc in next st and in each st around.

Rnd 8: Sc in next st and in each st around. Finish off; weave in ends.

Rnds 9 through 11: Rep Rnds 4 through 6.

Assembly

With right side of one end and body together, pin outside edge of end to long edge of body, leaving a 1/2" gap so that edges of body do not meet. With mint green, sc end and body together, working one sc through each sc of outer edge of end and into body. Rep for other end. Turn bag right side out with seams on inside.

Position zipper in 1/2" gap along length of bag. Note: Zipper is longer than bag opening. Place top zipper stop at one end of opening. Allow other end of zipper to hang down toward center of end on inside of bag. Do not cut off end of zipper. Pin zipper in place. Open zipper. With sewing needle and sewing thread, sew zipper in place. Tack end of zipper to inside of bag.

Position handle as shown in photograph so that outer edges of handle are 2 1/2" in from ends of bag. Pin handle in place beg 4" down from zipper on each side of bag. Stitch handle in place with tapestry needle and white nylon thread. Seal each knot with clear nail polish on inside of bag.

On each loose portion of handle at top, fold over center 4" and sc edges together with white thread as shown in photograph.

#31 FELTED PINWHEEL

Designed by Diane Moyer

SIZE

Before felting: about 15" wide x
  17" high (plus 16" handles)

After felting: about 12" x 12"
  (plus 16" handles);

MATERIALS

Worsted weight 100% wool yarn
  7 oz purple

Faux Fur yarn
  3 1/2 oz violet
  3 1/2 oz green

*Note: Photographed model made
with Patons® Classic Merino Wool
#77330 That's Purple and Lion
Brand® Fun Fur #191 Violet and
#132 Olive Green*

1 yd of 1/4" plastic tubing
  (available in plumbing dept
  of home improvement store)

Sewing needle

Violet sewing thread

Size N (9 mm) crochet hook (or
  size required for gauge)

GAUGE

Before felting: 12 sc = 6";
  7 rows = 3" with 1 strand each
  type yarn held tog

INSTRUCTIONS

Strips (make 4)

Make 2 with 1 strand each of wool yarn and violet fur yarn held tog.

Make 2 with 1 strand each of wool yarn and green fur yarn held tog.

With appropriate yarns held tog, ch 13.

Row 1: Sc in 2nd ch from hook and in each ch across: 12 sc; ch 1, turn.

Row 2: Sc in first sc and in each sc across: 12 sc; ch 1, turn.

Rep Row 2 until strip measures 18". At end of last row, do not ch 1. Finish off; weave in ends.

Handles (make two)

With 2 strands of wool yarn held together, ch 6, leaving 12" tail at beg.

Row 1: Sc in 2nd ch from hook and in each ch across: 5 sc; ch 1, turn.

Row 2: Sc in first sc and in each sc across: 5 sc; ch 1, turn.

Repeat Row 2 until piece measures 16". At end of last row, do not ch 1. Finish off, leaving 12" tail.

Whip long edges of each handle together. Cut tubing 14" long. Insert tubing into handle and tack handle closed at ends.

Assembling Purse

Mark one side of each strip as right side of fabric. Always sew pieces together with right sides facing. Measure up 6" on left-hand edge of one violet strip and mark this point. Sew 6" end of one green strip to violet strip between bottom and marked point, forming "L" shape. Repeat with second violet and green strips. Measure up 6" on left-hand edge of each green strip and mark this point. Sew 6" bottom end of each violet strip to other green strip between bottom and marked point, forming pinwheel shape (see Diagram).

Note: *All bottom left-hand corners should meet in middle. This becomes bottom of purse.*

Measure down 6" on right-hand edge of each strip and mark this point. Sew unsewn 12" on left-hand edge of each strip to right-hand edge of each adjacent strip between bottom and marked point. Sew ends of handles to top points of purse.

Felting Purse

Following instructions on page 252, felt purse.

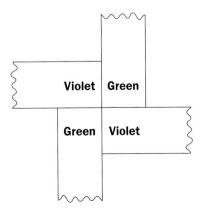

81

#32 STRING OF PEARLS

Designed by Mickie Akins for Coats & Clark

SIZE
7 1/4" wide x 4" high plus 18" or 29" strap

MATERIALS
Nylon yarn
   150 yds blue

Note: Photographed model made with J&P Coats® Crochet Nylon #49 Blue

Size E (3.5 mm) crochet hook (or size required for gauge)

2 1/4 yds strung 3 mm pearls

7" blue zipper

1/4 yd blue lining fabric (optional)

Needle and sewing thread to match lining fabric (optional)

GAUGE
(Sc, dc) 8 times = 3 3/4"; 14 rows in patt (sc, dc) = 4"

INSTRUCTIONS

Side (make 2)
Starting at bottom, ch 31.

Row 1 (wrong side): Working in back bar of chs, sc in 2nd ch from hook, dc in next ch; *sc in next ch, dc in next ch; rep from * across: 15 sc and 15 dc; ch 1, turn.

Row 2 (right side): Sc in first dc, dc in next sc; *sc in next dc, dc in next sc; rep from * across: 15 sc and 15 dc; ch 1, turn.

Rows 3 through 14: Rep Row 2 twelve times more. At end of Row 14, do not ch 1. Finish off; weave in ends.

Trim (make 2)
Ch 31.

Rows 1 and 2: Rep Rows 1 and 2 of Side. At end of Row 2, do not ch 1. Finish off; weave in ends.

Fringe
Cut 60 strands, each 8 pearls long, from strung pearls. With sewing needle and thread, sew 30 pearl strands evenly spaced across bottom of Row 1 on wrong side of each Trim, stitching between first and second pearls so 7 pearls dangle at bottom of Trim, skipping 2 sts at beg and end of Row 1. With tapestry needle and yarn, sew one Trim to each Side 1/2" down from top edge of Side along long edges of Trim with pearls dangling at bottom of Trim.

Gusset
Ch 1.

Row 1 (wrong side): (Sc, dc) in 2nd ch from hook: 1 sc and 1 dc; ch 1, turn.

Row 2 (right side): Sc in dc, dc in sc: 1 sc and 1 dc; ch 1, turn.

Row 3: (Sc, dc) in each st across: 2 sc and 2 dc; ch 1, turn.

Row 4: Sc in first dc, (dc, sc) in each of next 2 sts, dc in last sc: 3 sc and 3 dc.

Row 5: Sc in first dc, dc in next sc, (sc, dc) in each of next 2 sts, sc in next st, dc in last sc: 4 sc and 4 dc; ch 1, turn.

Row 6: (Sc in each dc, dc in each sc) across; ch 1, turn.

Rows 7 through 44: Rep Row 6 thirty-eight times more.

Row 45: Sc in first dc, dc in next sc, sc dec in next 2 sts, dc dec in next 2 sts, sc in next dc, dc in last sc; 3 sc and 3 dc; ch 1, turn.

Row 46: Rep Row 6.

Row 47: Sc in first dc, dc dec in next 2 sts, sc dec in next 2 sts, dc in last sc: 2 sc and 2 dc; ch 1, turn.

Row 48: Rep Row 6.

Row 49: Sc dec in first 2 sts, dc dec in last 2 sts: 1 sc and 1 dc; ch 1, turn.

Row 50: Sc dec in first 2 sts: 1 sc. Finish off; weave in ends.

Lining (optional)

Using crochet pieces as patterns and adding 1/2" extra on all edges for seams, cut 2 Side pieces and 1 Gusset piece from lining fabric.

Joining

With wrong sides together, matching sts on sides and bottom of one Side to edges of rows on Gusset, working through both layers (and Trim where joined), join with sc in top left corner of Side, sc Side and Gusset together across sides and bottom to top right corner of Side. Finish off; weave in ends. Rep with other Side and other edges of rows on Gusset. With right side of zipper facing wrong side of top edges of Sides, sew long edges of zipper in place along Sides; fold each end of zipper 1/4" to wrong side and sew to Gusset.

Lining Continued (optional)

With right sides of lining together, sew lining pieces together in same manner as crochet Sides and Gusset with 1/2" seam. Press top edges of lining 1/2" to wrong side. With wrong side of lining facing outward, insert lining into assembled Sides and Gusset; sew top edges of lining to wrong side of zipper along previous zipper seam on Sides and Gusset.

Strap

Ch 115 for shoulder strap or 71 for arm strap.

Row 1: Working in back bar of chs, sc in 2nd ch from hook, dc in next ch; *sc in next ch, dc in next ch; rep from * across: 57 sc and 57 dc (or 35 sc and 35 dc); ch 1, turn.

Rows 2 through 4: (Sc in each dc, dc in each sc) across; ch 1, turn. At end of Row 4, do not ch 1. Finish off; weave in ends.

Sew edges of rows on Strap to top edges of Gusset.

#33 TWO COLOR ROSE

Designed by Nancy Brown

SIZE
8" diameter plus 32" shoulder strap

MATERIALS
Chunky wool yarn
   3 ¹/₂ oz lavender
   3 ¹/₂ oz pink

Note: *Photographed model made with Mauch Chunky by Kraemer Yarns #Y1029 Juju Fruit and #Y1024 Cotton Candy*

Size K (6.5 mm) crochet hook
   (or size required for gauge)

GAUGE
Rnds 1 through 4 = 3 ¹/₄"

INSTRUCTIONS

Front

Starting at center of flower with pink, ch 2.

Rnd 1 (right side): Work 5 sc in 2nd ch from hook: 5 sc. Do not join.

Rnd 2: (Sl st, ch 1, 5 dc, ch 1, sl st) in next sc and in each sc around: 5 petals.

Rnd 3: Working behind petals on Rnd 2 and in sc on Rnd 1; *sc between 2nd and 3rd dc of next petal, ch 3; rep from * 4 times more; sl st in beg sc: 5 sc and 5 ch-3 sps.

Rnd 4: (Sl st, ch 1, 7 dc, ch 1, sl st) in next ch-3 sp and in each ch-3 sp around: 5 petals.

Rnd 5: Working behind petals on Rnd 4 and in ch-3 sps on Rnd 3; *sc between 3rd and 4th dc of next petal, ch 4; rep from * 4 times more; sl st in beg sc: 5 sc and 5 ch-4 sps.

Rnd 6: (Sl st, ch 1, 9 dc, ch 1, sl st) in next ch-4 sp and in each ch-4 sp around: 5 petals.

Rnd 7: Working behind petals on Rnd 6 and in ch-4 sps on Rnd 5; *sc between 1st and 2nd dc of next petal, ch 3, sc between 4th and 5th dc of same petal, ch 3, sc between 8th and 9th dc of same petal, ch 3; rep from * 4 times more; sc in beg sc: 15 sc and 15 ch-3 sps.

Rnd 8: 3 hdc in next ch-3 sp and in each ch-3 sp around: 45 hdc. Do not join.

Rnd 9: *2 hdc in next st, hdc in next 8 sts; rep from * 4 times more: 50 hdc.

Rnd 10: *2 hdc in next st, hdc in next 9 sts; rep from * 4 times more: 55 hdc.

Rnd 11: *2 hdc in next st, hdc in next 10 sts; rep from * 4 times more: 60 hdc. Do not finish off.

Top Opening

Sl st in next st, working from left to right; *ch 1, skip next st on right, sc in next st on right; rep from * 6 times more; ch 1, skip next st on right, sl st in next st on right. Finish off; weave in ends.

Back

Work same as Front with lavender.

Finishing

Place Front and Back with wrong sides together and top openings matching. With 1 strand each of lavender and pink, working from left to right through both thicknesses, join with sl st in st on right of top opening; *ch 1, skip next st on right, sc in next st on right; rep from * around, ending with sl st in st on left of top opening. Do not finish off.

Shoulder Strap

*Ch 2, sc in 2nd ch from hook; rep from * until strap measures about 32" or to desired length. Join with sl st in same st as joining on right of top opening. Finish off; weave in ends.

Flower Centers

With 2 strands of lavender, ch 4. Finish off. Tie ends together to form a ch-4 knot. Sew knot to center of lavender flower. Rep with pink, sewing knot to center of pink flower.

#34 STRIPES ON PARADE

Designed by Jodi Lewanda

SIZE
9 1/2" x 13 1/2"

MATERIALS
Worsted weight 100% wool yarn
  10 1/2 oz purple (A)
  3 1/2 oz lavender (B)
  3 1/2 oz gold (C)
  3 1/2 oz green (D)
  Seven 3/4" diameter shank buttons

Note: *Photographed model made with Tahki Donegal Tweed #806 Dark Purple (A), #841 Dark Lavender (B), #897 Gold (C) and #803 Grass Green (D); Zecca buttons #642B*

Size 11 (8 mm) straight knitting needles
  (or size required for gauge)

24" Size 11 circular knitting needle

Sharp pointed scissors or craft knife

GAUGE BEFORE FELTING
23 sts = 8" with 2 strands of yarn
  held tog in stock st (Knit 1 row,
  purl 1 row)

INSTRUCTIONS

Note: *Use 2 strands of yarn held tog throughout.*

Front

With 2 strands of color A, CO 42 sts.

Work in stock st (knit 1 row, purl 1 row) for 48 rows in following stripe pattern:

*Rows 1 through 4: Color A

Rows 5 through 8: Color B

Rows 9 through 12: Color C

Rows 13 through 16: Color D

Rep from * for stripe pattern.

Row 49: With Color A, knit.

Rows 50 through 52: With color A, work K1, P1 rib.

BO in rib.

Back

Work same as Front through Row 48.

Rows 49 through 52: With color A, work even in stock st.

Row 53: K2tog, K38, K2tog: 40 sts.

Row 54: P2tog, P36, P2tog: 38 sts.

Rows 55 through 62: Work even in stock st.

Shape Flap

Row 63: K2tog, knit to last 2 stitches, K2tog: 36 sts.

Row 64: P2tog, purl to last 2 stitches, P2tog: 34 sts.

Rep Rows 63 and 64 until 4 sts rem.

Work one row even. BO.

Strap

With 2 strands of A and circular needle, CO 260 sts. Knit 9 rows. BO.

Gusset

Center strap on Front and sew along sides and bottom of piece, forming gusset. Sew opposite edge of strap to Back in same manner, leaving Flap and top of Front open.

Felting

Felt bag following Felting Instructions on page 252.

Buttons and Buttonholes

On Front, sew one button centered and 3" down from top edge. With sharp, pointed scissors, cut a vertical slit centered on front flap 1" above point, and wide enough for button to slip through.

With front of bag facing, sew a button to the right side strap, 3" from top of bag. Sew another button 2" from loose end of the same strap. Sew 4 additional buttons, evenly spaced between the first two.

On the left side strap, carefully cut a vertical slit 3" from top of bag, then five other slits to line up with buttons on the right side strap, sized so that buttons will slip through.

#35 ALL THAT JAZZ

Designed by Patons Design Staff

SIZE
11 1/2" x 9 1/2" plus handles

MATERIALS
Sport weight cotton yarn
   3 1/2 oz blue

Eyelash yarn
   5 1/4 oz variegated

Note: *Photographed model made with Patons® Grace #60104 Azure and Patons® Cha Cha #02006 Jazz*

Size H (5 mm) crochet hook
   (or size required for gauge)

1 pair of 6" round Bamboo
   handles

Stitch markers

GAUGE
12 dc and 7 dc rows = 4"
   with one strand of each
   yarn held tog

INSTRUCTIONS

Body

Note: *Body of bag is worked from wrong side throughout.*

With 1 strand of each yarn held tog, ch 22.

Rnd 1: Sc in 2nd ch from hook, sc in each ch across to last ch, 5 sc in last ch; working in rem lps on opposite side of foundation ch: sc in next 19 chs, 4 sc in next ch: 48 sc; join with sl st in first sc.

Rnd 2: Ch 1, 2 sc in same sc as joining, sc in next 19 sc, 2 sc in each of next 5 sc, sc in next 19 sc, 2 sc in each of last 4 sc: 58 sc; join as before.

Rnd 3: Ch 1, 2 sc in same sc as joining, sc in next 20 sc, (2 sc in next sc, sc in next sc) 5 times, sc in next 19 sc, (2 sc in next sc, sc in next sc) 4 times: 68 sc; join.

Rnd 4: Ch 3 (counts as dc), dc in next sc and in each sc around: 68 dc; join with sl st in 3rd ch of beg ch-3.

Rep Rnd 4 until piece measures 9". At end of last rnd, finish off; weave in ends. Turn bag right side out if necessary.

Handle Extensions

With bag lying flat, place markers in last rnd 2" in from sides of bag on Front and Back to mark position for handle extensions. With right side of Front facing, join 1 strand of each yarn held tog with sl st in marked st on right.

Row 1: Ch 3 (counts as dc), dc in next dc and in each dc across to last marker; turn, leaving rem sts unworked.

Row 2: Ch 3, dc in next dc and in each dc across.

Rows 3 through 6: Rep Row 2 four times more. At end of last row, do not ch 3. Finish off; weave in ends.

With right side of Back facing, join 1 strand of each yarn held tog with sl st in marked st on right. Rep Rows 1 through 6 for Back handle extension.

Finishing

Wrap handle extensions around handles to inside of bag and sew in position.

#36 SOUTHWEST AMULET BAG

Designed by Susan Lowman

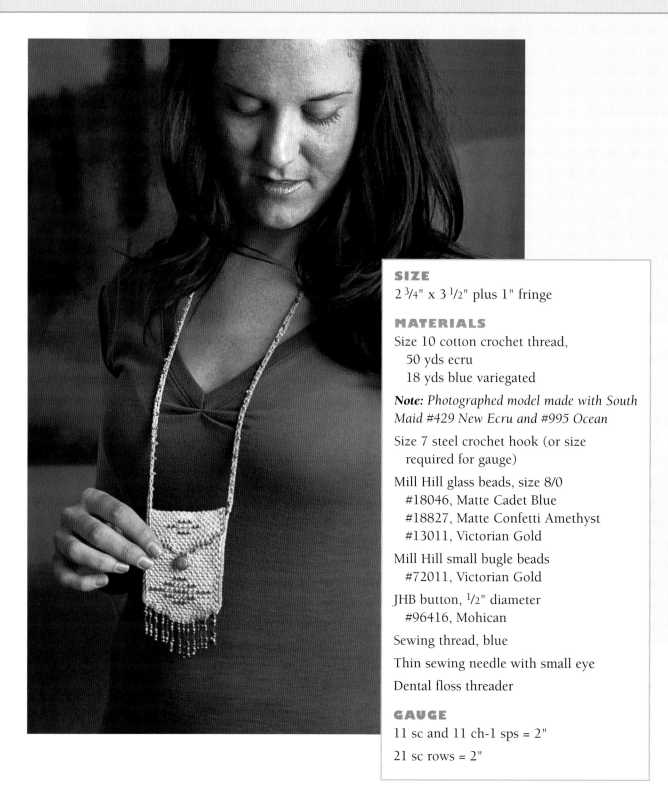

SIZE

2 ³/₄" x 3 ¹/₂" plus 1" fringe

MATERIALS

Size 10 cotton crochet thread,
　50 yds ecru
　18 yds blue variegated

Note: Photographed model made with South Maid #429 New Ecru and #995 Ocean

Size 7 steel crochet hook (or size
　required for gauge)

Mill Hill glass beads, size 8/0
　#18046, Matte Cadet Blue
　#18827, Matte Confetti Amethyst
　#13011, Victorian Gold

Mill Hill small bugle beads
　#72011, Victorian Gold

JHB button, ¹/₂" diameter
　#96416, Mohican

Sewing thread, blue

Thin sewing needle with small eye

Dental floss threader

GAUGE

11 sc and 11 ch-1 sps = 2"

21 sc rows = 2"

INSTRUCTIONS

Front

Using dental floss threader, string glass beads on ecru thread in this order: 5 amethyst, 3 gold, 5 amethyst, 2 gold, 3 blue, 2 gold, 5 amethyst, 3 gold, 5 amethyst.

Using ecru with strung beads, ch 30.

Row 1 (wrong side): Sc in 2nd ch from hook; (ch 1, skip next ch, sc in next ch) 14 times: 15 sc and 14 ch-1 sps; ch 1, turn.

Row 2 (right side): Sc in first sc and in next ch-1 sp; (ch 1, skip next sc, sc in next ch-1 sp) 13 times, sc in last sc: 16 sc and 13 ch-1 sps; ch 1, turn.

Row 3: Sc in first sc; (ch 1, skip next sc, sc in next ch-1 sp) 13 times, ch 1, skip next sc, sc in last sc: 15 sc and 14 ch-1 sps; ch 1, turn.

Rows 4 through 19: Rep Rows 2 and 3 eight times more.

Row 20: Rep Row 2.

Row 21: Sc in first sc; (ch 1, skip next sc, sc in next ch-1 sp) 5 times; (ch 1, skip next sc, BBsc in next ch-1 sp) 3 times; (ch 1, skip next sc, sc in next ch-1 sp) 5 times; ch 1, skip next sc, sc in last sc: 12 sc, 3 BBsc and 14 ch-1 sps; ch 1, turn.

Row 22: Rep Row 2.

Row 23: Sc in first sc; (ch 1, skip next sc, sc in next ch-1 sp) 3 times; (ch 1, skip next sc, BBsc in next ch-1 sp) 7 times; (ch 1, skip next sc, sc in next ch-1 sp) 3 times; ch 1, skip next sc, sc in last sc: 8 sc, 7 BBsc and 14 ch-1 sps; ch 1, turn.

Row 24: Rep Row 2.

Row 25: Sc in first sc; (ch 1, skip next sc, BBsc in next ch-1 sp) 13 times; ch 1, skip next sc, sc in last sc: 2 sc, 13 BBsc and 14 ch-1 sps; ch 1, turn.

Row 26: Rep Row 2.

Row 27: Rep Row 23.

Row 28: Rep Row 2.

Row 29: Rep Row 21.

Row 30: Rep Row 2.

Row 31: Sl st in first 2 sc, sl st in next ch-1 sp and in next sc, ch 1, sc in next ch-1 sp, (ch 1, skip next sc, sc in next ch-1 sp) 10 times: 11 sc and 10 ch-1 sps; ch 1, turn, leaving last 4 sts unworked.

Row 32: Sc in first sc and in next ch-1 sp, (ch 1, skip next sc, sc in next ch-1 sp) 9 times, sc in last sc: 12 sc and 9 ch-1 sps; ch 1, turn.

Row 33: Sl st in first 2 sc, (sl st in next ch-1 sp and in next sc) 2 times, ch 1, sc in next ch-1 sp, (ch 1, skip next sc, sc in next ch-1 sp) 4 times: 5 sc and 4 ch-1 sps; ch 1, turn, leaving last 6 sts unworked.

Instructions continue on next page. →

Row 34: Sc in first sc and in next ch-1 sp, (ch 1, skip next sc, sc in next ch-1 sp) 3 times, sc in last sc: 6 sc and 3 ch-1 sps. Finish off; weave in ends.

Back

With ecru, ch 30. Note: Row 1 on Back is right side and Row 2 is wrong side.

Rows 1 through 19: Rep Rows 1 through 19 of Front.

Rows 20 through 29: Rep Rows 2 and 3 of Front five times more.

Rows 30 through 34: Rep Rows 30 through 34 of Front.

Flap

Using dental floss threader, string glass beads on ecru thread in this order: 5 blue, 3 gold, 5 blue.

Row 1: With right side of Back facing, join ecru with strung beads with sc in free lp of first ch on Row 1, sc in next ch-1 sp, (ch 1, skip next ch, sc in next ch-1 sp) 13 times, sc in free lp of next ch: 16 sc and 13 ch-1 sps; ch 1, turn.

Rows 2 through 5: Rep Rows 3 and 2 of Front 2 times more.

Rows 6 through 9: Rep Rows 21 through 24 of Front.

Rows 10 through 15: Rep Rows 29 through 34 of Front.

Edging and Necklace

String 60 glass beads onto blue variegated in this order: (1 purple, 1 yellow, 1 blue) 20 times.

With wrong sides of Front and Back tog, with Front facing and working through Front and Back tog, join blue variegated with strung beads with sc in edge of last sc on Row 1 of Front (top left-hand corner of Front). Sc in edge of next row, work (ch 1, skip next row or st, sc in edge of next row or in next ch-1 sp) around, ending with sc in edge of last 2 rows at top right-hand corner of Front.

Ch 241 for neck chain; making sure ch is not twisted, sc in edge of Row 1 of Flap (top left-hand corner), sc in edge of next row, work (ch 1, skip next row or st, sc in edge of next row or in next ch-1 sp) around to center of Row 15, working (sc, ch 9, sl st in top of last sc) at center of Row 15, work (ch 1, skip next row or st, sc in edge of next row or in next ch-1 sp) around, ending with sc in edge of last 2 rows at top right-hand corner of Flap, sc in first ch of ch-241, (ch 1, skip next ch, BBsc in next ch, ch 1, skip next ch, sc in next ch) 60 times, join with sl st in first sc. Finish off; weave in ends.

Beaded Fringe

With thin needle and sewing thread, sew fringes of glass beads and bugle beads to bottom edges of Rows 30, 32 and 34 as shown in photograph or as desired.

Finishing

Using ecru crochet thread, sew button to Front at center of Row 16.

#37 MY TEDDY BEAR

Designed by Kathleen Stuart

SIZE
8 ¹/₂" diameter

MATERIALS
Super bulky weight chenille
   100 yds lt brown
   10 yds off-white

Note: *Photographed model made with Lion Brand® Chenille Thick & Quick® #124 Khaki and #98 Antique White*

2 yds black worsted weight yarn
   (for embroidered face)

7" lt brown zipper

Size K (6.5 mm) crochet hook
   (or size required for gauge)

Tapestry needle

Stitch markers

GAUGE
Rnds 1 through 4 = 3" diameter

STITCH GUIDE
To change color: Work st until 2 lps rem on hook, drop old color, pick up new color and draw through both lps on hook, cut dropped color.

Sc decrease (sc dec): (Insert hook in next st and draw up a lp) twice, YO and draw through all 3 lps on hook: sc dec made.

Instructions continue on next page. →

INSTRUCTIONS

Note: Do not join rnds, unless otherwise stated. Mark first st of each rnd.

Purse

Starting at center of muzzle on front, with off-white, ch 2.

Rnd 1 (right side): 6 sc in 2nd ch from hook: 6 sc.

Rnd 2: 2 sc in each st around: 12 sc.

Rnd 3: *Sc in next st, 2 sc in next st; rep from * around: 18 sc.

Rnd 4: Sc in each st around, changing to lt brown in last sc: 18 sc.

Rnd 5: Working in back lps only; *sc in next 2 sts, 2 sc in next st; rep from * around: 24 sc.

Rnd 6: *Sc in next 3 sts, 2 sc in next st; rep from * around: 30 sc.

Rnd 7: *Sc in next 4 sts, 2 sc in next st; rep from * around: 36 sc.

Rnd 8: *Sc in next 5 sts, 2 sc in next st; rep from * around: 42 sc.

Rnd 9: *Sc in next 6 sts, 2 sc in next st; rep from * around: 48 sc.

Rnds 10 and 11: Sc in each st around: 48 sc.

Rnd 12: Sc in next 12 sts, ch 16, skip next 16 sts (zipper opening made at top of Purse), sc in last 20 sts: 32 sc and 16 chs.

Rnd 13: Sc in next 12 sts, sc in next 16 chs, sc in last 20 sts: 48 sc.

Rnd 14: Sc in each st around: 48 sc.

Rnd 15: *Sc in next 6 sts, sc dec in next 2 sts; rep from * around: 42 sc.

Rnd 16: *Sc in next 5 sts, sc dec in next 2 sts; rep from * around: 36 sc.

Sew right side of zipper to wrong side of zipper opening on Rnd 12.

Rnd 17: *Sc in next 4 sts, sc dec in next 2 sts; rep from * around: 30 sc.

Rnd 18: *Sc in next 3 sts, sc dec in next 2 sts; rep from * around: 24 sc.

Rnd 19: *Sc in next 2 sts, sc dec in next 2 sts; rep from * around: 18 sc.

Rnd 20: *Sc in next st, sc dec in next 2 sts; rep from * around: 12 sc.

Rnd 21: *Sc dec in next 2 sts; rep from * around: 6 sc. Finish off. Weave end through 6 sc on Rnd 21 and pull tight to close hole. Weave in ends.

Ears (make 2)

With lt. brown, ch 2.

Rnds 1 through 3: Rep Rnds 1 through 3 on Purse.

Rnd 4: Sc in each st around: 18 sc. Finish off, leaving a 10" end for sewing.

Flatten ears. Sew Rnd 4 of Ears to top of Purse on Rnds 9 and 10 with about 2 ½" between ears and zipper behind ears.

Strap

With lt. brown, ch 2, sc in first ch; *insert hook under upper lp at left side of sc just made, draw up a lp, YO and draw through both lps; rep from * until strap measures about 32" or desired length. Sew ends of Strap to Rnd 12 of Purse at ends of zipper opening.

Finishing

With black yarn and tapestry needle, embroider nose with satin stitch and mouth with straight stitch on muzzle as shown in photograph. Embroider eyes with satin stitch above muzzle between Rnds 5 and 6 as shown in photograph.

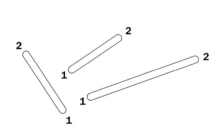

Come up at 1 and down at 2.
Straight Stitch

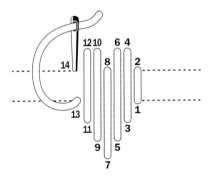

Satin Stitch

#38 LADYBUG, LADYBUG

Designed By Glenda Winkleman for Coats & Clark

SIZE
9" diameter x 9" high

MATERIALS
Nylon yarn
  300 yds red
  150 yds black

Note: *Photographed model made with J&P Coats® Crochet Nylon #6 Red and #19 Black*

Size G (4 mm) crochet hook
  (or size required for gauge)

7 Ladybug buttons

GAUGE
4 sc and 4 sc rows = 1"

INSTRUCTIONS

Handbag
Starting at bottom with Black, ch 4.

Rnd 1 (right side): 10 dc in 4th ch from hook (3 skipped chs count as dc): 11 dc; join with sl st in 3rd ch of beg ch-3.

Rnd 2: Ch 3 (counts as first dc now and throughout), dc in same ch as joining, 2 dc in next dc and in each dc around: 22 dc; join as before.

Rnd 3: Rep Rnd 2: 44 dc.

Rnd 4: Ch 3, dc in next dc; *2 dc in next dc, dc in next 2 dc; rep from * around: 58 dc; join.

Rnd 5: Ch 3, dc in next 2 dc, 2 dc in next dc; *dc in next 3 dc, 2 dc in next dc; rep from * around to last 2 dc; dc in last 2 dc: 72 dc; join.

Rnd 6: Ch 3, dc in next 3 dc, 2 dc in next dc; *dc in next 4 dc, 2 dc in next dc; rep from * around to last 2 dc; dc in last 2 dc: 86 dc; join.

Rnd 7: Ch 3, dc in next 6 dc, 2 dc in next dc; *dc in next 7 dc, 2 dc in next dc; rep from * around to last 6 dc; dc in last 6 dc: 96 dc; join.

Rnd 8: Ch 1, sc in same ch as joining, sc in next dc and in each dc around: 96 sc; join with sl st in first sc.

Rnd 9: Ch 1, sc in same sc as joining, sc in next sc and in each sc around; join with sl st in first sc.

Rnd 10: Rep Rnd 9, changing to Red in joining sl st. Finish off Black; weave in ends.

Rnds 11 through 22: With Red, rep Rnd 9 twelve times more.

Rnd 23: Ch 1, sc in same sc as joining, sc in next 4 sc; *sc dec in next 2 sc, sc in next 5 sc; rep from * around: 83 sc; join with sl st in first sc.

Rnds 24 through 29: Rep Rnd 9 six times more. At end of Rnd 29, change to Black in joining sl st. Finish off Red; weave in ends.

Rnds 30 through 37: With Black, rep Rnd 9 eight times more. At end of Rnd 37, change to Red in joining sl st. Finish off Black; weave in ends.

Rnds 38 through 44: With Red, rep Rnd 9 seven times more.

Rnd 45: Ch 1, sc in same sc as joining; *ch 1, skip next sc, sc in next sc; rep from * around; ch 1: 42 sc and 42 ch-1 sps; join with sl st in first sc, changing to Black. Finish off Red; weave in ends.

Rnd 46: With Black, ch 1, sc in same sc as joining, sc in each ch-1 sp and in each sc around: 84 sc; join with sl st in first sc. Finish off; weave in ends.

Strap

With Red, ch 5.

Row 1 (right side): Sc in 2nd ch from hook and in each ch across: 4 sc; ch 1, turn.

Rows 2 through 115: Sc in each sc across: 4 sc; ch 1, turn. At end of Row 115, do not ch 1. Finish off; weave in ends.

Strap Border

Rnd 1: With right side of Strap facing, join Black with sc in beg edge of Row 1, sc in edge of each row across same edge, sc in each sc on Row 115, sc in edge of each row on other edge of Strap, sc in each foundation ch; join with sl st in first sc. Finish off; weave in ends. With right side of strap facing outward, sew 1 1/2" at ends of strap to inside of Rows 39 through 44 of handbag at opposite sides as shown in photograph.

Drawstring

With Black, ch 100. Finish off. Weave drawstring in and out of ch-1 sps on Rnd 45, starting at center of handbag and weaving around to beg. Tie one ladybug button to each end of drawstring and weave in ends. Sew remaining ladybug buttons evenly spaced around handbag between Rnds 30 and 37.

#39 FELTED FUN

Designed by Donna Druchunas

SIZE
7" x 9" after felting

MATERIALS
Bulky weight wool yarn
   400 yds taupe
   50 yds black

Faux fur yarn
   50 yds taupe

Note: *Photographed model made with Brown Sheep Lamb's Pride Bulky #M08 Wild Oak and #M05 Onyx, and South West Trading Company Fur Real Mink*

4 stitch markers

16" size 15 (10 mm) circular knitting
   needle (or size required for gauge)

2 size 15 double point knitting needles

GAUGE BEFORE FELTING
8 sts = 4" in stock st (knit every row
   on circular needles)

INSTRUCTIONS

Sides

With circular needle and taupe wool yarn, CO 60 sts; join, being careful not to twist sts. Working in rnds, knit until piece measures 12".

Bottom

Rnd 1: *K15, place marker; rep from * 3 times more.

Rnd 2: (K2tog; knit to 2 sts before next marker, SSK, sl marker) 4 times.

Rep Rnd 2 until 12 sts rem. Cut yarn. Thread yarn end into a tapestry needle and draw through rem sts; pull up tightly and secure. Weave in yarn ends.

I-Cord Strap

With double-point needles and black wool and black faux fur yarn held tog, CO 3 sts.

Work I-Cord (see page 253) until strap measures 48". BO, weave in ends.

Felting

Place bag and strap in a zippered pillow case and felt according to instructions on Page 252. When felting is completed, place a small bowl or plate in bottom of bag to stretch flat. Following Fig, fold bag top like a paper lunch bag, and use 2 double point needles to make eyelet holes for the strap. Pierce all folded layers about 1" from outside edge of folds, and about $1/2$" down from top edge. If necessary, use an ice pick or craft knife to start the holes.

Let piece sit for about 8 hours to dry; then remove plate and needles and spread top open so that the inside will dry.

When completely dry, weave strap through eyelets as shown and sew strap ends tog inside bag.

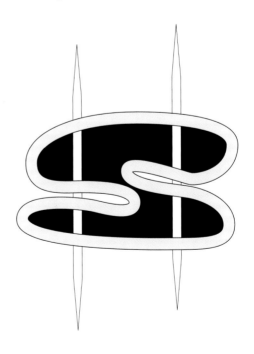

#40 LITTLE BLACK BAG

Designed by Carol Gleiberman for Judi & Co.

SIZE
6" x 6"

MATERIALS
Rayon cord
   288 yds black

Note: Photographed model made with Judi & Co. Rayon Cordé, Black

3/4" magnetic snap

5" plastic purse handles

Size F (3.75 mm) crochet hook
   (or size required for gauge)

GAUGE
14 sc = 3"

INSTRUCTIONS

Front

Starting at bottom, ch 29.

Row 1: Sc in 2nd ch from hook and in each rem ch: 28 sc; ch 1, turn.

Row 2: (Sc, dc) in first sc, * skip 2 sts; (sc, dc) in next sc; rep from * across; ch 1, turn.

Row 3: (Sc, dc) in each sc across; ch 1, turn.

Rep Row 2 until piece measures 6". Finish off; weave in ends.

Back

Make same as Front.

Side (make 2)

Ch 17.

Row 1: Sc in 2nd ch from hook and in each rem ch: 16 sc; ch 1, turn.

Row 2: (Sc, dc) in first st, * skip 2 sts; (sc, dc) in next sc; rep from * across; ch 1, turn.

Row 3: (Sc, dc) in each sc across; ch 1, turn.

Rep Row 3 until piece measures 3". Finish off; weave in ends.

Bottom

Ch 29.

Row 1: Sc in 2nd ch from hook and in each rem ch: 28 sc; ch 1, turn.

Row 2: Sc in each sc, ch 1, turn.

Rep Row 2 until piece measures 3". Finish off; weave in ends.

Finishing
Assembly

Sew front and back to side pieces; sew bottom to front, back and sides.

Base for Magnet Closure
(make 2)

Ch 3; join with sl st to form a ring.

Rnd 1: Ch 1, 6 sc in ring; join with sl st in beg sc.

Rnd 2: Ch 1, 2 sc in each sc: 12 sc; finish off, leaving long cord end for sewing to bag.

Attach one piece of closure to each base, pushing prongs through; bend with pliers to secure. Sew bases opposite each other on inside of bag, centered 1 3/4" below top of bag, one on front and one on back piece.

Sew handle to inside of bag.

Pinch each side in toward center at halfway point of side, making a pleat.

#4 BLACK TIE BUTTERCUPS

Designed by Vashti Braha

SIZE
About 8 1/2" wide x 8 1/2" high plus handles

MATERIALS
Sport weight yarn
  7 1/2 oz yellow

Note: *Photographed model made with Lion Brand® Microspun #158 Buttercup*

Size G (4 mm) crochet hook (or size required for gauge)

1 pair arched and curved black purse handles, 5 3/8" x 5 1/4" by Prym-Dritz

4" x 36" strip of black velvet fabric (or 1 yard of 2" black velvet ribbon)

4 heatproof stitch markers

Yellow fabric, two 10" x 17" pieces (optional)

9" x 16" piece of low-temp iron-on adhesive, plus scraps for hemming (optional)

Fabric glue or hot glue gun (optional)

Sewing needle (optional)

Yellow thread (optional)

GAUGE
10 hdc and 9 hdc rows = 3"

INSTRUCTIONS

Starting at top edge of front, ch 31 loosely.

Row 1 (wrong side): Sc in 2nd ch from hook and in each rem ch: 30 sc; ch 2, turn.

Row 2 (right side): Beg in first st; *RSB, hdc in next 3 sts; rep from * across: 5 RSB and 15 hdc; ch 2, turn.

Row 3: Beg in first st; *WSB in 3 hdc on previous row; working in RSB on previous row, hdc in last sc worked on top petal of

Right Side Buttercup (RSB): Hdc in next st, ch 1, skip next st, hdc in next st; working around 4 sides of ch sp just made; rotate piece 1/4 turn clockwise and work (ch 1, sc, ch 3, dc, ch 3, sc) around post of hdc just worked (petal made); rotate piece 1/4 turn clockwise and work petal in skipped st; rotate piece 1/4 turn clockwise and work petal around post of first of 2 hdc just worked; rotate piece 1/4 turn clockwise and work petal in ch-1 sp between 2 hdc just worked: RSB with 4 petals made.

Wrong Side Buttercup (WSB): Working over 3 hdc on previous row, hdc in next hdc, ch 1, skip next st, hdc in next hdc, turn to right side; working around 4 sides of ch sp just made; (ch 1, sc, ch 3, dc, ch 3, sc) in ch-1 sp between 2 hdc just worked (petal made); rotate piece 1/4 turn clockwise and work petal around post of first of 2 hdc just worked;

rotate piece 1/4 turn clockwise and work petal in skipped st; rotate piece 1/4 turn clockwise and work petal around post of hdc just worked; turn to wrong side and continue working across row: WSB with 4 petals made.

Front Post Single Crochet (FPsc): Insert hook from front to back under top 2 lps of specified sc, insert hook from back to front under top 2 lps of next sc, draw up a lp, YO and draw through both lps on hook: FPsc made.

Front Post Double Crochet (FPdc): YO, insert hook from front to back to front around post of specified st and draw up a lp, (YO and draw through 2 lps on hook) twice: FPdc made.

Back Post Double Crochet (BPdc): YO, insert hook from back to front to back around post of specified st and draw up a lp, (YO and draw through 2 lps on hook) twice: BPdc made.

Note: Buttercup rows are wider than hdc rows.

RSB, fold top petal of RSB down and away from you, hdc in ch-1 sp between 2 hdc on RSB, placing st between last sc worked and center dc of top petal; hdc in same ch-1 sp, placing st between center dc and first sc worked of top petal; rep from * across: 5 WSB and 15 hdc; ch 2, turn.

Row 4: Beg in first st; *RSB in 3 hdc on previous row; working in WSB on previous row, hdc in first sc worked on top petal of WSB; fold top petal of WSB down and toward you, hdc in ch-1 sp between 2 hdc on WSB, placing st between first sc worked and center dc of top petal; hdc in same ch-1 sp, placing st between center dc and last sc worked of top petal; rep from * across: 5 RSB and 15 hdc; ch 2, turn.

Rows 5 through 8: Rep Rows 3 and 4 two times more.

Rows 9 through 13: Hdc in first st and in each st across: 30 hdc; ch 2, turn.

Row 14: Rep Row 2.

Rows 15 through 30: Rep Rows 3 and 4 eight times more. Place st markers at each edge of Rows 20 and 24.

Rows 31 through 35: Rep Rows 9 through 13.

Row 36: Rep Row 2.

Rows 37 through 42: Rep Rows 3 and 4 three times more.

Row 43: Sc in first st and in each st across: 30 sc. Finish off; weave in ends.

Outer Lining (optional)

Note: Practice on a swatch first. Yarn is heat-sensitive. Never let yarn come in direct contact with iron.

Center iron-on adhesive on right side of one fabric piece and fuse, following manufacturer instructions. Shape crochet piece into 8 1/2" x 17" rectangle overall, allowing middle buttercup rows (which will become bag base) to measure 9 1/2" across and allowing solid hdc rows to measure 8 1/4" across. Center and fuse adhesive side of fabric to wrong side of crochet piece,

Instructions continue on next page. →

applying least amount of pressure necessary and avoiding sts at edges of each row to facilitate seaming sides. While still hot, gently flip piece over and fluff up buttercups, opening up flowers of first and last rows and those bordering hdc rows.

Side Seams

Fold bag in half with right sides tog, having first and last rows at top. Form a T-shaped bottom seam by flattening fold between markers at a 90-degree angle to side edges. Seam across bottom edges between markers, keeping fabric and petals away from seam; then seam up sides through yarn edges only. Trim away excess fabric from bag opening only. Turn bag right side out.

Handle Loops

With right side of bag facing, join with sc in top edge of right side seam on front; **FPsc in next 4 sc.

Row 1: *Working in nearest RSB one row below, fold top petal of RSB down and away from you, 2 hdc in ch-1 sp between 2 hdc on RSB, placing sts between first sc worked and center dc of top petal; 2 hdc in same ch-1 sp, placing sts between center dc and last sc worked of top petal; ch 2, turn.

Row 2: Skip first hdc, BPdc in next 2 hdc, hdc in next hdc; ch 2, turn.

Row 3: Skip first hdc, FPdc in next 2 sts, hdc in 2nd ch of turning ch-2; ch 2, turn.

Row 4: Skip first hdc, BPdc in next 2 sts, hdc in 2nd ch of turning ch-2; ch 2, turn.

Rows 5 and 6: Rep Rows 3 and 4. At end of Row 6, ch 1 instead of ch 2.

Fold this strip in half toward inside of bag. Sl st through 4 sts on Row 6 and 4 hdc on Row 1 of handle loop, skip one sc under

handle loop*; FPsc in next 17 sc on top edge of bag; rep from * on Row 1 of handle loops to *; FPsc in next 7 sc on top edge of bag to top of next side seam**; sc in side seam. Rep from * to ** across top edge of back, working both handle loops in nearest WSB 2 rows below instead of nearest RSB one row below: 4 handle loops made; sl st in first sc. Finish off; weave in ends. Note: Handle loops will be slightly offset from side seams. Side seams will twist slightly to adjust for handle offset.

Inner Lining (optional)

Fold other fabric piece in half crosswise, with right sides together. Seam 2 sides with 1/2" seam allowance to create a simple lining. Insert lining in bag. Decide best seam allowance along top lining opening so lining will be about 1/4" below top bag edge; remove lining. Fold top edges of lining to wrong side with chosen seam allowance and press; place lining inside bag and sew top of lining to bag just below top row of sts (or use fabric glue or scraps of iron-on adhesive to adhere top of lining inside bag).

Velvet Bow

If using velvet fabric, fold long edges of strip in to meet in center and seam (or use light amount of glue) to create double-thick 2" wide ribbon. Note: Make sure right side of velvet is facing outward. Wrap ribbon around hdc rows of bag snugly. Starting with one end of ribbon at center front of bag, glue down ribbon, making sure petals are not under ribbon as you glue. Cut excess ribbon and form into a bow. Glue bow over ribbon ends at center front.

Feed bag handle ends through handle loops.

#42 TASSELLATIONS

Designed by Patons Design Staff

SIZE
6" x 7"

MATERIALS
Super bulky eyelash yarn
  1 ³/₄ oz ruby

Bulky weight yarn
  3 ¹/₂ oz wine

Note: *Photographed model made with Patons® Allure #04405 Ruby and Patons® Shetland Chunky #03430 Wine*

1 yd wine drapery cord

Two 2" long wine tassels

Set of snap fasteners

¹/₂ yd lining fabric (optional)

Size 17 (12.75 mm) knitting needles
  (or size required for gauge)

GAUGE
8 sts and 9 rows = 4" with one strand of each yarn held together in stock st (knit 1 row, purl 1 row)

INSTRUCTIONS

Front and Back
(made in one piece)
With one strand of each yarn held tog, CO 15 sts.

Row 1: K1; *P1, K1; rep from * across.

Rows 2 and 3: Rep Row 1.

Row 4 (right side): Knit.

Row 5: Purl.

Rep Rows 4 and 5 until work from beg measures 11 ¹/₂", end by working a right-side row.

Next row: K1; * P1, K1; rep from * across.

Rep last row twice more.

BO in patt.

Finishing

Lining (optional)
Before sewing Front and Back tog, mark wrong side of lining fabric following Front and Back shape with ¹/₂" seam allowance. Cut out lining piece and sew sides of lining pieces tog.

With right sides of purse tog, fold work in half crosswise. Sew side seams, leaving a 2" opening at bottom for cord. Tuck end of drapery cord into opening at bottom of side seam, sew hole closed securely. Sew cord to side of purse, sew tassels to bottom corner of purse as illustrated.

Fold and stitch lining along top of Bag approximately ³/₈" from edge. Press lining to wrong side along this stitching line.

Sew snap fasteners on inside.

#43 OVERLAY MANDALAS

Designed by Melody MacDuffee
For the advanced crocheter

SIZE

19" wide x 11 ^{1}/$_2$" high x 3" deep

MATERIALS

Size 10 Cotton Crochet Thread
   200 yds dk brown
   200 yds cappuccino
   200 yds camel
   200 yds gold metallic
   200 yds lt pink
   200 yds rose

Eyelash Yarn
   21 oz brown
   21.6 oz tan

Note: *Photographed model made with J&P Coats® Aunt Lydia® Classic Crochet #131 Fudge Brown, J&P Coats® South Maid® # 434 Cappuccino, #433 Camel, #401 Lt Pink, #439 French Rose, J&P Coats® Metallic Knit-Cro-Sheen™ #90G Gold/Gold, Lion Brand® Fun Fur, #126 Chocolate and Yarn Bee Wild Child Eyelash Yarn Pecan*

Plastic canvas, three 22" x 13 ^{1}/$_4$" sheets

Pair of prefabricated purse handles

Tapestry needle

Lining fabric (optional)

Size 7 (1.65 mm) steel crochet hook (or size required for gauge)

Size H (5 mm) crochet hook (or size required for gauge)

GAUGE

Rnds 1 through 4 of Overlay Square = 1" diameter; finished Overlay Square = 5 ^{1}/$_4$" square with size 7 hook and cotton thread

15 sc = 4 ^{3}/$_4$" with H hook and one strand of each fur yarn

2 sc decrease (2 sc dec): *Insert hook in specified st and draw up a lp; rep from * once; YO and draw through all 3 lps on hook: 2 sc dec made.

2 tr decrease (2 tr dec): *YO twice, insert hook in specified st and draw up a lp, (YO and draw through 2 lps on hook) 2 times; rep from * once; YO and draw through all 3 lps on hook: 2 tr dec made.

3 tr decrease (3 tr dec): *YO twice, insert hook in specified st and draw up a lp, (YO and draw through 2 lps on hook) 2 times; rep from * 2 times more; YO and draw through all 4 lps on hook: 3 tr dec made.

4 tr decrease (4 tr dec): *YO twice, insert hook in specified st and draw up a lp, (YO and draw through 2 lps on hook) 2 times; rep from * 3 times more; YO and draw through all 5 lps on hook: 4 tr dec made.

Front post tr (FP tr): YO twice, insert hook from front to back to front around post of specified st and draw up a lp, (YO and draw through 2 lps on hook) 3 times: FP tr made.

Front post double tr (FP dtr): YO 3 times, insert hook from front to back to front around post of specified st and draw up a lp, (YO and draw through 2 lps on hook) 4 times: FP dtr made.

Front post triple tr (FP tr tr): YO 4 times, insert hook from front to back to front around post of specified st and draw up a lp, (YO and draw through 2 lps on hook) 5 times: FP tr tr made.

Front post 2 tr decrease (FP 2 tr dec): *YO twice, insert hook from front to back to front around post of specified st and draw up a lp, (YO and draw through 2 lps on hook) 2 times; rep from * once; YO and draw through all 3 lps on hook: FP 2 tr dec made.

Front post 2 dtr decrease (FP 2 dtr dec): *YO 3 times, insert hook from front to back to front around post of specified st and draw up a lp, (YO and draw through 2 lps on hook) 3 times; rep from * once; YO and draw through all 3 lps on hook: FP 2 dtr dec made.

Long sc (Lsc): Insert hook in indicated st or sp and draw up a lp to height of current row or rnd, YO and draw through 2 lps on hook: Lsc made.

Note: If you have chosen to use colors other than those indicated, be sure to make a color key to refer to as you work, since the instructions frequently refer to colors when describing where to anchor your Overlay stitches.

INSTRUCTIONS

Overlay Square
(make 4 using size 7 hook and cotton thread throughout)
With gold, ch 5; join with sl st to form a ring.

Rnd 1 (right side): 8 sc in ring: 8 sc; join with sl st in first sc.

Note: Throughout overlay squares, work sts in back lps only unless otherwise specified.

Rnd 2: Ch 1, 3 sc in same sc as joining, sc in next sc; *3 sc in next sc, sc in next sc; rep from * 2 times more: 16 sc; join as before.

Note: Corner sc is 2nd sc of 3-sc group.

Rnd 3: Ch 1, sc in same sc as joining; *3 sc in next corner sc, sc in next 3 sc; rep from * 2 times more; 3 sc in next sc, sc in next 2 sc: 24 sc; join.

Rnd 4: Ch 1, sc in same sc as joining, sc in next sc; *3 sc in next corner sc, sc in next 5 sc; rep from * 2 times more; 3 sc in next sc, sc in next 3 sc: 32 sc; join. Finish off; weave in ends.

Rnd 5: Join dk brown with sl st in sc before any corner sc, ch 1, sc in same sc; **3 sc in next corner sc, sc in next sc; *tr in corner gold sc on Rnd 2 almost straight down from current st, skip sc behind tr*; sc in next 3 sc; rep from * to * once***; sc in next sc; rep from ** 2 times more; rep from ** to *** once: 40 sts; join. Finish off; weave in ends.

107

Instructions continue on next page. →

Rnd 6: Join cappuccino with sl st in sc before any corner sc, ch 1, sc in same sc; **3 sc in next corner sc, sc in next sc; *working between 2 dk brown tr on Rnd 5 that form a "V", tr in same corner gold sc on Rnd 2 as dk brown tr on Rnd 5, skip sc behind tr*; sc in next 5 sts; rep from * to * once***; sc in next st; rep from ** 2 times more; rep from ** to *** once: 48 sts; join. Finish off; weave in ends.

Rnd 7: Join camel with sl st in sc before any corner sc, ch 1, sc in same sc; **3 sc in next corner sc, sc in next sc; *working between 2 cappuccino tr on Rnd 6 that form a "V", dtr in same corner gold sc on Rnd 2 as cappuccino tr on Rnd 6, skip sc behind dtr*; sc in next 7 sts; rep from * to * once***; sc in next st; rep from ** 2 times more; rep from ** to *** once: 56 sts; join. Finish off; weave in ends.

Rnd 8: Join pink with sl st in sc before any corner sc, ch 1, sc in same sc; *3 sc in next corner sc, sc in next 3 sts; working between 2 camel dtr on Rnd 7 that form a "V", dtr in corner gold sc on Rnd 4, tr in center gold sc of 5 sc worked on side of Rnd 4 (st straight down from center point of this side of current rnd), skip 2 sc behind dtr and tr, sc in next 3 sc, tr in same center gold sc on same side of Rnd 4 as last tr made, dtr in next corner gold sc on Rnd 4, skip 2 sc behind tr and dtr**; sc in next 3 sts; rep from * 2 times more; rep from * to ** once; sc in next 2 sts: 64 sts; join. Finish off; weave in ends.

Rnd 9: Join rose with sl st in sc before any corner sc, ch 1, sc in same sc; *3 sc in next corner sc, sc in next 6 sts; working between 2 pink tr on Rnd 8, tr in same center gold sc on side of Rnd 4 as pink tr on Rnd 8, skip sc behind tr, sc in next sc, tr in same center gold sc on side of Rnd 4 as last tr made, skip sc behind tr**; sc in next 6 sts; rep from * 2 times more; rep from * to ** once; sc in next 5 sts: 72 sts; join. Finish off; weave in ends.

Rnd 10: Join camel with sl st in sc before any corner sc, ch 1, sc in same sc; *3 sc in next corner sc, sc in next sc, tr in corner cappuccino sc on Rnd 6 almost straight down from current st, skip sc behind tr, sc in next 6 sts, working between two rose tr on Rnd 9, 2 tr dec in same center gold sc on side of Rnd 4 as rose tr on Rnd 9, skip sc behind 2 tr dec, sc in next 6 sts, tr in next corner cappuccino sc on Rnd 6 almost straight down from current st, skip sc behind tr**; sc in next sc; rep from * 2 times more; rep from * to ** once: 80 sts; join. Finish off; weave in ends.

Rnd 11: Join dk brown with sl st in any corner sc, ch 1, 3 sc in same corner sc; *tr in corner camel sc on Rnd 7 almost straight down from current st, skip sc behind tr, sc in next 3 sts, FP tr tr in next dk brown tr on Rnd 5, skip sc behind tr, sc in next 9 sts, FP tr tr in next dk brown tr on Rnd 5, skip sc behind tr, sc in next 3 sts, tr in next corner camel sc on Rnd 7 almost straight down from current st, skip sc behind tr**; 3 sc in next sc; rep from * 2 times more; rep from * to ** once: 88 sts; join. Finish off; weave in ends.

Rnd 12: Join cappuccino with sl st in any corner sc, ch 1, 3 sc in same corner sc; *working between 2 dk brown tr on Rnd 11, tr in same corner camel sc on Rnd 7 as dk brown tr on Rnd 11, skip sc behind tr, sc in next 2 sts, dtr in same corner cappuccino sc on Rnd 6 as camel tr on Rnd 10, skip sc behind dtr, sc in next sc, FP tr tr in next cappuccino tr on Rnd 6, skip st behind FP tr tr, sc in next 9 sc, FP tr tr in next cappuccino tr on Rnd 6, skip st behind FP tr tr, sc in next sc, dtr in same corner cappuccino sc on Rnd 6 as next camel tr on Rnd 10, skip sc behind dtr, sc in next 2 sts, working between 2 dk brown tr on Rnd 11, tr in same corner camel sc on Rnd 7 as dk brown tr on Rnd 11, skip sc behind tr**, 3 sc in next corner sc; rep from * 2 times more; rep from * to ** once: 96 sts; join. Finish off; weave in ends.

Rnd 13: Join gold with sl st in sc before any corner sc, ch 1, sc in same sc; *sc in next corner sc, working between two cappuccino tr on Rnd 12, 3 tr dec in same corner camel sc on Rnd 7 as cappuccino tr on Rnd 12, sc in same corner sc, sc in next 3 sts, dtr in same corner cappuccino sc on Rnd 6 as cappuccino dtr on Rnd 12, skip sc behind dtr, sc in next 15 sts, dtr in same corner cappuccino sc on Rnd 6 as next cappuccino dtr on Rnd 12, skip sc behind dtr**; sc in next 3 sts; rep from * 2 times more; rep from * to ** once; sc in next 2 sts: 104 sts; join. Finish off; weave in ends.

Rnd 14: Join cappuccino with sl st in sc before any 3 tr dec corner st, ch 1, sc in same sc; *sc in next corner st, FP 2 tr dec in previous cappuccino tr on Rnd 12 and in next cappuccino tr on Rnd 12, sc in same corner st, sc in next 2 sts, FP tr in next cappuccino dtr on Rnd 12, skip sc behind FP tr, sc in next 2 sts, FP tr in next cappuccino FP tr tr on Rnd 12, skip sc behind FP tr, sc in next 13 sts, FP tr in next cappuccino FP tr tr on Rnd 12, skip sc behind FP tr, sc in next 2 sts, FP tr in next cappuccino dtr on Rnd 12, skip sc behind FP tr**; sc in next 2 sts; rep from * 2 times more; rep from * to ** once; sc in next st: 112 sts; join. Finish off; weave in ends.

Rnd 15: Join dk brown with sl st in sc before any FP 2 tr dec corner st, ch 1, sc in same sc; *sc in next corner st, FP 2 dtr dec in previous dk brown tr on Rnd 11 and in next dk brown tr on Rnd 11, sc in same corner st, sc in next 2 sts, FP dtr in next dk brown FP tr tr on Rnd 11, skip sc behind FP dtr, sc in next 21 sts, FP dtr in next dk brown FP tr tr

on Rnd 11, skip sc behind FP dtr**; sc in next 2 sts; rep from * 2 times more; rep from * to ** once; sc in next st: 120 sts; join. Finish off; weave in ends.

Flowers (make 4)
With pink, ch 5; join with sl st to form a ring.

Rnd 1: 10 sc in ring: 10 sc; join with sl st in first sc.

Rnd 2: *Ch 2, skip next sc, sl st in next sc; rep from * 3 times more; ch 2, skip next sc, join with sl st in joining sl st: 10 chs and 5 sl sts.

Rnd 3: *(Sc, hdc, dc, tr, dc, hdc, sc) in next ch-2 sp, sl st in next sl st; rep from * 4 times more: 40 sts. Finish off; weave in ends.

Note: *Continue to work sts in back lps only unless otherwise instructed.*

Rnd 4: Join rose with sl st in dc before any tr, ch 1, sc in same st; *3 sc in tr, sc in next dc and in next hdc, Lsc in center ring, skip next (sc, sl st, sc)**; sc in next hdc and in next dc; rep from * 3 times more; rep from * to ** once; sc in next hdc: 40 sts; join with sl st in first sc. Finish off; weave in ends.

Overlay Square (continued)
Rnd 16: Join cappuccino with sl st in st before any corner st, ch 1, sc in same st; *3 sc in next corner st, sc in next 10 sts; holding flower and square with wrong sides together, sc in next st on square and in middle sc of 3 rose sc above any tr on flower together, sc in next 7 sts on both square and flower together, sc in next st on square and in middle sc of 3 rose sc above next tr on flower together**; sc in next 10 sts on square only; rep from * 2 times more; rep from * to ** once; sc in next 9 sts on square only: 128 sts; join. Finish off; weave in ends.

109

Instructions continue on next page. →

Rnd 17: Join gold with sl st in sc before any corner sc, ch 1, sc in same sc; *3 sc in next corner sc, sc in next 11 sts; working up side of flower, skip next sc, sc in next 2 sc, (skip next Lsc, sc in next 3 sc, 3 sc in next corner sc, sc in next 3 sc) 3 times, skip next Lsc, sc in next 2 sc, skip next sc**; sc in next 11 sts on square; rep from * 2 times more; rep from * to ** once; sc in next 10 sts on square: 224 sts; join. Finish off; weave in ends.

Rnd 18: Join cappuccino with sl st in sc before any corner sc; *sl st in next 5 sc, 2 sc dec in next 2 sc, sc in next 2 sc, hdc in next sc, dc in next sc, 4 tr dec in next 2 sts on square and in next 2 sts on flower, tr in next 2 sts, dc in next st, hdc in next st, 2 sc in next st, sc in next 8 sts, 3 sc in next st, sc in next 8 sts, 2 sc in next st, hdc in next st, dc in next st, tr in next 2 sts, 4 tr dec in next 2 sts on flower and in next 2 sts on square, dc in next sc, hdc in next sc, sc in next 2 sc, 2 sc dec in next 2 sc**; sl st in next 4 sc; rep from * 2 times more; rep from * to ** once; sl st in next 3 sc: 208 sts; join. Finish off; weave in ends.

Note: Corner sc is now 2nd sc in 3-sc group above center tip of flowers.

Rnd 19: Join dk brown with sl st in sc before any corner sc, ch 1, sc in same sc; *3 sc in next corner sc, sc in next 16 sts, hdc in next st, dc in next st, tr in next 3 sts, dc in next st, hdc in next st, sc in next 5 sts, hdc in next st, dc in next st, tr in next 3 sts, dc in next st, hdc in next st**; sc in next 16 sts; rep from * 2 times more; rep from * to ** once; sc in next 15 sts: 216 sts; join. Finish off; weave in ends.

Joining One Side of Squares

First Square: Join dk brown with sc in any corner sc; *ch 1, skip next st, sc in next st; rep from * to next corner sc: 28 sc and 27 ch-1 sps. Finish off; weave in ends.

Second Square: Join dk brown with sc in any corner sc, holding second square against first square with wrong sides together and lining corners and edges up; *sl st in corresponding ch-1 sp of first square, skip next st on second square, sc in next sc on second square; rep from * to next corner sc: 28 sc and 27 sl sts. Finish off; weave in ends.

Rep joining for other two squares.

Preparing Squares for Fur

Join dk brown with sl st in corner sc at right corner of either short end of joined squares; *ch 4, sl st in same corner sc (corner ch-4 lp made); **ch 3, skip next 2 sts, sl st in next st, (ch 3, skip next 3 sts, sl st in next st) 12 times, ch 3, skip next 2 sts, sl st in next st***; rep from * to *** once; sl st in corner sc of next square; rep from ** to *** once; rep from * to *** 2 times more; sl st in corner sc of next square; rep from ** to *** once, working last sl st in beg sl st: 84 ch-3 lps and 4 corner ch-4 lps. Finish off; weave in ends.

Rep for other joined squares.

Center Fur Panel

Row 1: With H hook and one strand of each eyelash yarn held together, join with sl st in ch-4 lp at right-hand corner of long edge of strip, ch 1, sc in same ch-4 lp, sc in next ch-3 lp and in each ch-3 lp to next corner ch-4 lp, sc in corner ch-4 lp: 30 sc; ch 1, turn.

Rows 2 through 5: Sc in first sc and in each sc across; ch 1, turn. At end of Row 5, do not ch 1. Finish off; weave in ends.

Rep Rows 1 through 5 for other strip.

Holding wrong sides of two strips together, sl st Row 5 of fur edges together. Finish off; weave in ends.

Surrounding Fur

Note: Work rows on left, bottom and right edges of assembled squares only.

Row 1: With H hook and one strand of each eyelash yarn held together, join with sl st in right-hand corner ch-4 lp on either non-furry long edge, ch 1, 2 sc in same corner ch-4 lp; *sc in next ch-3 lp and in each ch-3 lp to corner, 3 sc in corner ch-4 lp, sc in next ch-3 lp and in each ch-3 lp to corner*; sc in edge of each of 10 fur rows on center fur panel; rep from * to * once; 2 sc in corner ch-4 lp: 104 sc; ch 1, turn.

Note: Corner sc is 2nd sc of 3-sc group.

Rows 2 through 10: Sc in first sc and in each sc to corner, 3 sc in corner sc, sc in next sc and in each sc to corner, 3 sc in corner sc, sc in next sc and in each sc across; ch 1, turn. At end of Row 2: 108 sc. At end of Row 10: 140 sc.

Note: Measure work at this point and keep a record for use when cutting plastic canvas for front and back.

Rows 11 through 20: To form sides and bottom (gusset), sc in first sc and in each sc across: 140 sc; ch 1, turn. At end of Row 20, do not ch 1. Finish off; weave in ends.

Note: Measure these last 10 rows for use when cutting plastic canvas for sides and bottom.

Back

With H hook and one strand of each eyelash yarn held together, ch 61.

Row 1: Sc in 2nd ch from hook and in each ch across: 60 sc; ch 1, turn.

Rows 2 through 40: Sc in first sc and in each sc across; ch 1, turn. At end of Row 40, do not ch 1. Finish off; weave in ends.

Holding wrong side of back and front together, sl st back to front on 3 furry edges of front gusset.

Assembly

Keep in mind that crocheted sections should fit tightly across canvases, but not so tightly that canvases buckle. Cut two pieces of plastic canvas about 19" x 11 1/2"; two pieces about 11 1/2" x 3"; and one piece about 19" x 3" (or sizes to fit measurements of front, back, sides, and bottom of purse).

With dk brown cotton thread and tapestry needle, whipstitch one 3" edge of 11 1/2" x 3" canvas to 3" edge of 19" x 3" canvas. Whipstitch one 3" edge of other 11 1/2" x 3" canvas to other 3" edge of 19" x 3" canvas. This forms gusset of canvas "skeleton". Whipstitch side and bottom edges of front canvas to long edges of gusset pieces just assembled. Rep for back canvas.

Insert canvas "skeleton" into purse. It should fit snugly.

Using one strand of eyelash yarn and size 7 hook, work one rnd of sc along top edge of purse through top edge of "skeleton", joining "skeleton" to purse. Work a second rnd of sc along top edge, working loosely over first rnd of sc.

Attach handles with dk brown cotton thread. Add lining if desired.

#44 PRETTY PAISLEY

Designed by Judith Solomon

SIZE

12" wide x 11" high (with
   pointed top folded down)

MATERIALS

Super bulky chenille yarn
   100 yds rust
   100 yds teal
   100 yds brown
   100 yds blue
   100 yds black

Note: *Photographed model made
with Lion Brand® Chenille
Thick and Quick® #136 Russet,
#122 Peacock, #125 Chocolate,
#106 Monarch and #153 Black*

Size K (6.5 mm) crochet hook
   (or size required for gauge)

Stitch markers

GAUGE

Rnds 1 and 2 = 2 3/8" wide x
   3 1/4" high

INSTRUCTIONS

Sides (make 2)

With rust, ch 4 loosely.

Rnd 1 (right side): Work 8 dc in 4th ch from hook (3 skipped chs count as first dc): 9 dc; join with sl st in 4th ch of beg ch-4. Finish off; weave in ends.

Rnd 2: Join teal with sl st in any dc, ch 1, 2 sc in same st as joining, 2 sc in each of next 5 sts; work (sc, hdc) in next st; work (dc, tr, dc) in next st; work (hdc, sc) in next st: 19 sts; join with sl st in first sc. Finish off; weave in ends.

Note: Top of bag is tr on this rnd and center st of 3 sts worked in top st of bag on subsequent rnds.

Rnd 3: Join brown with sl st in first dc, ch 1, sc in same st as joining; work (sc, dc, sc) in top tr; sc in next 4 sts; *2 sc in next st, sc in next 2 sts; rep from * 3 times more; sc in next st: 25 sts; join with sl st in first sc. Finish off; weave in ends.

Rnd 4: Join blue with sl st in sc after top dc, ch 3 (counts as first dc), dc in same st as joining, dc in next 5 sts; *2 dc in next st, dc in next st; rep from * 5 times more; dc in next 5 sts, 2 dc in next st (place marker in 2nd dc); work (dc, tr, dc) in top dc: 35 sts; join with sl st in 3rd ch of beg ch-3. Finish off; weave in ends.

Rnd 5: Join black with sl st in marked st, ch 1, sc in same st as joining, sc in next st;

work (sc, dc, sc) in top tr; sc in next 7 sts; *2 sc in next st, sc in next 5 sts; rep from * 3 times more; sc in next st: 41 sts; join with sl st in first sc. Finish off; weave in ends.

Rnd 6: Join brown with sl st in sc after top dc, ch 1, sc in same st as joining, sc in next 8 sts; *2 sc in next st, sc in next 6 sts; rep from * 3 times more; sc in next 3 sts (place marker in 3rd sc); work (sc, dc, sc) in top dc: 47 sts; join with sl st in first sc. Finish off; weave in ends.

Rnd 7: Join rust with sl st in marked st, ch 3 (counts as first dc), 2 dc in next st; work (dc, tr, dc) in top dc; 2 dc in next st (place marker in 2nd dc), dc in next 11 sts; *2 dc in next st, dc in next 6 sts; rep from * 3 times more; dc in next 4 sts: 55 sts; join with sl st in 3rd ch of beg ch-3. Finish off; weave in ends.

Rnd 8: Join teal with sl st in marked st, ch 1, sc in same st as joining, sc in next 13 sts; *2 sc in next st, sc in next 6 sts; rep from * 3 times more; sc in next 10 sts (place marker in 10th sc); work (sc, dc, sc) in top tr; sc in next 2 sts: 61 sts; join with sl st in first sc. Finish off; weave in ends.

Rnd 9: Join black with sl st in marked st, ch 1, sc in same st as joining, sc in next st; work (sc, dc, sc) in top dc; sc in next 17 sts; *2 sc in next st, sc in next 11 sts; rep from * 2 times more; sc in next 5 sts: 66 sts; join with sl st in first sc. Finish off; weave in ends.

Instructions continue on next page. →

Rnd 10: Join blue with sl st in sc after top dc, ch 3 (counts as first dc), dc in same st as joining, dc in next 63 sts, 2 dc in next st; work (dc, tr, dc) in top dc: 70 sts; join with sl st in 3rd ch of beg ch-3. Finish off; weave in ends.

Edging

With right side facing, join brown with sl st in front lp of dc before top tr, ch 1, sc in front lp of same st, sc in front lp of top tr, work picot; *sc in front lp of next 2 sts, work picot; rep from * around: 70 sc and 35 picots; join with sl st in first sc. Finish off; weave in ends. Rep on second side.

Joining Rnd

With wrong sides together and top tr lined up, working through both thicknesses, join black with sc in back lp of 12th st after top tr on Rnd 10, sc in back lp of each st around, working last sc in 12th st before top tr: 47 sc. Finish off; weave in ends.

Dangles (make 4)

With rust, ch 4 loosely.

Rnds 1 and 2: Rep Rnds 1 and 2 of Sides.

With wrong sides of 2 Dangles together and top tr lined up, working through both thicknesses, join brown with sc in back lp of 8th st before top tr, work picot; *sc in back lp of next 2 sts, work picot; rep from * 7 times more; sc in back lp of next st: 18 sc and 9 picots. Finish off; weave in ends. Rep with other 2 Dangles.

Ties

Join black with sl st in unworked st at rounded bottom of Dangle, make 36" ch. Finish off, leaving 6" end. Starting at right edge on Front of bag at end of joining rnd (12th st before top tr), weave ch through bag straight across to beg of joining rnd (12th st after top tr) and across Back of bag to end of joining rnd. Sew end of ch to bottom of same Dangle next to beg of ch. Rep with other Dangle, starting at right edge on Back of bag at beg of joining rnd. Adjust chains; weave in ends.

#45 FUN FUR BAG

SIZE
9 1/2" x 10"

MATERIALS
Bulky weight faux fur yarn
3 1/2 oz red

Super bulky weight yarn
5 oz multi-color (red, gold,
orange, cerise, turquoise)

Note: *Photographed model made
with Lion Brand® Jiffy® Thick &
Quick® #208 Rocky Mountains and
Lion Brand® Fun Fur #113 Red*

Size 35 (19 mm) knitting needles
(or size required for gauge)

One 1" dimeter button (optional)

GAUGE
6 sts and 8 rows = 4" with one
strand of super bulky and two
strands of faux fur in stock st
(knit 1 row, purl 1 row)

INSTRUCTIONS

Note: *Bag is worked with one strand of super
bulky yarn and two strands of faux fur held
together throughout.*

Purse

With 3 strands of yarn held tog, CO 15 sts.
Work 2 rows in garter st. Work in stock st
until piece measures 18", ending by working a purl row. Work 2 rows of garter st.
BO all sts.

Finishing

Fold piece in half and sew side seams.

Strap

CO 40 sts.

Next Row: BO all sts.

Sew strap to side seams at top of purse.
Weave in loose ends.

Closure

Sew on button, if desired. Insert through
fabric for buttonhole.

#46 BLUE ELEGANCE

Designed by Glenda Winkleman for Coats & Clark

SIZE

9" wide x 8" high without handles
  (14" high with handles)

MATERIALS

Super bulky weight novelty yarn
  5 1/4 oz multi-color

Super bulky weight yarn
  1 oz black

Note: *Photographed model made
with Moda Dea™ Orbit™ #3934
Moonbeam and Red Heart® Light &
Lofty™ #9312 Onyx*

Size K (6.5 mm) crochet hook (or
  size required for gauge)

1 Pair Antique Silver Beaded handles

Decorative Heart Pin (optional)

2" x 1" black hook & loop fastener

9 1/2" x 17" piece of fabric for lining
  (optional)

Needle and sewing thread to match
  lining fabric (optional)

Stitch markers

GAUGE

8 sc and 9 sc rows = 3"

INSTRUCTIONS

Handbag

Starting at bottom with multi-color yarn, ch 23.

Rnd 1: 3 sc in 2nd ch from hook, sc in next 20 chs, 3 sc in last ch; working in free lps on other side of foundation ch, sc in next 20 chs: 46 sc; do not join. Mark beg of each rnd.

Rnds 2 through 21: Sc in next sc and in each sc around. At end of Rnd 21, join with sl st in first sc. Finish off; weave in ends.

Rnd 22: Join black with sl st in first sc, ch 1, sc in same sc as joining, sc in next sc and in each sc around: 46 sc; join with sl st in first sc. Finish off; weave in ends.

Flap

Starting at top with black, ch 12.

Row 1 (right side): Sc in 2nd ch from hook, sc in next ch and in each ch across: 11 sc; ch 1, turn.

Rows 2 through 8: Sc in first sc and in each sc across; ch 1, turn.

Row 9: Sc dec in first 2 sc, sc in next 7 sc, sc dec in last 2 sc: 9 sc; ch 1, turn.

Row 10: Sc dec in first 2 sc, sc in next 5 sc, sc dec in last 2 sc: 7 sc. Finish off; weave in ends.

Flap Border

Rnd 1: With right side of Flap facing, join multi-color with sl st in edge of st at top left-hand corner of Flap, ch 1, sc in same st, sc in edge of each row down left side, sc in each sc across Row 10, sc in edge of each row up to top right-hand corner. Finish off; weave in ends.

Assembly

With right sides facing, center Row 1 of Flap with Rnd 22 on back of Handbag. Sew in place. Center handles on each side of top of handbag, sew in place. Fold Flap to front of Handbag. Sew hook & loop fastener to underside of flap and to front of Handbag, aligning pieces to match. Attach decorative pin to center of Front Flap, if desired.

Lining (optional)

Fold short ends ½" to wrong side twice, press. Sew folded ends. Fold lining in half with right sides together and folded ends aligned at top, sew along raw edges with ¼" seam allowance, leaving top folded edges open. Insert lining into handbag; hand sew in place along top edge.

#47 BLACK AND WHITE HOBO BAG

Designed by Judi & Co.

SIZE
11" x 25" (with handle)

MATERIALS
1/8" wide flat braid (soutache) 288 yds (2 spools) black and white mix

Note: Photograhed model made with Judi & Co's Soutache

2 glass beads, 3/4" diameter, with large openings

Size F (3.75 mm) crochet hook

Size 8 (5 mm) knitting needles

GAUGE
16 sts and 24 rows = 4" in stock st (knit 1 row, purl 1 row)

INSTRUCTIONS

Straps

With one spool of soutache, CO 7 sts for one strap; with another spool of soutache, CO 7 sts for 2nd strap. Work both straps at the same time with the separate spools.

Row 1: K3, sl 1, K3.

Row 2: Purl.

Rep Rows 1 and 2 until each strap measures 7".

Increase Rows

Working in (K3, sl 1) patt, inc one st each side on every odd-numbered row, and purl every even row, until there are 47 sts on each strap. Then increase at one edge only: 48 sts in each strap. Slip all 96 sts onto one needle.

Sides

Row 1: *K3, sl 1; rep from * across.

Row 2: Purl.

Rep Rows 1 and 2 until piece measures 9 3/4", ending by working a purl row. Dec 6 sts evenly spaced across next row, then purl one row.

Bottom

Row 1: *K8, K2 tog; rep from * across.

Row 2 and all even rows: Purl.

Row 3: *K7, K2 tog; rep from * across.

Row 5: *K6, K2 tog; rep from * across.

Row 7: *K5, K2 tog; rep from * across.

Row 9: *K4, K2 tog; rep from * across.

Row 11: *K3, K2 tog; rep from * across.

Row 13: *K2, K2 tog; rep from * across.

Row 15: *K1, K2 tog; rep from * across.

Row 17: *K2 tog; rep from * across.

Finish off, leaving an 18" length for sewing. Thread soutache into a yarn needle and draw through rem sts. Pull up tightly and secure.

Finishing

With wrong sides tog, sew center seam. Sew ends of handles together. With crochet hook, work one row of single crochet around each edge of handle.

Bag Ties

With crochet hook, join soutache with a sl st to center of one side of bag opening on outside.

Ch 28; sl st in each ch, finish off. Slip one bead over end of tie.

Make a 2nd tie in same manner on opposite side of bag opening.

#48 FLAPPER

Designed by Susan McCreary

FINISHED SIZE
7 ½" x 6 ½"

MATERIALS
Worsted weight yarn
  2 oz yellow/orange

Note: *Photographed model was made with Caron® Wintuk® #3256 Jonquil*

3 yards 4 mm gold facet
  pre-strung beads

1 set ¾" hook and loop round
  fasteners.

Sewing needle and thread

Size J (6 mm) crochet hook
  (or size required for gauge)

GAUGE
(Sc, ch-1 sp, sc, ch-1 sp) = 1"

STITCH GUIDE
Sc2tog: (Insert hook in next st, yo and pull up a lp) twice, YO and pull through all 3 lps on hook.

INSTRUCTIONS

Front Panel
Starting at top, ch 24.

Row 1: Sc in 2nd ch from hook and in next ch; *ch 1, skip next ch, sc in next ch: rep from * to last 3 chs, ch 1, skip next ch, sc in last 2 chs, ch 1, turn: 13 sc, 10 ch-1 sps.

Row 2: Sc in first 2 sc; *ch 1, skip ch-1 sp, sc in next st; rep from * across, ending with ch 1, skip next ch-1 sp, sc in last 2 sc, ch 1, turn.

Rows 3 through 15: Rep Row 2.

Row 16: Sc2tog, skip ch-1 sp; *sc in next sc, ch 1, skip next ch-1 sp; rep from * to last 2 sc, sc in last 2 sc, ch 1, turn: 12 sc, 9 ch-1 sps.

Row 17: Sc2tog, skip ch-1 sp; *sc in next sc, ch 1, skip next ch-1 sp; rep from * to last 2 sc, sc in last 2 sc, ch 1, turn: 11 sc, 8 ch-1 sps.

Row 18: Sc2tog, skip ch-1 sp; *sc in next sc, ch 1, skip next ch-1 sp; rep from * to last 2 sc, sc in last 2 sc, ch 1; turn: 10 sc, 7 ch-1 sps

Row 19: Sc2tog, skip ch-1 sp; *sc in next sc, ch 1, skip next ch-1 sp; rep from * to last 2 sc, sc in last 2 sc, ch 1, turn: 9 sc, 6 ch-1 sps.

Row 20: Sc2tog, skip ch-1 sp; *sc in next sc, ch 1, skip next ch-1 sp; rep from * to last 2 sc, sc in last 2 sc, ch 1, turn: 8 sc, 5 ch-1 sps.

Row 21: Rep Row 2. Finish off; weave in all ends.

Back Panel
Work same as Front Panel

Flap
Ch 20

Row 1: Sc in 2nd ch from hook and in next ch; * ch 1, skip next ch, sc in next ch: rep from * to last 3 chs, ch 1, skip next ch, sc in last 2 chs, ch 1, turn: 11 sc, 8 ch-1 sps.

Row 2: Sc in first 2 sc; *ch 1, skip ch-1 sp, ch 1, sc in next st; rep from * across, ending with ch 1, skip next ch-1 sp, sc in last 2 sc, ch 1, turn.

Row 3: Sc2tog, skip ch-1 sp; *sc in next sc, ch 1, skip next ch-1 sp; rep from * to last 2 sc, sc in last 2 sc, ch 1; turn: 10 sc, 7 ch-1 sps.

Row 4: Sc2tog, skip ch-1 sp; *sc in next sc, ch 1, skip next ch-1 sp; rep from * to last 2 sc, sc in last 2 sc, ch 1, turn: 9 sc, 6 ch-1 sps.

Row 5: Sc2tog, skip ch-1 sp; *sc in next sc, ch 1, skip next ch-1 sp; rep from * to last 2 sc, sc in last 2 sc, ch 1, turn: 8 sc, 5 ch-1 sps. Finish off. Weave in all ends.

Assembly
Sew Front and Back panels tog, leaving top open. Cut 16" length of gold facet beads, sew each end to wrong side of side seam for handle.

Sew wide end of flap to top back panel. Pull flap forward to front. Sew half of fastener to flap, half to bag front.

Cut seven 8" lengths of gold facet beads. Pull one length through each of the 5 ch-1 sps on edge of flap, and one length through each end sc. Align so that each length of chain measures 4". Tack in place.

Cut five 7" lengths of beads. Pull one length through each of the 5 ch-1 sps on bottom of bag, pull all lengths together to meet at center bottom of bag, and tie them security together with thread.

#49 PINK ELEPHANT

Designed by Noreen Crone-Findlay

SIZE
9" x 17" (including trunk)

MATERIALS
Super bulky weight yarn
  12 oz pink
  6 oz multi-color

Note: Photographed model made with Lion Brand® Big #146 Panoramic Pink and #202 Spectacular Sunset.

Size 19 (15 mm) knitting needles
  (or size required for gauge)

Two ½" diameter black beads or
  buttons for eyes

Fifteen ½" diameter beads to trim
  elephant's hat and blanket

GAUGE
5 sts and 10 rows = 4" in garter st
  (knit every row)

INSTRUCTIONS

Body
Beginning at elephant's bottom with pink, CO 10 sts.

Rows 1 and 2: Knit.

Row 3: (K1, P1) in each st across: 20 sts.

Rows 4 through 19: Knit.

Shape Neck
Row 20: *K2tog; rep from * across: 10 sts.

Rows 21 through 23: Knit.

Shape Head
Row 24: (K1, P1) in each st across: 20 sts.

Rows 25 through 35: Knit.

Shape Trunk
Row 36: * K2tog; rep from * across: 10 sts.

Row 37: K10.

Row 38: * K2tog; rep from * across: 5 sts.

Rows 39 through 46: Knit.

BO, leaving an 18" yarn end for sewing. The center seam runs along upper edge of elephant. Sew edges of trunk together. Pull up firmly on end of yarn to curl trunk. Sew edges of head together. Tack head in place several times at neck to anchor. Leaving an 8" opening, sew rem upper edge closed. Gather stitches of first row and pull up. Tack first row in place several times to anchor.

Ear (make 2)
With pink, CO 5 sts. Work 10 rows of garter st. At end of Row 10, do not BO. Leaving an 8" yarn end, cut yarn. Thread yarn into a tapestry needle and draw through all 5 sts on needle. Pull up to gather. Thread yarn tail through sts one more time. Pull up firmly and sew ear to side of elephant's head.

Leg (make 4)
With pink, CO 5 sts. Work 6 rows of garter st. At end of Row 6, do not BO. Leaving an 8" yarn end, cut yarn. Thread yarn into a tapestry needle and draw through all 5 sts on needle. Pull up to gather. Thread yarn through sts one more time. Pull up firmly to form sole of foot. Sew edges together, then sew top of each leg to elephant's body.

Hat
With multi-color yarn, CO 5 sts. Work 8 rows of garter st. BO, leaving an 18" yarn end for sewing. With one point of square on elephant's forehead, sew the square to the top of the head. Sew one bead to the front and side points of the hat.

123

Instructions continue on next page. →

Blanket and Handle

With multi-color, CO 2 sts.

Rows 1 and 2: Knit.

Rows 3: (K1, P1) in each st across: 4 sts.

Rows 4, 6 and 8: Knit.

Rows 5, 7 and 9: (K1, P1) in first st; knit across to last st; (K1, P1) in last st.

Row 10: Knit.

Rows 11 through 13: K2tog; knit across to last 2 sts, K2tog.

Row 14: K2tog, K2: 3 sts.

Rows 15 through 55 (Handle): K3.

Row 56: (K1, P1) in first st, K2: 4 sts.

Rows 57 through 59: Rep Row 5 three times.

Row 60: K10.

Rows 61, 63, 65 and 67: Rep Row 11: 2 sts.
Rows 62, 64, 66 and 68: Knit.

BO, leaving a 30" yarn end for sewing.

Finishing

Sew two black beads or buttons to face for eyes.

Tail: Cut two 11" pieces of pink yarn. Thread ends into needle and pull them through bottom of elephant. Fold in half and hold two strands at center as one, then braid the tail. Wrap yarn around the tail and stitch in place to secure. Trim and fluff tail ends.

With handle coming straight up from elephant's neck, sew blanket square to sides of elephant's body. Leave the upper edges of the blanket open for pockets. Stitch six beads along lower edge of each side of blanket. Sew one or two sts through both layers of the handle at the neck edge to secure.

#50 BEACH BAG

Designed by Susan McCreary

SIZE
14" x 14"

MATERIALS
Super bulky yarn
  8 oz bright pink

Note: Photographed model made with Red Heart® Bright and Lofty™ #9727 Bubblegum

Sewing thread to match yarn

Sewing needle.

Three 4" artificial painted
  daisies in coordinating colors

Size N (10 mm) crochet hook
  (or size required for gauge)

GAUGE
6 sc = 4"

INSTRUCTIONS

Front Panel
Ch 23.

Row 1: Dc in 4th ch from hook and in each sc across, ch 3 (counts as first dc of following row throughout), turn: 21 dc.

Row 2: Dc in next dc across; ch 3, turn.

Rows 3 through 12: Rep Row 2. At end of last row, finish off; weave in ends.

Back Panel
Work same as Front Panel

Shoulder Strap
Ch 3.

Row 1: Sc in 2nd ch from hook and in next ch, ch 1, turn.

Row 2: Sc in each sc, ch 1; turn.

Rows 3 through 47: Rep Row 2. At end of last row, finish off; weave in ends.

Finishing
Hold Front and Back panels tog; with matching sewing thread and needle, sew tog along 3 edges, leaving top open.

Sew each end of strap to inside of bag, overlapping 3 rows. Sew daisies on one side of bag as shown in photograph.

#51 YOGA MAT TOTE

Designed by Marty Miller

SIZE
Approx 7 1/2" diameter x 31" long

MATERIALS
Worsted weight cotton yarn
   420 yds blue/green variegated

Note: *Photographed model made with Plymouth Fantasy Naturale #9936 Tropical*

Stitch markers

Size H (5 mm) crochet hook (or
   size required for gauge)

GAUGE
Rnds 1 through 4 = 2" diameter

INSTRUCTIONS

Note: *Do not join rnds of sc. Place marker at end of rnd and move marker up with each round.*

Starting at bottom, ch 2.

Rnd 1: 6 sc in 2nd ch from hook: 6 sc. DO NOT JOIN. Place marker.

Rnd 2: 2 sc in each sc around: 12 sc.

Rnd 3: 2 sc in first sc, sc in next sc; *2 sc in next sc, sc in next sc; rep from * 4 times more: 18 sc.

Rnd 4: 2 sc in first sc, sc in next 2 sc; *2 sc in next sc, sc in next 2 sc; rep from * 4 times more: 24 sc.

Rnds 5 through 12: Rep Rnd 4 eight times more, increasing numbers between increases by one more in each rnd: 6 more sc in each rnd than in previous rnd. At end of Rnd 12: 72 sc.

Rnd 13: Sc in first sc and in each sc around: 72 sc.

Rnds 14 through 24: Rep Rnd 13 eleven times more or until bottom measures about 6" from center to edge. At end of last rnd, join with sl st in first sc of rnd.

Side

Rnd 1: Ch 1, sc in same sc as joining; *ch 5, skip 3 sc, sc in next sc; rep from * around, ending with ch 2, dc in first sc (ch 2 and dc counts as ch-5 sp now and throughout): 18 ch-5 sps.

Rnd 2: *Ch 5, sc in next ch-5 sp; rep from * around, ending with ch 2, dc in dc of prev rnd: 18 ch-5 sps.

Rnds 3 through 35: Rep Rnd 2 thirty-three times more.

Top Edge

Rnd 1: Ch 1, sc around post of last dc, sc in next sc; *3 sc in next ch-5 sp, sc in next sc; rep from * around, ending with 2 sc in last ch-2 sp: 72 sc. DO NOT JOIN. Place marker.

Rnd 2: Sc in first sc and in each sc around: 72 sc.

Rnds 3 through 12: Rep Rnd 2 ten times more. Do not finish off.

Handle

Row 1: Sc in next 6 sc: 6 sc; ch 1, turn.

Row 2: Sc in first sc and in each sc across: 6 sc; ch 1, turn.

Row 3: Sc in first sc and in each sc across. DO NOT TURN.

Note: Begin to crochet in rnds.

Rnd 4: Sc in first sc and in each sc around: 6 sc. Place marker.

Rnds 5 through 97: Rep Rnd 4 ninety three times more or until handle measures about 29".

Note: Handle should reach to last rnd of bottom.

Handle Joining

Fold bag in half widthwise so first row of handle is at fold. Place markers in 3 sc sts on fold on last rnd of bottom. Fold handle flat.

Row 1: Sc in next 3 sts through both layers of handle and in marked sts: 3 sc; ch 1, turn.

Handle Continued

Row 1: Sc in first sc and in each sc across: 3 sc; ch 1, turn.

Rows 2 through 25: Rep Row 1 twenty four times more.

Attaching Handle to Bottom of Bag

Sc in first 3 sts on Rnd 1 at bottom of bag. Finish off; weave in ends.

#52 TAPESTRY CROCHET DIAMONDS

Designed by Carol Ventura for Coats & Clark

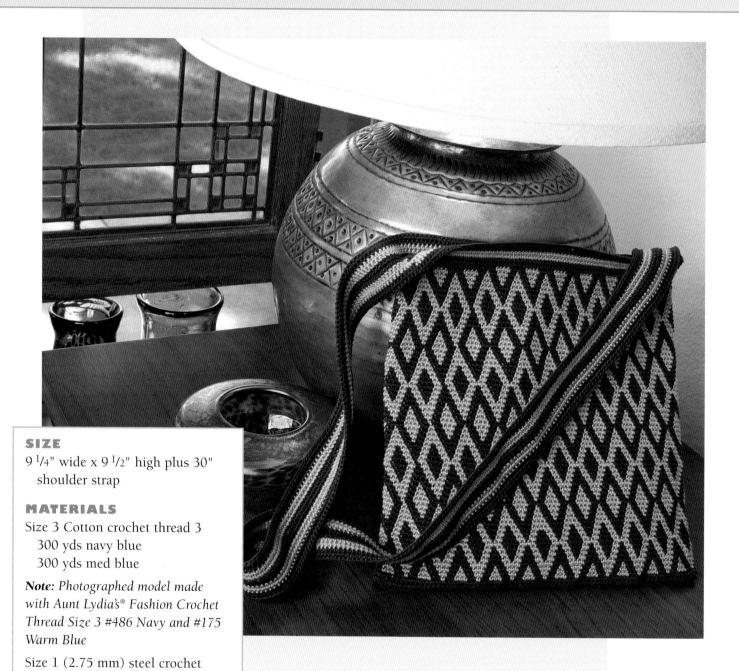

SIZE

9 1/4" wide x 9 1/2" high plus 30" shoulder strap

MATERIALS

Size 3 Cotton crochet thread 3
   300 yds navy blue
   300 yds med blue

Note: Photographed model made with Aunt Lydia's® Fashion Crochet Thread Size 3 #486 Navy and #175 Warm Blue

Size 1 (2.75 mm) steel crochet hook (or size required for gauge)

Stitch marker

GAUGE

35 sc and 30 sc rows = 4"

To carry tail: Lay tail over top of sts being worked into, then sc across as usual, encasing carried tail within sts (see diagram). If done correctly, carried tail will not be visible from front or back of work.

Tapestry crochet st: While carrying non-working thread over top of sts in rnd below, insert hook in next st and draw up a lp with working thread, YO and draw through 2 lps on hook, encasing carried (non-working) thread within sts (see diagram): tapestry crochet st made.

To change color in tapestry crochet: Work st until 2 lps rem on hook, drop working thread, pick up non-working (carried) thread and draw through both lps on hook. Non-working thread now becomes working thread. Working thread now becomes non-working thread and is carried over top of sts in rnd below.

INSTRUCTIONS

Starting at bottom, ch 79 with navy, leaving 14" tail at beg of ch.

Rnd 1: Sc in 2nd ch from hook and in next 76 chs, 4 sc in last ch; working in free lps on other side of foundation ch and carrying navy tail, sc in next 76 chs, 3 sc in last ch: 160 sc. Do not join. Insert stitch marker in last st and move up to last st of each rnd.

Note: Work rest of bag in tapestry crochet sts, changing colors as necessary and carrying non-working thread on top of sts in rnd below (see diagram).

Rnd 2: Cut navy tail close to work and start to carry warm blue thread under sts being worked. Tapestry crochet 160 navy blue: 160 sts.

Rnd 3: *Tapestry crochet 1 med blue, 2 navy, 3 med blue, 2 navy; rep from * 19 times more.

Rnd 4: *Tapestry crochet 2 med blue, 2 navy; rep from * around.

Rnd 5: *Tapestry crochet 3 med blue, 2 navy, 1 med blue, 2 navy; rep from * around.

Rnd 6: *Tapestry crochet 4 med blue, 4 navy; rep from * around.

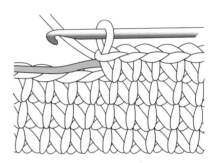

Tapestry crochet

Rnd 7: *Tapestry crochet 2 med blue, 1 navy, 2 med blue, 3 navy; rep from * around.

Rnd 8: Rep Rnd 4.

Rnd 9: *Tapestry crochet 2 med blue, 3 navy, 2 med blue, 1 navy; rep from * around.

Rnd 10: *Tapestry crochet 2 med blue, 4 navy, 2 med blue; rep from * around.

Rnd 11: *Tapestry crochet 1 navy, 2 med blue, 3 navy, 2 med blue; rep from * around.

Rnd 12: *Tapestry crochet 2 navy, 2 med blue; rep from * around.

Instructions continue on next page. →

Rnd 13: *Tapestry crochet 3 navy, 2 med blue, 1 navy, 2 med blue; rep from * around.

Rnd 14: *Tapestry crochet 4 navy, 4 med blue; rep from * around.

Rnd 15: *Tapestry crochet 2 navy, 1 med blue, 2 navy, 3 med blue; rep from * around.

Rnd 16: Rep Rnd 12.

Rnd 17: *Tapestry crochet 2 navy, 3 med blue, 2 navy, 1 med blue; rep from * around.

Rnd 18: *Tapestry crochet 2 navy, 4 med blue, 2 navy; rep from * around.

Note: *Notice that motif is slightly diagonal. This is normal, since tapestry crochet sts are not exactly on top of sts immediately below.*

Rnds 19 through 66: Rep Rnds 3 through 18 three times more. At end of Rnd 66, tapestry crochet 22 navy to end at side of handbag. Cut carried med blue thread close to work. Do not cut navy thread.

Top Edge and Shoulder Strap

First Side of Bag
With navy, ch 250, or desired length, for shoulder strap.

Rnd 1: Skip 80 sts on Rnd 66, making sure ch is not twisted, sc in next st. Tapestry crochet 80 navy across Rnd 66 while carrying med blue.

Rnd 2: Tapestry crochet 250 navy across ch for strap and 80 navy across top of bag while carrying med blue.

Rnds 3 and 4: Tapestry crochet 250 med blue across strap and 80 med blue across top of bag while carrying navy.

Rnds 5 and 6: Tapestry crochet 250 navy across strap and 80 navy across top of bag while carrying med blue. At end of Rnd 6, cut med blue close to work. Sl st in next st with navy. Finish off navy; weave in ends.

Second Side of Bag
Rnd 1: Turn shoulder bag over. Join navy with sl st in first skipped st on Rnd 66, leaving a 2" tail, ch 1, sc in same st, tapestry crochet 79 navy across Rnd 66 while carrying med blue thread and navy tail.

Rnd 2: Tapestry crochet 250 navy in free lps on other side of ch for strap and 80 navy across top of bag while carrying med blue.

Rnds 3 through 6: Rep Rnds 3 through 6 on First Side of Bag.

Finishing
Block shoulder bag with steam iron set on cotton.

#53 PRETTY FELTED PATCHWORK

Designed by Patons Design Staff

SIZE
14" wide x 16" high

MATERIALS
Worsted weight wool yarn
  7 oz gold
  7 oz brown
  7 oz rust
  3 ¹/₂ oz orange

Note: *Photographed model made with Patons® Classic Merino Wool #204 Old Gold, #205 Deep Olive, #206 Russet and #238 Paprika*

Size G (4 mm) crochet hook
  (or size required for gauge)

Awl tool, 4 mm diameter

GAUGE
Granny Square Motif = 3 ¹/₂"
  square

16 sc and 16 sc rows = 4"

Instructions continue on next page. →

INSTRUCTIONS

Granny Square (make 12)

With gold, ch 4; join with sl st to form a ring.

Rnd 1: Ch 3 (counts as dc), 2 dc in ring; *ch 1, 3 dc in ring; rep from * 2 times more; ch 1: 12 dc and 4 ch-1 sps; join with sl st in 3rd ch of beg ch-3.

Rnd 2: Ch 4 (counts as dc and ch-1 sp); *(3 dc, ch 1) twice in next ch-1 sp; rep from * 2 times more; (3 dc, ch 1, 2 dc) in last ch-1 sp: 24 dc and 8 ch-1 sps; join with sl st in 3rd ch of beg ch-4.

Rnd 3: Ch 3 (counts as dc), 2 dc in next ch-1 sp, ch 1; *(3 dc, ch 1) twice in next ch-1 sp, 3 dc in next ch-1 sp, ch 1; rep from * two times more; (3 dc, ch 1) twice in last ch-1 sp: 36 dc and 12 ch-1 sps; join with sl st in 3rd ch of beg ch-3. Finish off; weave in ends.

Piece A

(make 1 each with brown, rust and orange)

With appropriate color, ch 46.

Row 1: Sc in 2nd ch from hook, sc in each ch across: 45 sc; ch 1, turn.

Row 2: Sc in each sc across; ch 1, turn.

Rep Row 2 until piece measures 12". At end of last row, do not ch 1. Finish off; weave in ends.

Piece B

With rust, ch 30.

Row 1: Sc in 2nd ch from hook, sc in each ch across: 29 sc; ch 1, turn.

Row 2: Sc in each sc across; ch 1, turn.

Rep Row 2 until piece measures 15". At end of last row, do not ch 1. Finish off; weave in ends.

Handle/Gusset

With brown, ch 10.

Row 1: Sc in 2nd ch from hook, sc in each ch across: 9 sc; ch 1, turn.

Row 2: Sc in each sc across; ch 1, turn.

Rep Row 2 until piece measures 95". At end of last row, do not ch 1. Finish off; weave in ends.

Finishing

Following felting instructions on page 252, felt Pieces A, B and Handle/Gusset. Felted Piece A should measure about 8" x 8". Felted Piece B should measure about 5 1/2" x 11". Felted Handle/Gusset should measure about 1 1/2" x 72".

Squares

Cut four 3 1/2" squares from each Piece A (12 squares total). With awl tool, make 4 corner holes 1/4" in from both edges. Make 3 more holes evenly spaced between corner holes along each side of square, 1/4" in from edges. Join gold with sl st in any corner hole, ch 1; *(2 sc, ch 1, 2 sc) in corner hole, 3 sc in each hole along side; rep from * around; join with sl st in first sc. Finish off; weave in ends.

Triangle Motifs

Cut four Triangle Motifs 4 1/2" wide x 5" high from Piece B, cutting angles in opposite directions to have 2 right triangles and 2 left triangles. With awl tool, make corner hole 1/4" in from both edges at right angle. Make 1 hole at each point 1/2" below both edges. Make 6 holes along the shortest (bottom) side, 10 holes along the longest side and 8 holes along last side of Triangle Motif evenly spaced between corner holes, 1/4" in from edges.

Right Triangle Motif

Join gold with sl st in bottom right corner hole, ch 1, (2 sc, ch 1, 2 sc) in corner hole, 3 sc in each hole up right side of Triangle Motif, (2 sc, ch 2, 2 sc) in next point hole, 3 sc in each hole down longest side of Triangle Motif, (2 sc, ch 2, 2 sc) in next point hole, 3 sc in each hole along bottom side of Triangle Motif; join with sl st in first sc. Finish off; weave in ends.

Left Triangle Motif

Join gold with sl st in bottom left corner hole of Triangle Motif, ch 1, (2 sc, ch 1, 2 sc) in corner hole, 3 sc in each hole along bottom side of Triangle Motif, (2 sc, ch 2, 2 sc) in next point hole, 3 sc in each hole up longest side of Triangle Motif, (2 sc, ch 2, 2 sc) in next point hole, 3 sc in each hole down left side of Triangle Motif; join with sl st in first sc. Finish off; weave in ends.

Handle/Gusset

Trim Handle/Gusset to measure 70" long. With an awl tool, make 4 corner holes 1/4" in from both edges. Make 2 holes evenly spaced between corner holes along short sides of Handle/Gusset, 1/4" in from edges. Make remaining holes 1/2" apart along long sides of Handle/Gusset, 1/4" in from edges. Join gold with sl st in any corner hole, ch 1, *(2 sc, ch 1, 2 sc) in corner hole, work 3 sc in each hole along sides and (2 sc, ch 1, 2 sc) in each corner hole; join with sl st in first sc. Finish off; weave in ends.

Assembly

With right sides facing and gold, sew together 12 Squares for Front and 12 Squares for Back in 3 rows of 4 squares each as shown in photograph or as desired. Sew shortest side of Triangle Motifs to Front and Back as shown in photograph. Sew short sides of Handle/Gusset together to form a ring, taking care not to twist gusset. Pin Handle/Gusset to Front, with gusset seam at center bottom of bag. Starting at top of Triangle Motif, with right sides facing and gold, sew Handle/Gusset and Front together. Repeat for Back.

#54 BELTED BAG

Designed by Bernat Design Staff

SIZE
6" x 9"

MATERIALS
Bulky weight eyelash yarn,
  1 3/4 oz brown (MC)
  1 3/4 oz multicolor (A)

Note: Photographed model made with Bernat® Disco #68013 Mr Brown (MC) and #68526 Jungle Jive (A)

1 1/2" wide belt, at least 32" long

Size 9 (5.5 mm) knitting needles
  (or size required for gauge)

Spare knitting needle Size 9

GAUGE
16 sts and 25 rows = 4" in patt

INSTRUCTIONS

Notes: *(1) Slip all sts as to purl. (2) Carry yarn not in use loosely up side of work.*

Front

With MC, CO 41 sts.

Row 1 (wrong side): With MC, K1; *sl 1, K1; rep from * across.

Row 2: Purl.

Row 3: With A, K1; *K1, sl 1; rep from * to last 2 sts, K2.

Row 4: Purl.

Rep Rows 1 through 4 of pattern until piece measures about 5", ending by working a Row 1. Place markers at each end of last row.

Handles

Row 1 (right side): P14, turn; place rem sts on a spare needle.

Row 2: Sl 1, K1, PSSO, K1; work in patt across: 13 sts.

Row 3: Purl to last 2 sts, P2tog: 12 sts.

Row 4: Work in patt across.

Rep Rows 2 and 4, two times more: 10 sts.

Work even in patt until piece measures 3" from marked row, ending by working a right-side row. BO.

With right side of work facing, join appropriate color to rem sts on spare needle and BO next 13 sts; purl to end of row: 14 sts.

Row 1: Work in patt across.

Row 2: P2tog, purl across: 13 sts.

Row 3: Work in patt across.

Row 4: Rep Row 2: 12 sts.

Rep Rows 3 and 4 two times more: 10 sts.

Work even in patt until piece measures 3" from marked row, ending by working a right-side row. BO.

Back

Work same as Front.

Finishing

Sew side and bottom seams.

Cut desired length of belt (without buckle) for handle. Sew handle to top of crocheted handles. Buckle rem length of belt around purse as shown in photo. Shake purse to fluff up yarn.

#55 CAGED TOTE

Designed by Vashti Braha

SIZE
About 10" wide x 10 ½" high plus 24" shoulder straps

MATERIALS
Worsted weight yarn
  6 oz black

Super bulky ribbon yarn
  8 ¾ oz rainbow

Note: *Photographed model made with Caron® Simply Soft® #9727 Ebony and Caron® Pizazz, #0001 Birthday*

Straight dowel-type tote handles, 15 ½" long

Black cotton fabric for interlining, about 15" x 30" (optional)

Medium or heavy weight colorful fabric for lining, about 15" x 30" (optional)

Low-temp iron-on adhesive, about 15" x 30" plus scrap pieces (optional)

Sewing needle (optional)

Black thread (optional)

Stabilizer, 8" x 10" piece (optional)

Hot glue gun or fabric glue (optional)

Iron (optional)

Quilter's mini-iron, recommended (optional)

Size G (4 mm) crochet hook (or size required for gauge)

Size K (6.5 mm) crochet hook (or size required for gauge)

GAUGE
10 sc plus 10 chs = 4" with G hook and worsted weight yarn

2 picots plus 2 ch-7 sps = 4" with K hook and ribbon yarn

INSTRUCTIONS

Inner Bag

Note: Inner bag is worked with G hook throughout in one piece (except for handle lps), then seamed to create 2"-wide gussets and a 2" x 10" base.

Top of First Side

Starting at top with black, ch 47.

Row 1 (right side): Sc in back bar of 2nd ch from hook and in back bar of each rem ch across: 46 sc; ch 1, turn.

Row 2: Sc in first sc; *ch 1, skip next sc, sc in next sc; rep from * across to last sc; sc in last sc: 24 sc and 22 ch-1 sps; ch 1, turn.

Row 3: Sc in first sc; *ch 1, skip next sc, sc in next ch-1 sp; rep from * across to last sc; sc in last sc; ch 1, turn.

Rows 4 through 8: Rep Row 3 five times more. At end of Row 8, ch 7 instead of ch 1.

First Side and Gusset

Row 9: Sc in 2nd ch from hook and in next 5 chs, sc in next sc; *ch 1, skip next sc, sc in next ch-1 sp; rep from * across to last sc; sc in last sc; work beg Csc, work 5 Csc: 58 sts; ch 1, turn.

Row 10: Sc in first sc; *ch 1, skip next sc, sc in next sc*; rep from * to * 2 times more; **ch 1, skip next sc, sc in next ch-1 sp; rep from ** 21 times more; rep from * to * 3 times more; sc in last sc: 30 sc and 28 ch-1 sps; ch 1, turn.

Rows 11 through 39: Rep Row 3 twenty nine times more. At end of Row 39, turn, but do not ch 1.

Bottom

Row 40: Sl st across first 7 sts, ch 1, sc in same st as last sl st; *ch 1, skip next sc, sc in next ch-1 sp; rep from * across to last 7 sts; sc in next st: 24 sc and 22 ch-1 sps; ch 1, turn, leaving last 6 sts unworked.

Rows 41 and 50: Rep Row 3 ten times more. At end of Row 50, ch 7 instead of ch 1.

Second Side and Gusset

Rows 51 through 81: Rep Rows 9 through 39.

Top of Second Side

Row 82: Rep Row 40.

Rows 83 through 88: Rep Row 3 six times more.

Row 89: Sc in first sc, sc in each ch-1 sp and in each sc across: 46 sc; ch 1, turn.

First Handle Loop

Row 90: Sc in first sc; *ch 1, skip next sc, sc in next sc; rep from * 2 times more; sc in next sc: 5 sc and 3 ch-1 sps; ch 1, turn, leaving rem sts unworked.

Rows 91 through 102: Rep Row 3 twelve times more, or until handle loop measures 3" long. Finish off; weave in ends.

Instructions continue on next page. ➡

Second Handle Loop

Row 90: With wrong side facing, skip next 11 sc on Row 89, join black with sl st in next sc, ch 1, sc in same sc as joining; *ch 1, skip next sc, sc in next sc; rep from * 2 times more; sc in next sc: 5 sc and 3 ch-1 sps; ch 1, turn, leaving rem sts unworked.

Rows 91 through 102: Rep Rows 91 through 102 on First Handle Loop.

Third Handle Loop

Rows 90 through 102: Rep Rows 90 through 102 on Second Handle Loop, working in last 8 sts on Row 89.

Fourth Handle Loop

Row 1: With wrong side facing and working in free lps of foundation ch, join black with sl st in first ch, ch 1, sc in same ch as joining; *ch 1, skip next ch, sc in next ch; rep from * 2 times more; sc in next ch: 5 sc and 3 ch-1 sps; ch 1, turn, leaving rem chs unworked.

Rows 2 through 13: Rep Rows 91 through 102 on First Handle Loop.

Fifth Handle Loop

Row 1: With wrong side facing and working in free lps of foundation ch, skip next 11 chs, join black with sl st in next ch, ch 1, sc in same ch as joining; *ch 1, skip next ch, sc in next ch; rep from * 2 times more; sc in next ch: 5 sc and 3 ch-1 sps; ch 1, turn, leaving rem chs unworked.

Rows 2 through 13: Rep Rows 91 through 102 on First Handle Loop.

Sixth Handle Loop

Rows 1 through 13: Rep Rows 1 through 13 on Fifth Handle Loop, working in last 8 chs on foundation ch.

Cage

Note: The rectangular base of this outer layer is worked first, then sides and handle loops are worked in the rnd; there is no seaming or rein-forcements.

With K hook and rainbow, ch 42.

Row 1 (right side): Tr in back bar of 9th ch from hook (skipped chs count as tr and ch-2 sp); *ch 2, skip next 2 chs, tr in back bar of next ch; rep from * across: 13 tr and 12 ch-2 sps; ch 5 (counts as dc and ch-2 sp on next row), turn.

Row 2: *Dc in next tr, ch 2; rep from * across; skip next 2 chs, dc in next ch: 13 dc and 12 ch-2 sps; ch 6 (counts as tr and ch-2 sp on next row), turn: bottom made.

Row 3: *Tr in next dc, ch 2; rep from * across; skip next 2 chs, tr in next ch: 13 tr and 12 ch-2 sps; ch 1, turn.

Rnd 1 (wrong side): Picot in first tr; *ch 7, skip next tr, FPsc in next tr; rep from * 4 times more**; ch 7, picot in 4th ch of turning ch-6 on Row 2; ch 7, sc around post of dc on Row 2; ch 7, picot in 3rd ch of foundation ch after base of next tr; rep from * to ** once; ch 7, picot in free lps of first ch of foundation ch; ch 7, sc around post of dc on Row 2; ch 3, tr in first sc of first picot to form last ch-7 sp: 16 ch-7 sps and 4 picots; ch 1, turn.

Rnd 2 (right side): Picot in ch-3 sp after tr; *ch 6, picot in next ch-7 sp; rep from * around; ch 3, dc in first sc of first picot to form last ch-6 sp: 16 ch-6 sps and 16 picots; ch 1, do not turn.

Rnds 3 through 8: Picot around post of dc; *ch 6, picot in next ch-6 sp; rep from * around; ch 3, dc in first sc of first picot to form last ch-6 sp; ch 1, do not turn.

Rnd 9: Picot around post of dc; *ch 9, picot in next ch-6 sp; rep from * around; ch 9, sl st in first sc of first picot: 16 ch-9 sps and 16 picots. Finish off; weave in ends.

Lining (optional)

Note: Yarn is heat-sensitive so practice on a swatch first. Never let yarn come in direct contact with iron.

Cut piece of iron-on adhesive 1/4" smaller on all sides than inner bag, including handle loops. Fuse to wrong side of inner bag. Let cool and remove paper backing.

Cut piece of black fabric 1/4" smaller on all sides than inner bag except same size as all 6 handle loops. Hem 2 sides of each handle loop 1/4" to wrong side of fabric. Fuse wrong side of black fabric to wrong side of inner bag. Let cool.

Cut 2 pieces of stabilizer 1 3/4" x 9 3/4". Fuse one piece to right side of black fabric at bottom of bag (Rows 40 through 50.) Fuse second piece to first piece to reinforce bottom of bag. Cut 2 pieces of stabilizer 2" x 7" each for gussets. Fold pieces in half lengthwise and iron halfway along fold so half of length of fold is creased. Cut two pieces of iron-on adhesive 2" x 7" each. Fuse iron-on adhesive to inward-bending side of each stabilizer gusset piece. Leave paper on. While still hot, fold again along creased part of fold. Set aside.

Cut colorful lining fabric to same size and shape as inner bag, 1/2" past top edges that will form opening of bag, but not including handle loops.

Seaming

With black yarn and G hook, with right sides of inner bag together, seam tog sides of gusset flaps (Rows 9 through 39 & 51 through 81) and bottom edges of gusset flaps to bottom edge of bag; rep for other gusset.

Note: Finished seam on each side looks like an upside-down "T".

Lining continued (optional)

Fuse stabilizer gusset piece to seam on gusset with inward-folding crease against seam at top of bag; rep for other gusset. Turn bag right side out.

Seam colorful lining with right sides tog in same boxy shape as inner bag, with 1/4" seam allowance on all sides except 1/2" seam allowance at top opening of bag. Insert lining into inner bag and seam or glue lining opening to bag opening. Fold each of 6 handle loops in half toward inside of bag and seam or glue last row of each handle loop to first row of handle loop.

Finishing

Weave one dowel through half of ch-9 sps on last row of cage and through inner bag handle loops for one side of bag, as shown in photo; rep with second dowel for other side of bag.

Shoulder Straps (make 2)

With K hook and ribbon yarn, ch 80; sc tightly in 2nd ch from hook and in next 7 chs; fold sc sts so first sc is behind 8th sc, sl st 8th sc and first sc tog tightly to form a loop, sc tightly in rem chs across; fold sc sts so 8th sc from end is behind last sc, sl st last sc and 8th sc from end tog tightly to form a loop, sl st in next 3 sc tightly. Finish off; weave in ends. Slide looped ends of straps onto dowel ends and secure in place with drop of glue.

#56 GOING GREEN

Designed by Mickie Akins for Coats & Clark

SIZE
6" wide x 4" high at center
   plus 11" or 25" strap

MATERIALS
Nylon yarn
   200 yds lt green

Note: *Photographed model made with J&P Coats® Nylon Crochet #51 Lt Green*

Size E (3.5 mm) crochet hook
   (or size required for gauge)

46 green pony beads

¼ yd lt green lining fabric
   (optional)

7" lt green zipper

Needle and sewing thread to
   match lining fabric (optional)

GAUGE
18 sc and 18 sc rows = 4"

Sc decrease (sc dec): (Insert hook in next st and draw up a lp) twice, YO and draw through all 3 lps on hook: sc dec made.

Sc bead st: Slide bead up to hook; working behind bead, insert hook in next st and draw up a lp, YO and draw through 2 lps on hook: sc bead st made.

Note: Thread 23 beads onto yarn before beginning each side.

INSTRUCTIONS

Side (make 2)

Starting at top, ch 30.

Row 1 (wrong side): Working in back lp and back bar of chs, sc in 2nd ch from hook, sc in next 8 chs, (2 sc in next ch, sc in next 8 chs) 2 times, sc dec in last 2 chs: 30 sc; ch 1, turn.

Row 2 (right side): Sc dec in first 2 sc, sc in next sc and in each sc across to last 2 sc, sc dec in last 2 sc: 28 sc; ch 1, turn.

Row 3: Sc dec in first 2 sc, sc in next 3 sc, 2 sc in next sc, (sc in next 7 sc, 2 sc in next sc) 2 times, sc in next 4 sc, sc dec in last 2 sc: 29 sc; ch 1, turn.

Row 4: Sc dec in first 2 sc, sc in next 3 sc, sc bead st, (sc in next 5 sc, sc bead st) 3 times, sc in next 3 sc, sc dec in last 2 sc: 23 sc and 4 sc bead sts; ch 1, turn.

Row 5: Sc dec in first 2 sc, sc in next 5 sc, (2 sc in next sc, sc in next 5 sc) 3 times, sc dec in last 2 sc: 28 sc; ch 1, turn.

Row 6: Sc dec in first 2 sc, sc in next 3 sc, (sc bead st, sc in next 2 sc, sc bead st, sc in next 3 sc) 3 times, sc dec in last 2 sc: 20 sc and 6 sc bead sts; ch 1, turn.

Row 7: Sc dec in first 2 sc, sc in next 3 sc, (2 sc in next sc, sc in next 7 sc) 2 times, 2 sc in next sc, sc in next 2 sc, sc dec in last 2 sc: 27 sc; ch 1, turn.

Row 8: Sc dec in first 2 sc, sc in next 3 sc, sc bead st, sc in next 2 sc, (sc bead st, sc in next sc) 5 times, sc bead st, sc in next 2 sc, sc bead st, sc in next 3 sc, sc dec in last 2 sc: 17 sc and 8 sc bead sts; ch 1, turn.

Row 9: Sc dec in first 2 sc, (sc in next 5 sc, 2 sc in next sc) 3 times, sc in next 3 sc, sc dec in last 2 sc: 26 sc; ch 1, turn.

Row 10: Sc dec in first 2 sc, sc in next 9 sc, sc bead st, sc in next 2 sc, sc bead st, sc in next 9 sc, sc dec in last 2 sc: 22 sc and 2 sc bead sts; ch 1, turn.

Row 11: Sc dec in first 2 sc, sc in next 4 sc, 2 sc in next sc, (sc in next 5 sc, 2 sc in next sc) 2 times, sc in next 3 sc, sc dec in last 2 sc: 25 sc; ch 1, turn.

Row 12: Sc dec in first 2 sc, sc in next 10 sc, sc bead st, sc in next 10 sc, sc dec in last 2 sc: 22 sc and 1 sc bead st; ch 1, turn.

Row 13: Sc dec in first 2 sc, sc in next 2 sc, (2 sc in next sc, sc in next 4 sc) 3 times, 2 sc in next sc, sc in next sc, sc dec in last 2 sc: 25 sc; ch 1, turn.

Row 14: Sc dec in first 2 sc, sc in next 9 sc, sc bead st, sc in next sc, sc bead st, sc in next 9 sc, sc dec in last 2 sc: 21 sc and 2 sc bead sts; ch 1, turn.

Row 15: Sc dec in first 2 sc, sc in next 3 sc, (2 sc in next sc, sc in next 5 sc) 2 times, 2 sc in next sc, sc in next 3 sc, sc dec in last 2 sc: 24 sc; ch 1, turn.

Row 16: Rep Row 2: 22 sc.

Instructions continue on next page. →

Row 17: Sc dec in first 2 sc, sc in next 3 sc, (2 sc in next sc, sc in next 5 sc) 2 times, 2 sc in next sc, sc in next 2 sc, sc dec in last 2 sc: 23 sc; ch 1, turn.

Row 18: Rep Row 2: 21 sc.

Row 19: Rep Row 2: 19 sc.

Row 20: Rep Row 2: 17 sc. At end of row, do not ch 1. Finish off; weave in ends.

Gusset

Ch 62.

Row 1 (wrong side): Sc in 2nd ch from hook and in each rem ch across: 61 sc; turn.

Row 2 (right side): Skip first sc, sl st in next 2 sc, sc in next sc and in each sc across to last 3 sc, sl st in next sc, leaving last 2 sc unworked: 55 sc; turn.

Row 3: Skip first sl st, sl st in next 11 sc, sc in next 33 sc, sl st in next sc, leaving last 10 sc unworked: 33 sc; turn.

Row 4: Skip first sl st, sl st in next 8 sc, sc in next 17 sc, sl st in next sc, leaving last 7 sc unworked: 17 sc. Finish off; weave in ends.

Row 5: With wrong side facing and working in free lps on opposite side of foundation ch, skip first 2 chs, join with sl st in next ch, sc in next ch and in each ch across to last 3 chs, sl st in next ch, leaving last 2 chs unworked: 55 sc; turn.

Rows 6 and 7: Rep Rows 3 and 4. At end of Row 7, finish off; weave in ends.

Strap

Ch 112 for shoulder strap or 49 for arm strap.

Row 1 (right side): Working in back bar of chs, sc in 2nd ch from hook and in each ch across: 111 or 48 sc; ch 1, turn.

Rows 2 and 3: Sc in first sc and in each sc across; ch 1, turn. At end of Row 3, do not ch 1. Finish off; weave in ends.

Lining (optional)

Using crochet pieces as patterns, cut 2 Side pieces and 1 Gusset piece from lining fabric with 1/2" added on all edges for seams. With right sides together and 1/2" seam allowance, sew side and bottom edges of Side linings to long edges of Gusset lining. Press top edges of Side linings 1/2" to wrong side.

Joining

With wrong sides together, matching side and bottom edges of one Side to one long edge of Gusset, working through both layers, join with sc at top left corner of Side, work sc evenly across left side, bottom and right side to top right corner of Side. Finish off; weave in ends.

Repeat with other Side and other long edge of Gusset.

Finishing

Sew right side of zipper in place along wrong side of top edge of Sides at base of Row 1; fold each short end of zipper 1/4" to wrong side and sew to top of Gusset.

Optional

With lining wrong side out, insert lining into assembled Sides and Gusset; sew top folded edges of Lining to wrong side of zipper along previous zipper seam.

Sew short edges of Strap to top edges of Gusset about 1/4" down from top edge.

#57 NIGHT ON THE TOWN

Designed by Patons Design Staff

SIZE
5 1/2" wide x 6 1/2" high plus
   8" strap

MATERIALS
DK weight yarn
   1 3/4 oz burgundy

Note: *Photographed model made
with Patons® Brilliant #4430
Beautiful Burgundy*

Purse clasp, 3 1/2" wide

1/4 yd burgundy lining fabric
   (optional)

Size F (3.75 mm) crochet
   hook (or size required for
   gauge)

GAUGE
18 hdc and 16 hdc rows = 4"

SPECIAL STITCHES
Front post dc (FPdc): YO, insert hook from
front to back to front around post of specified st on previous row and draw up a lp,
(YO and draw through 2 lps on hook) 2
times: FPdc made.

Back post dc (BPdc): YO, insert hook from
back to front to back around post of specified st on previous row and draw up a lp,
(YO and draw through 2 lps on hook) 2
times: BPdc made.

Picot: Ch 3, sl st in top of last dc: picot
made.

INSTRUCTIONS

Note: *Work first hdc in each row in last hdc
of previous row. Do not work any sts in turning ch-2.*

Front
Starting at top, ch 23.

Row 1 (wrong side): Hdc in 3rd ch from hook,
hdc in next ch and in each ch across: 21
hdc; ch 2, turn.

Row 2 (right side): Hdc in first 9 hdc, skip
next hdc, (FPdc, ch 3, FPdc) in next hdc,
skip next hdc, hdc in last 9 hdc: 18 hdc, 2
FPdc and 1 ch-3 sp; ch 2, turn.

143

Instructions continue on next page. →

Row 3: Hdc in first 9 hdc, BPdc in next FPdc, ch 2, sc in next ch-3 sp, ch 2, BPdc in next FPdc, hdc in last 9 hdc: 18 hdc, 2 BPdc, 1 sc and 2 ch-2 sps; ch 2, turn.

Row 4: Hdc in first 8 hdc, skip next hdc, FPdc in next BPdc, ch 2, sc in next ch-2 sp, ch 3, sc in next ch-2 sp, ch 2, FPdc in next BPdc, skip next hdc, hdc in last 8 hdc: 16 hdc, 2 FPdc, 2 sc, 2 ch-2 sps and 1 ch-3 sp; ch 2, turn.

Row 5: Hdc in first 8 hdc, BPdc in next FPdc, ch 3, skip next ch-2 sp, sc in next ch-3 sp, ch 3, skip next ch-2 sp, BPdc in next FPdc, hdc in last 8 hdc: 16 hdc, 2 BPdc, 1 sc and 2 ch-3 sps; ch 2, turn.

Row 6: Hdc in first 7 hdc, skip next hdc, FPdc in next BPdc, (ch 3, sc in next ch-3 sp) twice, ch 3, FPdc in next BPdc, skip next hdc, hdc in last 7 hdc: 14 hdc, 2 FPdc, 2 sc and 3 ch-3 sps; ch 2, turn.

Row 7: Hdc in first 7 hdc, BPdc in next FPdc, ch 2, sc in next ch-3 sp, (ch 3, sc in next ch-3 sp) twice, ch 2, BPdc in next FPdc, hdc in last 7 hdc: 14 hdc, 2 BPdc, 3 sc, 2 ch-2 sps and 2 ch-3 sps; ch 2, turn.

Row 8: Hdc in first 6 hdc, skip next hdc, FPdc in next BPdc, ch 2, sc in next ch-2 sp, (ch 3, sc in next ch-3 sp) twice, ch 3, sc in next ch-2 sp, ch 2, FPdc in next BPdc, skip next hdc, hdc in last 6 hdc: 12 hdc, 2 FPdc, 4 sc, 2 ch-2 sps and 3 ch-3 sps; ch 2, turn.

Row 9: Hdc in first 6 hdc, BPdc in next FPdc, skip next ch-2 sp, (ch 3, sc in next ch-3 sp) 3 times, ch 3, skip next ch-2 sp, BPdc in next FPdc, hdc in last 6 hdc: 12 hdc, 2 BPdc, 3 sc and 4 ch-3 sps; ch 2, turn.

Row 10: Hdc in first 5 hdc, skip next hdc, FPdc in next BPdc, (ch 3, sc in next ch-3 sp) 4 times, ch 3, FPdc in next BPdc, skip next hdc, hdc in last 5 hdc: 10 hdc, 2 FPdc, 4 sc and 5 ch-3 sps; ch 2, turn.

Row 11: Hdc in first 5 hdc, BPdc in next FPdc, ch 2, sc in next ch-3 sp, (ch 3, sc in next ch-3 sp) 4 times, ch 2, BPdc in next FPdc, hdc in last 5 hdc: 10 hdc, 2 BPdc, 5 sc, 2 ch-2 sps and 4 ch-3 sps; ch 2, turn.

Row 12: Hdc in first 4 hdc, skip next hdc, FPdc in next BPdc, ch 2, sc in next ch-2 sp, (ch 3, sc in next ch-3 sp) 4 times, ch 3, sc in next ch-2 sp, ch 2, FPdc in next BPdc, skip next hdc, hdc in last 4 hdc: 8 hdc, 2 FPdc, 6 sc, 2 ch-2 sps and 5 ch-3 sps; ch 2, turn.

Row 13: Hdc in first 4 hdc, BPdc in next FPdc, skip next ch-2 sp, (ch 3, sc in next ch-3 sp) 5 times, ch 3, skip next ch-2 sp, BPdc in next FPdc, hdc in last 4 hdc: 8 hdc, 2 BPdc, 5 sc and 6 ch-3 sps; ch 2, turn.

Row 14: Hdc in first 3 hdc, skip next hdc, FPdc in next BPdc, (ch 3, sc in next ch-3 sp) 6 times, ch 3, FPdc in next BPdc, skip next hdc, hdc in last 3 hdc: 6 hdc, 2 FPdc, 6 sc and 7 ch-3 sps; ch 2, turn.

Row 15: Hdc in first 3 hdc, BPdc in next FPdc, ch 2, sc in next ch-3 sp, (ch 3, sc in next ch-3 sp) 6 times, ch 2, BPdc in next FPdc, hdc in last 3 hdc: 6 hdc, 2 BPdc, 7 sc, 2 ch-2 sps and 6 ch-3 sps; ch 2, turn.

Row 16: Hdc in first 2 hdc, skip next hdc, FPdc in next BPdc, ch 2, sc in next ch-2 sp, (ch 3, sc in next ch-3 sp) 6 times, ch 3, sc in next ch-2 sp, ch 2, FPdc in next BPdc, skip next hdc, hdc in last 2 hdc: 4 hdc, 2 FPdc, 8 sc, 2 ch-2 sps and 7 ch-3 sps; ch 2, turn.

Row 17: Hdc in first 2 hdc, BPdc in next FPdc, skip next ch-2 sp, (ch 3, sc in next ch-3 sp) 7 times, ch 3, skip next ch-2 sp, BPdc in next FPdc, hdc in last 2 hdc: 4 hdc, 2 BPdc, 7 sc and 8 ch-3 sps; ch 2, turn.

Row 18: Hdc in first hdc, skip next hdc, FPdc in next BPdc, (ch 3, sc in next ch-3 sp) 8 times, ch 3, FPdc in next BPdc, skip next hdc, hdc in last hdc: 2 hdc, 2 FPdc, 8 sc and 9 ch-3 sps; ch 2, turn.

Row 19: Hdc in first hdc, BPdc in next FPdc, ch 2, sc in next ch-3 sp, (ch 3, sc in next ch-3 sp) 8 times, ch 2, BPdc in next FPdc, hdc in last hdc: 2 hdc, 2 BPdc, 9 sc, 2 ch-2 sps and 8 ch-3 sps.

Row 20: Skip first hdc, FPdc in next BPdc, ch 2, sc in next ch-2 sp, (ch 3, sc in next ch-3 sp) 8 times, ch 3, sc in next ch-2 sp, ch 2, FPdc in next BPdc: 2 FPdc, 10 sc, 2 ch-2 sps and 9 ch-3 sps. Finish off; weave in ends.

Back

Work same as Front.

Lining (optional)

Using Front and Back as patterns, mark wrong side of lining fabric, adding ¹/₂" seam allowance. Cut out lining pieces. With right sides together, sew sides and bottom of lining pieces together. Fold and press top of lining ¹/₂" to wrong side.

Joining Front and Back

With right sides of Front and Back together, join with sl st in edge of Row 4 on left side, ch 1, working through both thicknesses, sc in edge of each row and in top of each st down left side of Bag. Finish off; weave in ends. Rep on right side, leaving bottom unworked. Turn Bag right side out. With right side of Bag facing, join with sl st in ch-2 sp at bottom left-hand corner, ch 1, working through both thicknesses, sc in same sp as joining; (3 dc, picot, 3 dc) in next ch-3 sp, sc in next ch-2 sp; rep from * 4 times more. Finish off; weave in ends.

Optional: Stitch top of lining to inside of Bag ¹/₂" down from top of Bag.

Sew top edge of Bag to holes in clasp.

Strap

Ch 50, sl st in 2nd ch from hook, sl st in next ch and in each ch across, working in free lps on opposite side of foundation ch, sl st in each lp across. Finish off. Sew ends of Strap to notches on clasp.

#58 GUSSIED UP

Designed by Anne Rubin for Judi & Co.

SIZE
7" x 9"

MATERIALS
Rayon cord
   288 yds taupe

Note: *Photographed model made with Judi & Co's Cordé taupe*

One ³/4" magnetic snap

Size G (4 mm) crochet hook
   (or size required for gauge)

Size 5 (3.75 mm) knitting
   needles (optional) (or size
   required for gauge)

GAUGE
8 dc = 2"

9 sts = 2" in garter stitch (knit
   every row) (optional)

INSTRUCTIONS

Front

Starting at side edge, ch 29.

Foundation Row: Dc in 4th ch from hook and in each rem ch: 27 dc; ch 3 (counts as first dc of following row), turn.

Row 1: BPdc around each of next 2 sts; *FPdc around each of next 3 sts, BPdc around each of next 3 sts; rep from * across to last 3 sts, BPdc in 2 sts, dc in top of turning ch; ch 3, turn.

Row 2: FPdc around each BPdc, BPdc around each FPdc to last 3 sts, BPdc around last 2 FPdc, dc in top of turning ch; ch 3, turn.

Row 3: Rep Row 1.

Row 4: BPdc around each of next 2 sts; *FPdc around each of next 3 sts, BPdc around each of next 3 sts; rep from * across, FPdc around last 2 sts, dc in last st; ch 3, turn.

Row 5: BPdc around each FPdc, FPdc around each BPdc; dc in last st; ch 3, turn.

Rows 6: Rep Row 4.

Rep Rows 1 through 6 until piece measures 9". At end of last row, work one row sc around all four edges, working 3 sc in each corner.

Finish off, weave in ends.

Back

Work same as Front.

Gusset

Optional Knitted Gusset (shown in photo)
With knitting needles, CO 9 sts. Knit every row until piece measures 46". BO.

Crocheted Gusset (not shown)
Ch 9.

Row 1: Sc in 2nd ch from hook and in each rem ch: 8 sc; ch 1, turn.

Row 2: Sc in each sc, ch 1, turn.

Rep Row 2 until piece measures 46".

Assembly

Turn Front sideways with long edge horizontal. Starting at top left corner, sew gusset to left side edge (short edge) with whipstitch, continue along bottom edge and up remaining right side edge, leaving remaining long edge loose for top opening. Join Back in same manner to opposite edge of gusset; rem gusset forms strap. Sew rem end of gusset to opposite side of opening.

Stabilizer (make 2)

Ch 5.

Row 1: Sc in 2nd ch from hook and in each rem ch; ch 1, turn.

Row 2: Sc in each sc, ch 1, turn.

Rep Row 2 until piece measures 1" long. Finish off.

Attach one piece of magnetic snap to each stabilizer. Sew stabilizers inside of purse, centered at top opening about 1/2" down from top edge.

#59 A TRIBUTE TO COCO

Designed by Vashti Braha

SIZE
9" wide x 5 1/2" high x 2" deep

MATERIALS
Super bulky weight chenille yarn
   7 oz mango with metallic flecks

Note: Photographed model made with Caron® Glimmer #0007 Mango

Matching medium weight fabric for lining,
   16" x 20" piece

Non-fusible stiff stabilizer, two 13" x 18"
   pieces

Iron-on adhesive, 16" x 20" piece, 13" x 18"
   piece, 3" x 8 1/4" piece

3 magnetic snaps

5 extra-large eyelets, 7/16" diameter

4 large eyelets, 1/4" diameter

Eyelet-setting tools for 7/16" and 1/4" eyelets

Hammer and pliers

Mini iron and regular iron

Metal zinc-plated jack chain that fits
   through 7/16" eyelets, 36" to 48" long

Sewing needle and matching thread

Flat-backed round white rhinestones: one
   18mm and four 9mm or 10mm

Tweezers

Aleene's Platinum Bond Super Fabric textile
   glue

Small clamps to hold seams while shaping
   (optional)

Size J (6 mm) crochet hook (or size
   required for gauge)

Size H (5 mm) crochet hook

GAUGE
10 sc = 4" with J hook,

Front Post sc (FPsc): Insert hook from front to back to front around post of specified st and draw up a lp, YO and draw through both lps on hook: FPsc made.

Front Post dc (FPdc): YO, insert hook from front to back to front around post of specified st and draw up a lp, (YO and draw through 2 lps on hook) twice: FPdc made.

Front Post tr (FPtr): YO twice, insert hook from front to back to front around post of specified st and draw up a lp, (YO and draw through 2 lps on hook) 3 times: FPtr made.

Work in rows below: Current row is worked in stitches of the previous row.

Work 1 row below: Work in stitches of the row that is 1 row below previous row.

Work 2 rows below: Work in stitches of row that is 2 rows below previous row.

INSTRUCTIONS

Note: When placing a st 1 or 2 rows below working row, skip sc of working row that is directly behind the long st. In Rows 3 and 21, FPdc are worked over horizontal ridge formed by previous FPsc row and around post of sc just under ridge. First and last 6 sts on Rows 1 through 14 form gussets.

Front and Gussets

Starting at top front with J hook, ch 35 loosely.

Row 1 (right side): Sc in 2nd ch from hook and in each rem ch: 34 sc; ch 1, turn.

Row 2: FPsc in first st and in each st across to last st, sc in last st: 33 FPsc and 1 sc; ch 1, turn.

Row 3: Sc in first FPsc, FPdc in next sc 1 row below; sc in next 4 FPsc, FPdc in next sc 1 row below; *sc in next 5 FPsc, FPdc in next sc 1 row below; rep from * 2 times more; sc in next 2 FPsc, FPdc in next sc 1 row below; sc in next 4 FPsc, FPdc in next sc 1 row below; sc in last FPsc: 7 FPdc and 27 sc; ch 1, turn.

Row 4: Sc in first st and in each st across: 34 sc; ch 1, turn.

Row 5: Sc in first sc, FPdc in next FPdc 1 row below; sc in next 2 sc, FPtr in next FPsc 2 rows below; sc in next sc, FPdc in next FPdc 1 row below; *sc in next 2 sc, FPtr in next FPsc 2 rows below; sc in next 2 sc, FPdc in next FPdc 1 row below; rep from * 2 times more; sc in next 2 sc, FPdc in next FPdc 1 row below; sc in next sc, FPtr in next FPsc 2 rows below; sc in next 2 sc, FPdc in FPdc 1 row below; sc in last sc: 7 FPdc, 5 FPtr and 22 sc; ch 1, turn.

Row 6: Rep Row 2.

Row 7: Sc in first 4 FPsc, FPdc in next FPtr 1 row below, sc in next FPsc, FPdc in next FPdc 1 row below, sc in next 2 FPsc; *FPdc in next FPtr 1 row below, sc in next 5 FPsc; rep from * 2 times more; FPdc in next FPdc 1 row below, sc in next FPsc, FPdc in next FPtr 1 row below, sc in last 4 FPsc: 7 FPdc and 27 sc; ch 1, turn.

Row 8: Rep Row 4.

Row 9: Sc in first sc, FPtr in next FPsc 2 rows below; sc in next 2 sc, FPdc in next FPdc 1 row below; sc in next sc, FPdc in next FPdc 1 row below; *sc in next 2 sc, FPdc in next FPdc 1 row below; sc in next 2 sc, FPtr in next FPsc 2 rows below; rep from * 2 times more; sc in next 2 sc; FPdc in next FPdc 1 row below; sc in next sc, FPdc in next FPdc 1 row below, sc in next 2 sc, FPtr in next FPsc 2 rows below, sc in last sc: 7 FPdc, 5 FPtr and 22 sc; ch 1, turn.

Instructions continue on next page. →

Row 10: Rep Row 2.

Row 11: Sc in first FPsc, FPdc in next FPtr 1 row below; sc in next 4 FPsc, FPdc in next FPdc 1 row below; *sc in next 5 FPsc, FPdc in next FPtr 1 row below; rep from * 2 times more; sc in next 2 FPsc; FPdc in next FPdc 1 row below, sc in next 4 FPsc; FPdc in next FPtr 1 row below, sc in last FPsc: 7 FPdc and 27 sc; ch 1, turn.

Rows 12 through 14: Rep Rows 4 through 6.

Bottom

Row 15: Sl st in first 5 FPsc, ch 1, sc in next FPsc, FPdc in next FPdc 1 row below, sc in next 2 FPsc; *FPdc in next FPtr 1 row below, sc in next 5 FPsc; rep from * 2 times more; FPdc in next FPdc 1 row below, sc in next FPsc, leaving last 5 sts unworked: 5 FPdc and 19 sc; ch 1, turn.

Row 16: Sc in first st and in each st across: 24 sc; ch 1, turn.

Rows 17 through 19: Rep Row 16 three times more.

Back and Flap

Row 20: FPsc in first st and in each st across to last st, sc in last st: 24 sc; ch 1, turn.

Row 21: Sc in first FPsc, FPdc in next sc 1 row below; *sc in next 5 FPsc, FPdc in next sc 1 row below; rep from * 2 times more; sc in next 2 FPsc, FPdc in next sc 1 row below, sc in last FPsc: 5 FPdc and 19 sc; ch 1, turn.

Row 22: Rep Row 16.

Row 23: Sc in first sc; *FPdc in next FPdc 1 row below, sc in next 2 sc, FPtr in next FPsc 2 rows below, sc in next 2 sc; rep from * 2 times more; FPdc in next FPdc 1 row below, sc in next 2 sc, FPdc in next FPdc 1 row below, sc in last sc: 5 FPdc, 3 FPtr and 16 sc; ch 1, turn.

Row 24: Rep Row 20.

Row 25: Sc in first FPsc; FPdc in next FPdc 1 row below, sc in next 2 FPsc; *FPdc in next FPtr 1 row below, sc in next 5 FPsc; rep from * 2 times more; FPdc in next FPdc 1 row below, sc in last FPsc: 5 FPdc and 19 sc; ch 1, turn.

Row 26: Rep Row 16.

Row 27: Sc in first sc; FPdc in next FPdc 1 row below, sc in next 2 sc; *FPdc in next FPdc 1 row below, sc in next 2 sc, FPtr in FPsc 2 rows below, sc in next 2 sc; rep from * 2 times more; FPdc in next FPdc 1 row below, sc in last sc: 5 FPdc, 3 FPtr, 16 sc; ch 1, turn.

Row 28: Rep Row 20.

Row 29: Sc in first FPsc, FPdc in next FPdc 1 row below; *sc in next 5 FPsc, FPdc in next FPtr 1 row below; rep from * 2 times more; sc in next 2 FPsc, FPdc in next FPdc 1 row below; sc in last FPsc: 5 FPdc and 19 sc; ch 1, turn.

Row 30: Rep Row 16.

Row 31: Rep Row 23.

Rows 32 through 47: Rep Rows 24 through 31 two times more.

Rows 48 through 52: Rep Rows 24 through 28. At end of Row 52, do not ch 1.

Scallop

Row 53: Skip first st; *4 hdc in next st; skip next st, sl st in next st*; skip next st; rep from * to * once; skip next 3 sts, (3 tr, 3 dc, 3 tr) in next st; skip next 3 sts, sl st in next st; skip next st; rep from * to * once; skip next st; rep from * to * once: 16 hdc, 3 dc, 6 tr and 5 sl sts; turn.

Row 54: Sl st in first st and in each st across. Finish off; weave in ends.

Chain Strap

With H hook, make a chain 60" long, leaving a 5" tail at beg. Do not finish off. Thread tail through yarn needle and weave chain back and forth through one end of every link of metal chain along full length. Add or remove ch sts to yarn as necessary for preferred length of strap. Note: Strap will be half its length when added to handbag. Finish off and set aside.

Finishing
Eyelets

Insert 5 larger eyelet tops (tube-shaped, not pronged) between strands of yarn from right side to wrong side in st at base of center scallop of flap and in beg and end squares (formed by post sts) on 3rd and 4th rows of squares from end of flap. Fit will be snug. Work in eyelets patiently to avoid cutting yarn with them. Following package instructions and working in center scallop of flap only, hammer pronged eyelet bottom to eyelet top. Leave other 4 eyelet tops in place but set aside 4 pronged eyelet bottoms for later. Insert smaller eyelet tops from right side to wrong side in st at base of each small scallop and hammer eyelet bottoms to them.

Snaps

Cut piece of stabilizer 1 1/2" x 8 1/4". Place on wrong side of crochet along Row 6 to reinforce snaps. On right side, place bottom of snaps over ridge on Row 6 and 9th st in from each end. Cut slits in stabilizer for prongs. Follow package instructions to secure snap to crochet and stabilizer. Rep with 3rd snap in center of Row 6.

Stabilizer

Note: Practice first on a swatch. Never let yarn come in direct contact with iron. Read instructions on all packaging.

Cut stabilizer 1/4" smaller than crocheted piece (about 12 1/2" across gusset Rows 1 through 14, 8 1/2" across Rows 15 through 54, and 18" from Row 1 through Row 53). Do not cut stabilizer edge to match scallop edge until later. If crocheted piece is not 1/4" larger on every side than stabilizer, it can be coaxed to fit shape closely enough. With hot iron and minimum gliding, press 4 sharp creases into stabilizer corresponding to where crocheted piece will be folded to form bag: along first and last sc rows of bottom (Rows 15 and 19) and sides which will form gussets (6 sts from each edge of Rows 1 through 14). Flap does not need a crease. Side with creases folded inward becomes right side of stabilizer. Heat area of stabilizer where flap will bend to close with hot iron to soften it, then gently bend right side over log-shaped item such as rolled up fabric and apply more heat to set. Let cool with flap in curved position. Line up creases of stabilizer with fold rows of crochet piece and fold into bag shape; crochet should stretch a bit to fit. Trim top and bottom edges of stabilizer to 1/4" less than crocheted edges as necessary. Every crochet edge should still extend past every edge of stabilizer by 1/4" after folding into bag shape. Set aside.

Cut piece of stabilizer and piece of iron-on adhesive 3" x 8 1/4" for reinforcing magnetic snaps at scallop end. Line up 3" x 8 1/4" piece of stabilizer with scalloped end of shaped stabilizer on wrong side and fuse together.

Instructions continue on next page. →

Fabric Lining

Cut fabric and iron-on adhesive ¾" larger on all sides than shaped stabilizer. Fuse adhesive to wrong side of fabric according to package instructions, then fuse wrong side of fabric to right side of stabilizer. Avoid heating fabric edges which extend past stabilizer and avoid scalloped edge. While fusing to fabric, fold along creases of stabilizer allowing fabric to shift slightly for a snug fit along creases to reduce wrinkling. Fold fabric edges (except for scalloped edge) over stabilizer edges and press to hem on wrong side. Let cool folded into bag shape with curved flap closed.

Cut piece of iron-on adhesive same size as shaped stabilizer. Fuse adhesive to wrong side of stabilizer. Lay wrong side of stabilizer on top of wrong side of crocheted piece, positioning stitches and edges evenly. Fuse together bottom of bag first. While fusing, take extra care to stretch Rows 15 through 19 (sc rows) evenly over bottom folds of stabilizer while stabilizer is folded so that ridges on Rows 14 and 20 show at front and back of bag. Fuse front of bag, evenly stretching Rows 1 through 14 if necessary so that Row 1 extends past stabilizer's edge just enough to be rolled a bit over edge later, then fuse gussets. Fuse back of bag, stopping before 4 eyelets still needing their backings. Cut snug holes into lined stabilizer corresponding to eyelets and hammer pronged eyelet bottoms to tube-shaped eyelet tops through all thicknesses. Continue fusing toward scalloped edge, preserving curve in stabilizer and stretching crochet over stabilizer as necessary. Make sure sides have just enough crochet edges extending past stabilizer to be sewn or glued over stabilizer edge later. Stop fusing 4" before scalloped edge.

Clip stabilizer to ¼" smaller than crochet scalloped edge, following scallops. Clip lining fabric to ½" past scalloped stabilizer edge. Fold fabric over scalloped edge of stabilizer and fuse lining to stabilizer. Close bag and mark best placement for magnetic snap tops. Attach magnetic snap tops to right side of lining through both thicknesses of stabilizer. Fuse fabric scraps over backs of snaps to protect yarn from abrasion. Fuse rest of lined stabilizer to crochet up to scalloped edge.

Seaming

With needle and thread, sew gusset seams invisibly from outside of bag through all layers. Reinforce seams from inside with fabric glue (recommended). Apply thin line of fabric glue to all unseamed edges of lined stabilizer and fold crocheted edges over stabilizer or hand sew for a finished look.

Rhinestones and Strap

Apply minimum amount of fabric glue necessary to back of large rhinestone and affix onto front of center eyelet of flap. Rep with small rhinestones onto front of small eyelets, using tweezers for precision. Feed metal chain through 4 eyelets at top of bag so that chain forms a double strap. With pliers, open an end link of chain enough to connect with link at other end of chain and close link securely. Remove any excess crochet chs as necessary and sl st to join. Finish off; weave in ends.

#60 & 61 A PAIR OF PACKS

Instructions continue on next page. →

CROCHET BACKPACK

INSTRUCTIONS

Front
Ch 28.

Row 1 (right side): Sc in 2nd ch from hook and in each ch across: 27 sc; ch 1, turn.

Row 2: Sc in each st across; ch 1, turn.

Rows 3 through 6: Rep Row 2 four times more. At end of Row 6, ch 2 (counts as dc on next row), turn.

Row 7: Dc in next 2 sc; *ch 1, skip next sc, dc in next 3 sc; rep from * across: 21 dc and 6 ch-1 sps; ch 1, turn.

Rep Row 2 until piece measures 12" from beg. At end of last row, ch 2 (counts as dc on next row), turn.

Rep Row 7.

Rep Row 2 six times more. At end of last row, do not ch 1. Finish off; weave in ends.

Back
Work same as Front.

Strap
With 2 strands held together, make a chain 80" long. Finish off; weave in ends.

Finishing
With wrong sides facing, sew front and back together at sides and bottom. Tie overhand knot in center of strap. With front facing, place knot at center and weave ends of strap in and out of ch-1 sps on top dc row, beginning at ch-1 sps to left and right of center on front, and ending at ch-1 sps to left and right of center on back. Tie overhand knot 8" from each end of strap. With front facing, working thought both layers, weave ends of strap from back to front in outermost ch-1 sps on bottom dc row, weave in and out of remaining ch-1 sps toward center. Tie ends in a square knot at center front.

KNIT BACKPACK

SIZE
9" x 14"

MATERIALS
Bulky weight yarn
  3 oz royal blue

Note: *Photographed model made with Lion Brand® Jiffy® #109 Royal Blue*

Size 9 (5.5 mm) knitting needles (or size required for gauge)

Size 9 (5.5 mm) double-pointed knitting needles (dpns)

GAUGE
15 sts and 20 rows = 4" in Check Pattern.

STITCH GUIDE

Check Pattern (multiple of 4 + 2)

Rows 1 and 5: Knit.

Rows 2 and 6: Purl.

Row 3: K1, (K2, P2) across, end K1.

Row 4: P1, (K2, P2) across, end P1.

Row 7: K1, (P2, K2) across, end K1.

Row 8: P1, (P2, K2) across, end P1.

ssk (slip, slip, knit): Sl next 2 sts as to knit, one at a time, to right needle; insert left needle into fronts of these 2 sts and knit them tog.

INSTRUCTIONS

Back

CO 34 sts. Work 8 rows in Check Patt.

Eyelet Row: K4; * YO, ssk, K3; rep from * across.

Work in Check Patt until piece measures 12" from beg.

Rep Eyelet Row.

Work in Check Patt until piece measures 14". BO; weave in ends.

Front

Work same as Back.

Strap

Make an I-cord strap as follows: With dpns, cast on 4 sts.

*Slide work to other end of needle, K4.

Rep from * until 80" long. Cut yarn. Pull end through last row.

Finishing

Sew backpack pieces together at sides and bottom. Tie an overhand knot in the center of the strap. At the top of bag with front facing, place knot at center and weave strap in and out of bag in Eyelet Row, beginning at the hole to the left of center, and ending at hole halfway around on the back side. Rep with other end of strap on right side.

Tie an overhand knot 8" from the end of each strap. With front of bag facing and left strap, working through both layers, go in leftmost hole from back to front, weave in and out towards center. Rep with right strap. Tie ends in a square knot at center front.

#62 IN THE RED

Designed by Glenda Winkleman Designs for Coats & Clark

SIZE
8" wide x 9" high x 5" deep

MATERIALS
Bulky weight suede-look ribbon
   7 1/4 oz variegated (A)

Crochet nylon cord
   150 yds contrasting color,
   wound into 2 equal balls (B)

Note: *Photographed model was made with Moda Dea™ Ticker Tape™ #9727 Charade (A) and J&P Coats® Crochet Nylon #06 Red (B)*

One Red button, 1" diameter

Size K (6.5 mm) crochet hook
   (or size required for gauge)

GAUGE
9 sc = 3"

INSTRUCTIONS

Starting at bottom of bag with A, ch 19.

Rnd 1: 3 sc in 2nd ch from hook, sc in next 16 chs, 3 sc in last ch; working on opposite side of foundation ch, sc in next 16 chs, join with sl st in beg sc: 38 sc.

Rnd 2: Ch 1, 2 sc in first 3 sc, sc in next 16 sc, 2 sc in next 3 sc, sc in next 16 sc; join in beg sc: 44 sc.

Rnd 3: Ch 1, sc in first 2 sc, 2 sc in next 3 sc, sc in next 18 sc; 2 sc in next 3 sc, sc in next 18 sc, join: 50 sc.

Rnd 4: Ch 1, sc in next 2 sc, (2 sc in next sc, sc in next sc) 3 times, sc in next 19 sc; (2 sc in next sc, sc in next sc) 3 times, sc in next 17 sc, join: 56 sc.

Rnd 5: Ch 1, sc in first 2 sc, 2 sc in next sc; (sc in next 2 sc, 2 sc in next sc) 3 times, sc in next 19 sc; (2 sc in next sc, sc in next 2 sc) twice, 2 sc in next sc, sc in each of next 18 sc, join: 63 sc.

Note: For Rnds 6 through 23, do not join at end of the rnd. Place marker in first stitch of rnd to identify beginning of next rnd and move marker up as you work.

Rnd 6: Ch 1, sc in each sc around.

Rnd 7: * Sc in next sc, dc in next sc; rep from * around to last st, sc in last st.

Rnds 8 through 23: Dc in each sc, sc in each dc around. After last rnd, finish off. Weave in ends.

Rnd 24: With 2 strands of B held tog, join in beg st from previous rd, ch 1; sc in each st around, do not join.

Rnd 25: Sc in each sc around. Do not fasten off. Start Center Flap.

Center Flap

Row 1: Sc in next 3 sc, ch 1; turn.

Row 2: Sc in next 10 sc, ch 1; turn.

Rows 3 through 8: Sc in each sc across, ch 1, turn: 10 sc.

Row 9: Sc dec, sc in next 6 sc, sc dec, ch 1, turn: 8 sc.

Row 10: Sc dec, sc in next 4 sc, sc dec, ch 1, turn: 6 sc.

Row 11: Sc dec, sc in each of next 2 sc, sc dec, ch 1, turn: 4 sc.

Row 12: Sc dec 2 times, ch 1, turn: 2 sc.

Row 13: Sc dec, turn: 1 sc.

Row 14: Ch 8, sl st in first ch, forming button lp. Finish off; weave in ends.

Strap

With A, ch 3.

Row 1: Sc in 2nd ch from hook and in next ch, ch 1, turn: 2 sc.

Rows 2 through 100: Sc in each sc, ch 1: turn: At end of last row, finish off. Weave in ends.

Strap Border

Rnd 1: With 2 strands of B held tog, join in beg sc, ch 1; sc in first 2 sc, ch 1; *working down length, sc in each row end to next corner, ch 1*; sc in next 2 sc, ch 1; rep from * to * once, join with sl st in beg sc. Finish off. Weave in ends.

Assembly

Sew strap ends inside the sides of handbag. Align button on front of handbag with corresponding ch-8 lp of flap, sew in place.

#6 LITTLE PINK PROM PURSE

Designed by Nancy Brown

SIZE
6 ³/4" wide x 4 ¹/2" high plus
  4 ¹/4" handle

MATERIALS
Eyelash yarn
  80 yds pink

Note: *Photographed model made*
with Erdal Yarns Eyelash Tweed
#70 Pink

Plastic handle from Sunbelt
  Fasteners

Magnetic fastener

Stitch markers

Size H (5 mm) crochet hook
  (or size required for gauge)

GAUGE
10 sc = 4"

INSTRUCTIONS

Starting at bottom, ch 17.

Rnd 1 (wrong side): Sc in 2nd ch from hook and in next 14 chs, 3 sc in last ch; working in free lps on opposite side of foundation ch, sc in next 14 chs, 2 sc in next ch: 34 sc. Do not join. Place stitch marker in last sc and move stitch marker up to last sc in each rnd.

Rnd 2: Sc in next sc and in each sc around: 34 sc.

Rep Rnd 2 until piece measures about 4".

Last Rnd: *(Sc in next 4 sc, sc dec in next 2 sc) 2 times, sc in next 3 sc, sc dec in next 2 sc; rep from * once: 28 sc; join with sl st in beg sc. Finish off; weave in ends.

Snap Fastener Base (make 2)
Ch 5.

Row 1: Sc in 2nd ch from hook and in each ch across: 4 sc; ch 1, turn.

Rows 2 through 4: Sc in next sc and in each sc across: 4 sc; ch 1, turn. At end of Row 4, do not ch 1. Finish off.

Attach one half of magnetic fastener to center of each Snap Fastener Base. Turn purse right side out. Sew one Snap Fastener Base to inside top center on each side of bag.

Handle
Sew handle to inside top edges of purse.

#64 STRIPED CLUTCH

Designed by Rona Feldman for Judi & Co.

SIZE

8" x 10"

MATERIALS

Twisted nylon cord
  500 yds brown (Color A)
  125 yds beige (Color B)

Note: Photographed model made with Judi & Co's Groovy brown and Groovy beige

One ³/₄" diameter magnetic
  snap

SIze G (4 mm) crochet hook
  (or size required for gauge)

GAUGE

4 sc = 1"

INSTRUCTIONS

Front

With Color A, ch 10.

Row 1: Sc in 2nd ch from hook and in next 7 chs, 3 sc in last ch; working in unused lps on opposite side of ch, sc in 8 chs; ch 1, turn.

Note: Work in back lp only of each st from here on.

Row 2 (right side): Working in back lp only, sc in 8 sc, 3 sc in next sc, sc in next sc, 3 sc in next sc, sc in rem 8 sc; change to Color B, ch 1 turn.

Note: From here on, alternate two rows of each color for stripe pattern.

Row 3: Sc in 9 sc, 3 sc in next sc, sc in 3 sc; 3 sc in next sc, sc in rem 9 sts sc, ch 1, turn.

Continue working in this manner, having 1 more st at each side and 2 more sts at lower edge on every row, until there are 26 sts at sides and 37 sts at lower edge. Finish off; weave in ends.

Note: To determine length of gusset to be worked later, measure along edge of last row worked and note.

Top Border

Hold piece with right side facing and ends of rows at top. You will now work across this top edge. Join Color A in first st at right, ch 2.

Row 1: Hdc in each row across, ch 2, turn.

Row 2: Hdc in front lps only of each st across, ch 2, turn.

Row 3 (right side): Hdc into back lps only across; finish off; weave in ends.

Back

Work same as front.

Gusset

With Color A, ch 7.

Row 1: Sc in 2nd ch from hook and in each rem ch; ch 1, turn.

Row 2: Sc in back lps only across, ch 1, turn.

Rep Row 2 until piece is length previously measured for gusset.

Assembly

Attach one long edge of gusset to Front, starting just below the Top border on one side, across bottom, and up opposite side, ending just below Top border. To join, use Color A and sc, working through side edge of gusset and edge of top, working 3 sc in each corner. Finish off.

Join opposite side of gusset to Back. Gently steam bag all around to hold shape; do not touch iron to bag surface.

Snap Stabilizer (make 2)

With brown, ch 6.

Row 1: Sc in 2nd ch from hook and each rem ch; ch 1, turn.

Row 2: Sc in each sc across; ch 1, turn.

Rows 3 through 5: Rep Row 2; finish off.

Attach one piece of each snap to a stablizer; sew stablizers opposite each other on inside of top, centered and placed at top edge of opening.

#65 SHOPPER'S TOTE

Designed by Marty Miller

SIZE
11" x 16"

MATERIALS
Worsted weight cotton yarn
  7 oz white

Note: Photographed model made with Tahki Cotton Classic #3001 White

Size G (4 mm) crochet hook
  (or size required for gauge)

GAUGE
4 sc rnds = 1 ³/₄"

STITCH GUIDE
Sc3tog (decrease): (Insert hook in next st, YO and draw up a lp) 3 times, YO and draw through all 4 lps on hook.

INSTRUCTIONS

Starting at bottom, ch 2.

Rnd 1: 6 sc in 2nd ch from hook: 6 sc; join with sl st in first sc, ch 1.

Rnd 2: 2 sc in each sc around: 12 sc; join, ch 1.

Rnd 3: 2 sc in first sc, sc in next sc; *2 sc in next sc, sc in next sc; rep from * 4 more times: 18 sc; join, ch 1.

Rnd 4: 2 sc in first sc, sc in next 2 sc; *2 sc in next sc, sc in next 2 sc; rep from * 4 more times: 24 sc; join, ch 1.

Rnd 5: Sc in first sc; *ch 4, skip one st, sc in next st; rep from * around, ending last rep with ch 1, dc in first sc of rnd (counts as a ch-4 sp): 12 ch-4 sps.

Rnd 6: *Ch 5, sc in next ch-4 sp; rep from * around, ending last rep with with ch 2, dc in dc of previous rnd (counts as ch-5 space here and throughout): 12 ch-5 sps.

Rnd 7: *Ch 5, sc in next ch-5 sp; in next ch-5 sp work (ch 5, sc) twice; place marker in this sp; rep from * around, ending last rep with ch 5, sc in next ch-5 sp, ch 5, sc in next ch-2/dc sp, ch 2, dc in dc of previous rnd: 18 ch-5 sps.

Rnd 8: *Ch 5, sc in next ch-5 sp; rep from * around to marker, (ch 5, sc in same ch-5 sp, place marker in this ch-5 sp) 5 times; (ch 5, sc in next ch-5 sp) twice; ch 5, sc in next ch-2/dc sp, ch 2, dc in dc of previous rnd: 24 ch-5 sps.

Rnd 9: *Ch 5, sc in next ch-5 sp; rep from * around to marker, (ch 5, sc in same ch-5 sp, place marker in this ch-5 sp) 5 times; (ch 5, sc in next ch-5 sp) 3 times, ch 5, sc in next ch-2/dc sp, ch 2, dc in dc of previous rnd: 30 ch-5 sps.

Rnd 10: *Ch 5, sc in next ch-5 sp; rep from * around to marker, (ch 5, sc in same ch-5 sp) five times; (ch 5, sc in next ch-5 sp) four times, ch 5, sc in next ch-2/dc sp, ch 2, dc in dc of previous rnd: 36 ch-5 sps.

Rnd 11: *Ch 5, sc in next ch-5 sp; rep from * around, ending last rep with ch 2, dc in dc of previous rnd: 36 ch-5 sps.

Rnds 12 through 39: Rep Rnd 11.

Rnd 40: *Ch 4, sc in next ch-5 sp; rep from * around, ending last rep with ch 1, dc in dc of previous rnd.

Top Edging

Rnd 1: Ch 1, 2 sc in sp created by (ch-1, dc); *4 sc in next ch-4 sp; rep from * around, ending last rep with 2 sc in same sp as first 2 sc: 144 sc; join with sl st in first sc, ch 1.

Rnds 2 through 4: Sc in each sc around; join, ch 1.

Handles

Rnd 1: Sc in first 6 sc, place marker in last st; ch 100, skip 30 sc, sc in next sc and place marker; sc in next 41 sc, place a marker in the last sc; ch 100, skip next 30 sc; sc in next sc, place a marker in last sc; sc in last 35 sc; join, ch 1.

Decrease Rnds

Note: *Start (sc3tog) dec one st (or ch) before each marker.*

Rnd 1: Sc in each sc and ch around, working a sc3tog dec at each marked st. Move the markers to these sts to indicate where to dec on following rnds. On this rnd, your sc3tog will include 1 ch st and 2 sc sts; join, ch 1.

Rnds 2 and 3: Sc in each sc, working a sc3tog dec at markers as before.

At end of Rnd 3, finish off; weave in all ends.

#66 FELTED BACKPACK

Designed by Patons Design Staff

SIZE

11" by 24" after felting

MATERIALS

Worsted weight wool yarn

   3 1/2 oz red (MC)

   10 1/2 oz black (A)

   3 1/2 oz gold (B)

   3 1/2 oz russet (C)

Note: Photographed model made with Patons® Classic Merino Wool #207 Rich Red (MC), #226 Black (A), #204 Old Gold (B) and #206 Russet (C)

Size 7 (4.5 mm) straight knitting needles

16" Size 7 (4.5 mm) circular knitting needle (or size required for guage)

GAUGE

20 sts and 26 rows = 4" in stock st (knit 1 row, purl 1 row) before felting

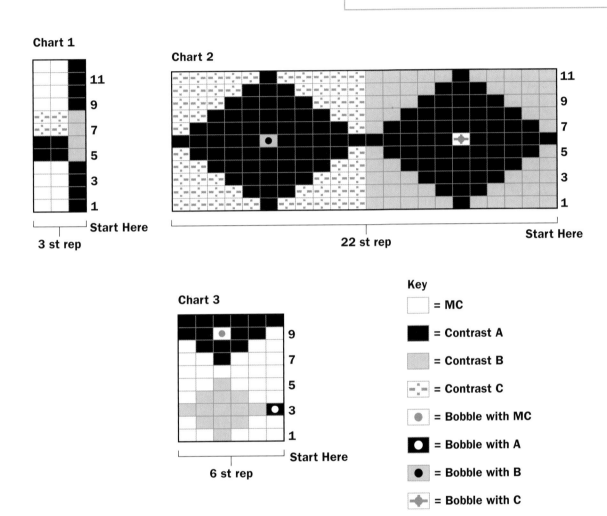

STITCH GUIDE

Bobble: [(K1, YO) 3 times, K1] in next st: 7 sts. Slip 6th, 5th, 4th, 3rd, 2nd and 1st sts separately over 7th st: 1 st remains: Bobble made.

WORKING FROM CHARTS

Bag is worked in rnds, so read all rows from right to left.

Carry yarn not in use loosely across wrong side of work but never over more than 3 sts. When yarn must pass over more than 3 sts, weave it over and under color in use on next st or at center point of sts it passes over.

Chart 1

11
9
7
5
3
1

Start Here

3 st rep

Chart 2

11
9
7
5
3
1

Start Here

22 st rep

Chart 3

9
7
5
3
1

Start Here

6 st rep

Key

☐ = MC

■ = Contrast A

▨ = Contrast B

⊡ = Contrast C

⦿ = Bobble with MC

◖ = Bobble with A

● = Bobble with B

✦ = Bobble with C

INSTRUCTIONS

Main Section

With MC and circular needle, cast on 156 sts. Join, being careful not to twist sts; mark beg of rnds.

Knit Rnds 1 through 12 of Chart 1.

Rep Rnds 5 through 12 of Chart 1 once, dec 2 sts evenly across last rnd: 154 sts.

Knit Rnds 1 through 11 of Chart 2, inc 2 sts evenly across last rnd: 156 sts.

Knit Rnds 1 through 12 of Chart 1.

Rep Rows 5 through 12 of Chart 1 once.

With MC, knit 3 rnds.

Knit Rnds 1 through 10 of Chart 3.

Knit Rnds 1 to 12 of Chart 1.

165

Instructions continue on next page. →

Ribbing

Rnd 1: *With B, K2; with A, K2; rep from * around.

Rnd 2: *With B, P2; with A, K2; rep from * around.

Rnd 3: *With A, P2; with C, K2; rep from * around.

Rnd 4: Rep Rnd 3.

Rnd 5: *With MC, P2; with A, K2; rep from * around.

Rnd 6: Rep Rnd 5.

Rnds 7 and 8: Rep Rnd 3.

Rnds 9 and 10: Rep Rnd 2.

Rep Rnds 3 through 10 two more times.

With A, knit one rnd. BO.

Base

With A and straight of needles, CO 48 sts.

Work in stock st for 15", ending by working a purl row. BO.

Strap (make 2)

With A and straight needles, CO 9 sts.

Row 1: *K1, P1; rep from * to last st, K1.

Rep Row 1 for 27". BO in patt.

Finishing

Felt all pieces following instructions on page 252.

After felting, pieces should measure:

Main Section: 11" high and 24" around.

Base: 8" x 11".

Cut base to an oval shape 9" x 7". Pin base to bottom of main section. With 2 strands of A, blanket st base to main section. With punch or ice pick, make small holes around top edge of bag for drawstring, placed 1 1/4" down from top edge, spaced about 1" apart.

Trim straps to 24". Mark center st at top and at base of bag (center back). Sew ends of straps on either side of marked st at top of bag, under row of drawstring holes. Sew other ends of straps 4" either side of marked st at base.

Drawstring

With 2 strands of MC cut 95" long, make a twisted cord (see page 253) 38" long. Weave through drawstring holes of bag having cords meet at center front.

#67 PETITE PEARLY

Designed by Mickie Akins for Coats and Clark

SIZE

6" wide x 6" high plus 16" or
25" strap

MATERIALS

Nylon yarn
200 yds red

Note: *Photographed model made
with J&P Coats® Crochet Nylon
#6 Red*

Size E (3.5 mm) crochet hook
(or size required for gauge)

44 ivory pearl pony beads

7" red zipper

1/4 yd red lining fabric
(optional)

Needle and sewing thread
to match lining fabric
(optional)

GAUGE

17 sc and 21 sc rows = 4"

STITCH GUIDE

Sc bead st: Slide bead up to hook; working
behind bead, insert hook in next st and
draw up a lp, YO and draw through 2 lps on
hook: sc bead st made.

Sc decrease (sc dec): (Insert hook in next st
and draw up a lp) twice, YO and draw
through all 3 lps on hook: sc dec made.

INSTRUCTIONS

Front

Thread beads onto yarn. Starting at bottom,
ch 25.

Row 1 (right side): Working in back bar of
chs, sc in 2nd ch from hook, sc in next
ch and in each ch across: 24 sc; ch 1, turn.

Row 2: Sc in first st and in each st across;
ch 1, turn.

Rows 3 through 6: Rep Row 2 four times
more.

Instructions continue on next page. →

Row 7: Sc in first 8 sts, sc bead st, sc in next 6 sts, sc bead st, sc in last 8 sts: 22 sc and 2 sc bead sts; ch 1, turn.

Rows 8, 10, 12, 14, 16 and 18: Rep Row 2.

Row 9: Sc in first 9 sts, sc bead st, sc in next 4 sts, sc bead st, sc in last 9 sts: 22 sc and 2 sc bead sts; ch 1, turn.

Row 11: Sc in first 10 sts, sc bead st, sc in next 2 sts, sc bead st, sc in last 10 sts: 22 sc and 2 sc bead sts; ch 1, turn.

Row 13: Sc in first 7 sts, sc bead st, sc in next st, sc bead st, sc in next 4 sts, sc bead st, sc in next st, sc bead st, sc in last 7 sts: 20 sc and 4 sc bead sts; ch 1, turn.

Row 15: Rep Row 11.

Row 17: Rep Row 9.

Row 19: Rep Row 7.

Rows 20 through 25: Rep Row 2 six times more. At end of Row 25, do not ch 1 and turn.

Note: Change to working in rnds for rest of front.

Rnd 26: Working around outer edge, work 2 more sc in same st as last st on Row 25, sc in edge of each row down left side from Row 24 to Row 2; working in free lps of foundation chs: 3 sc in first ch at bottom left corner, sc in each ch across bottom to last ch, 3 sc in last ch at bottom right corner; sc in edge of each row up right side from Row 2 to Row 24, 3 sc in first st on Row 25*, sc in next st, (sc bead st, sc in next st) 11 times.

Note: Second sc of 3 sc at corners is corner st.

Rnd 27: 3 sc in corner st, sc in each st down to next corner st, 3 sc in corner st, sc in next st, (sc bead st, sc in next st) 11 times across bottom, sc in next st, 3 sc in corner st, sc in each st up to next corner st, 3 sc in corner st, sc in each st across top to next corner st; join with sl st in next sc. Finish off; weave in ends.

Back

Starting at bottom, ch 25.

Row 1 (right side): Working in back bar of chs, sc in 2nd ch from hook, sc in next ch and in each ch across: 24 sc; ch 1, turn.

Row 2: Sc in each st across; ch 1, turn.

Rows 3 through 25: Rep Row 2 twenty three times more. At end of Row 25, do not ch 1 and turn.

Note: Change to working in rnds for rest of back.

Rnd 26: Work same as Rnd 26 on Front to *; sc in each st across top to next corner.

Rnd 27: 3 sc in corner st, sc in each st around to top left corner, working 3 sc in corner st of each of next 3 corners; join with sl st in next sc. Finish off; weave in ends.

Gusset

Ch 2.

Row 1 (wrong side): Sc in 2nd ch from hook: 1 sc; ch 1, turn.

Row 2 (right side): Sc in st; ch 1, turn.

Row 3: 2 sc in st: 2 sc; ch 1, turn.

Row 4: Sc in each st across; ch 1, turn.

Row 5: 2 sc in first st, sc in next st: 3 sc; ch 1, turn.

Rows 6, 8, 10, 12 and 14: Rep Row 4.

Row 7: Sc in first st, 2 sc in next st, sc in last st: 4 sc; ch 1, turn.

Row 9: Sc in first 2 sts, 2 sc in next st, sc in last st: 5 sc; ch 1, turn.

Row 11: Sc in first 2 sts, 2 sc in next st, sc in last 2 sts: 6 sc; ch 1, turn.

Row 13: Sc in first 2 sts, 2 sc in next st, sc in last 3 sts: 7 sc; ch 1, turn.

Row 15: Sc in first 3 sts, 2 sc in next st, sc in last 3 sts: 8 sc; ch 1, turn.

Rows 16 through 64: Rep Row 4.

Row 65: Sc in first 3 sts, sc dec in next 2 sts, sc in last 3 sts: 7 sc; ch 1, turn.

Rows 66, 68, 70, 72, 74 and 76: Rep Row 4.

Row 67: Sc in first 2 sts, sc dec in next 2 sts, sc in last 3 sts: 6 sc; ch 1, turn.

Row 69: Sc in first 2 sts, sc dec in next 2 sts, sc in last 2 sts: 5 sc; ch 1, turn.

Row 71: Sc in first st, sc dec in next 2 sts, sc in last 2 sts: 4 sc; ch 1, turn.

Row 73: Sc in first st, sc dec in next 2 sts, sc in last st: 3 sc; ch 1, turn.

Row 75: Sc dec in first 2 sts, sc in last st: 2 sc; ch 1, turn.

Row 77: Sc dec in first 2 sts: 1 sc; ch 1, turn.

Row 78: Sc in st. Finish off; weave in ends.

Lining (optional)

Using crochet pieces as patterns and adding 1/2" extra on all edges for seams, cut 2 Side pieces and 1 Gusset piece from lining fabric.

Joining

With wrong sides together, matching sts on edges of sides and on bottom of one Side to edges of rows on Gusset, working through both layers, join with sc in first sc at top of left corner of Side, sc Side and Gusset together across sides and bottom to last sc at top right corner of Side, easing if needed. Finish off; weave in ends. Rep with other Side and other edge of rows on Gusset. With right side of zipper facing wrong side of top edges of Sides, sew long edges of zipper in place along Sides; fold each end of zipper 1/4" to wrong side and sew to Gusset.

Lining Continued (optional)

With right sides of lining together, sew lining pieces together in same manner as crochet Sides and Gusset with 1/2" seams. Press top edges of lining 1/2" to wrong side. With wrong side of lining facing outward, insert lining into assembled Sides and Gusset; sew top edges of lining to wrong side of zipper along previous zipper seam on Sides and Gusset.

Strap

Ch 112 for shoulder strap or 70 for arm strap.

Row 1: Working in back bar of chs, sc in 2nd ch from hook, sc in next ch and in each ch across: 111 or 69 sc; ch 1, turn.

Rows 2 through 4: Sc in first st and in each st across: 111 or 69 sc; ch 1, turn. At end of Row 4, do not ch 1. Finish off; weave in ends.

Sew ends of Strap to Gusset about 1" down from top; sew 3 pony beads to each end of Strap.

#68 COMING UP ROSES

Designed by Suzanne Atkinson
For the advanced knitter

SIZE BEFORE FELTING
Bottom diameter: 14"; handles: 33"

SIZE AFTER FELTING
Bottom diameter, 11"; circumference: 32"; handles: 29"

MATERIALS
Worsted weight 100 per cent wool yarn

10 $^1/_2$ oz lt rose (A)

7 oz red (B)

25 yds contrasting waste yarn

Note: Photographed model made with Plymouth Yarn™ Galway Worsted #114 Lt Rose (A) and #44 Red (B)

Tapestry needle size 14 (or large-eyed yarn needle)

24" Size 7 (4.5 mm) circular knitting needle (spare)

24" Size 8 (5 mm) circular knitting needle

24" Size 10 $^1/_2$ (6.5 mm) circular knitting needle

Size 9 (5.5 mm) straight knitting needles (or size required for gauge)

GAUGE
Before felting: 16 sts = 4" with Size 9 needles in garter st (knit every row)

INSTRUCTIONS

Note: Bag begins at bottom with a circular pinwheel design in garter st short row wedges.

With size 9 needles and waste yarn, CO 28 sts. Knit two rows with waste yarn, which will be removed later; finish off waste yarn.

With A, and leaving an 18" length of yarn for grafting later, knit one row.

Row 1 (right side): **Knit to last 2 sts, turn, leaving 2 sts unworked. Mark this row as right side.

Row 2: YO, knit across.

Row 3: Knit to last 4 sts (not counting YO from previous row), turn.

Row 4: YO, knit across.

Continue in pattern as established, working 2 fewer sts on each odd-numbered row, until all the sts have been worked.** Finish off A.

Next Row: With B, K1; *K1, knit YO tog with next st; rep from * across to last st, K1: 28 sts. Rep from ** to **. Finish off B, join A. Rep as established, alternating A and B, until 12 wedges have been worked in total. Finish off B.

With waste yarn, K1; *K1, knit YO tog with next st; rep from * to last st, K1: 28 sts. Knit 2 more rows with waste yarn and finish off yarn. Remove knitting from needles.

Using cast-on yarn tail and yarn needle, graft the first row of knitting to the last row of knitting, following the paths of the waste yarn stitches. Remove waste yarn from both rows by picking out sts, snipping carefully with scissors as needed. Using a length of A, sew closed the hole in the center of the circle. Weave in all ends securely with blunt yarn needle.

Tuck

With right side facing, with size 8 circular needle and A, pick up and knit 168 sts around the edge of the bag bottom (14 sts for each garter st wedge). Mark beg of rnd. Knit 8 rnds.

With spare circular needle, working on the wrong side, pick up the horizontal bars from pick-up rnd sts and place on needle: 168 sts on size 7 needle and 168 sts on size 8 needle. With size 8 needle and A, working around knit tog one st from each needle until all sts have been worked: tuck completed. Finish off A: 168 sts.

Chart Instructions

With size 10 ½ circular needle and B, join and knit one rnd, inc 8 sts evenly spaced: 176 sts. Knit 2 rnds.

The bag is now worked from charts. Work each row of chart from right to left, beginning at bottom right corner, working each row of chart twice (work Row 1 of chart once, then work Row 1 again). Each row of each chart is repeated 8 times around. Always sl sts purlwise, with yarn carried across wrong side of work. Keep carried yarn loose. There will be some natural puckering, but this will disappear in the felting process.

Chart 1

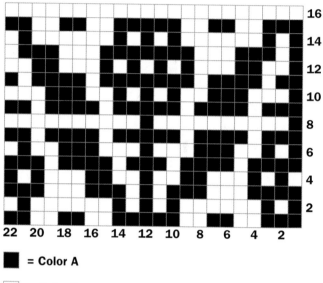

■ = Color A

☐ = Color B

Working Chart 1: White squares are worked in B, black squares in A. On odd-numbered rows, black squares are sts knitted in A; white squares are slipped sts. On even-numbered rows, black squares are slipped sts, white squares are knitted in B.

Working Chart 2: White squares are worked in A, black squares in B. On odd numbered rows, black squares are sts knitted in B; white squares are slipped sts. On even numbered-rows, black squares are slipped sts; white squares are knitted in A.

Chart 2

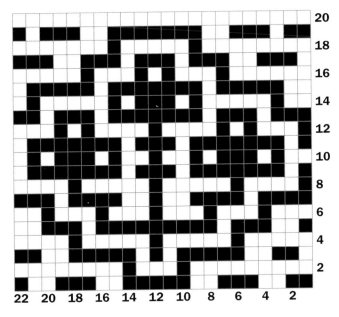

= Color A
= Color B

Sides Instructions

Work Chart 1.

Knit 2 rnds in A.

Work Chart 2.

Knit 2 rnds in B.

Work Chart 1. Finish off B.

With size 8 circular needle and A, (knit one rnd, purl one rnd) five times, then knit one rnd. Finish off A.

I-Cord Bind-Off Trim

Leave sts on circular needle. Join B and CO 4 sts onto left needle. Work I-cord bind off: *K3, ssk with one st from CO and one st from bag top, do not turn, sl 4 sts back onto left-hand needle; rep from * around top edge of the bag. Do not BO, finish off A, leaving a 12" end.

Thread end into tapestry needle and sew last row to CO edge of I-cord trim, matching sts. Weave in all ends securely.

Handle (make 2)

With size 8 needles and A, CO 8 sts. Do not join. Knit every row until handle measures 33". BO.

Felting

Follow Felting Instructions on page 252. When desired size is reached, remove from washer and rinse in cold water by hand, squeezing out excess moisture when rinsing is complete. Stand bag up to dry. Lay handles flat to dry. If required, place a canister or wastebasket of similar dimensions inside the bag while drying, to give it more shape.

Finishing

When bag is completely dry, lay it flat and mark positions along top edge, about 3 1/2" from each side fold, for placement of handles. With sharp needle and A, stitch handles in place on the inside at these marked positions, beginning at the first row of A, stitching along the end of the handle and the sides to the top edge.

#69 BUTTERCUP CANISTER

Designed by Vashti Braha

SIZE

4 1/2" diameter x 9 1/2" long

MATERIALS

Sport weight yarn
  5 oz yellow
  2 1/2 oz black

Note: Photographed model made with Lion Brand® Microspun #158 Buttercup and #153 Ebony

Two 4" diameter circles plastic canvas

Yellow fabric, 9" x 14 3/4" and 10" x 16"

Four 4" diameter black fabric circles (thick or fleecy fabric is preferred)

Stiff heavyweight stabilizer, two 4" diameter circles, two 1" x 8 1/2" strips, two 1 1/2" squares, and one 9" x 14 3/4" rectangle

Two 9" x 14 3/4" pieces low-temp iron-on adhesive

Mini-iron and regular iron

3 magnetic snaps

1 pair arched clear acrylic purse handles, 5 3/4" x 4 1/2" by Prym-Dritz

2" wide metal buckle

4" x 30" strip black velvet fabric (or 30" of 2" wide black velvet ribbon)

Hot glue gun or fabric glue

Sewing needle

Yellow thread

Size G (4 mm) crochet hook (or size required for gauge)

GAUGE

16 sc = 4"

INSTRUCTIONS

Body

With yellow, ch 36.

Row 1 (wrong side): Sc in 2nd ch from hook and in each rem ch: 35 sc; ch 2 (counts as hdc on next row now and throughout), turn.

Row 2 (right side): Skip first sc; RSB, hdc in next 3 sc, RSB, hdc in next 4 sc, tr in next 7 sc, hdc in next 4 sc, RSB, hdc in next 3 sc, RSB, hdc in last sc: 4 RSB, 7 tr and 16 hdc; ch 2, turn.

SPECIAL STITCHES

Right Side Buttercup (RSB): Hdc in next st, ch 1, skip next st, hdc in next st; working around the 4 sides of ch sp just made; rotate piece 1/4 turn clockwise and work (ch 1, sc, ch 3, dc, ch 3, sc) around post of hdc just worked (petal made); rotate piece 1/4 turn clockwise and work petal in skipped st; rotate piece 1/4 turn clockwise and work petal around post of first of 2 hdc just worked; rotate piece 1/4 turn clockwise and work petal in ch-1 sp between 2 hdc just worked: RSB with 4 petals made.

Wrong Side Buttercup (WSB): Hdc in next hdc, ch 1, skip next hdc, hdc in next hdc, turn to right side; working around 4 sides of ch sp just made; (ch 1, sc, ch 3, dc, ch 3, sc) in ch-1 sp between 2 hdc just worked (petal made); rotate piece 1/4 turn clockwise and work petal around post of first of 2 hdc just worked; rotate piece 1/4 turn clockwise and work petal in skipped st; rotate piece 1/4 turn clockwise and work petal around post of hdc just worked; turn to wrong side and continue working across row: WSB with 4 petals made.

Hdc Puff: YO, insert hook in next st and draw up a lp, YO, insert hook in same st and draw up a lp, YO and draw through all 5 lps on hook: hdc puff made.

Front Post Double Crochet (FPdc): YO, insert hook from front to back to front around post of specified st and draw up a lp, (YO and draw through 2 lps on hook) twice: FPdc made.

Back Post Double Crochet (BPdc): YO, insert hook from back to front to back around post of specified st and draw up a lp, (YO and draw through 2 lps on hook) twice: BPdc made.

To change color: Work st until 2 lps rem on hook, drop old color, pick up new color and draw through both lps on hook, cut dropped color.

Row 3: Skip first hdc; *working in RSB on previous row, hdc in last sc worked on top petal of RSB, fold top petal of RSB down and away from you, hdc in ch-1 sp between 2 hdc on RSB, placing st between last sc worked and center dc of top petal; hdc in same ch-1 sp, placing st between center dc and first sc worked of top petal**; WSB*; rep from * to * once; hdc in next st, BPdc in next 7 tr, hdc in next st, WSB; rep from * to * once; rep from * to ** once; hdc in 2nd ch of turning ch-2: 4 WSB, 7 BPdc and 16 hdc; ch 2, turn.

Row 4: Skip first hdc; *RSB; working in WSB on previous row, hdc in first sc worked on top petal of WSB; fold top petal of WSB down and toward you, hdc in ch-1 sp between 2 hdc on WSB, placing st between first sc worked and center dc of top petal; hdc in same ch-1 sp, placing st between center dc and last sc worked of top petal*; rep from * to * once; hdc in next st, FPdc in next 7 BPdc, hdc in next 4 sts; rep from * to * once; RSB; hdc in 2nd ch of turning ch-2: 4 RSB, 7 FPdc and 16 hdc; ch 2, turn.

Rep Rows 3 and 4 until piece measures 13 1/4" long. Finish off; weave in ends.

Bottom Flap

Row 1: With right side facing, join yellow with sc around first foundation ch and into sc on Row 1 of Body; *sc around next foundation ch and into sc on Row 1 of Body; rep from * across: 35 sc; ch 1, turn.

Rows 2 through 9: Sc in first sc and in each sc across: 35 sc; ch 1, turn. At end of Row 9, do not ch 1. Finish off; weave in ends.

Gusset (make 2)

Lightly glue stabilizer circle to each plastic circle. Glue black fabric circle to both sides of each plastic circle.

Circle (make 4)

With black, ch 4; join with sl st to form a ring.

Rnd 1: Ch 1, work 6 sc in ring: 6 sc; join with sl st in first sc.

Instructions continue on next page. →

Rnd 2: Ch 1, work 2 sc in same sc as joining and in each sc around: 12 sc; join as before.

Rnd 3: Ch 1, sc in same sc as joining, 2 sc in next sc; *sc in next sc, 2 sc in next sc; rep from * 4 times more: 18 sc; join.

Rnd 4: Ch 1, sc in same sc as joining, sc in next sc, 2 sc in next sc; *sc in next 2 sc, 2 sc in next sc; rep from * 4 times more: 24 sc; join.

Rnd 5: Ch 1, sc in same sc as joining, sc in next 2 sc, 2 sc in next sc; *sc in next 3 sc, 2 sc in next sc; rep from * 4 times more: 30 sc; join.

Rnd 6: Ch 1, sc in same sc as joining, sc in next 3 sc, 2 sc in next sc; *sc in next 4 sc, 2 sc in next sc; rep from * 4 times more: 36 sc; join.

Rnd 7: Ch 1, sc in same sc as joining, sc in next 4 sc, 2 sc in next sc; *sc in next 5 sc, 2 sc in next sc; rep from * 4 times more: 42 sc; join.

Rnd 8: Ch 1, sc in same sc as joining, sc in next 5 sc, 2 sc in next sc; *sc in next 6 sc, 2 sc in next sc; rep from * 4 times more: 48 sc; join.

Rnd 9: Ch 1, sc in same sc as joining, sc in next 6 sc, 2 sc in next sc; *sc in next 7 sc, 2 sc in next sc; rep from * 4 times more: 54 sc; join. Finish off; weave in ends.

Sandwich covered plastic circle between wrong sides of 2 crochet circles to form gusset. With yellow, working through both crochet circles, sc in each sc on Rnd 9. Finish off; weave in ends. Rep for second gusset.

Finishing

Note: *Yarn is heat-sensitive so practice on a swatch first. Never let yarn come in direct contact with iron.*

Fuse iron-on adhesive to right side of 9" x 14 ¾" fabric piece. Shape crochet body with wrong side up to be 9 ½" x 15 ¼". Fuse adhesive side of fabric to wrong side of buttercups. Turn over gently and fluff petals of buttercups. Trim excess fabric edges.

Heat 9" x 14 ¾" rectangle of stabilizer with iron without gliding and curl it into canister shape, making 9" ends overlap. Clamp ends and let stabilizer cool in this shape. Outside of curved stabilizer becomes wrong side. Iron 2 creases into stabilizer for bag flap opening: fold each 9" end down 1 ¼" toward wrong side and press with hot iron. Unfold creases. Fuse iron-on adhesive to wrong side of stabilizer. Form into canister shape again while hot. Clamp and let cool.

Clip wedges into ¾" seam allowance on long edges of 10" x 16" yellow fabric piece. Center wrong side of fabric on right side (inside) of curved stabilizer. Beg halfway down length of stabilizer, wrap seam allowance around stabilizer to wrong side and fuse with mini-iron over a rounded ironing surface. Starting in center of long edges, work out to 9" ends, maintaining curve of stabilizer so that wrinkles in fabric are minimized. Leave 9" ends unfused.

Fuse wrong side (outside) of curved stabilizer to wrong side of fabric-lined crochet body, but do not fuse 1 ½" from both 9" ends.

Note: *Fabric-hemmed long edges of stabilizer may not fuse to crochet. Trim 9" ends of stabilizer ¼" shorter than 9 ½" ends of crochet body. Glue each 1" x 8 ½" stabilizer strip to wrong side of each 9" end of stabilizer.*

Handles

Center and attach handles through all thicknesses to 2nd row of buttercup petals from end sc rows and to 6th row of buttercup petals from first row, according to instructions for type of handles purchased.

Gusset Assembly

With right side of buttercups facing, crochet gussets to body. Join yellow with sl st in long curved edge of body 2" from 9" end, sl st through both thicknesses along edge of body and edge of gusset to join gusset to body, ending 2" from other 9" end of body. Finish off; weave in ends. Rep for other gusset seam.

Note: *Flaps of body should overlap by 1 1/2" to 2". It may help to clamp flaps in place while you seam gusset. Apply glue along seam crevice on inside of bag and press gusset firmly against stabilized edge of body.*

Edging

With wrong side (inside) of bag facing, join yellow with sl st at beg of top unjoined edge of either gusset, sl st in each st along top unjoined edge of gusset, then work hdc puff in each st along edges and end of flap of body, sl st in each st along top unjoined edge of other gusset, work hdc puff in each st along edges and end of other flap of body, join with sl st in first sl st. Finish off; weave in ends.

Attaching Magnetic Snaps

Center one pair of magnetic snaps on each side of center dc column of purse over 1" stabilizer strip about 2" in from long curved edge of body. Attach bottom half of snap to right side of sc rows at end of body through all layers except unfused fabric which lines stabilizer. Match placement of other half of snap on other flap. Attach snap to wrong side of beg buttercup flap through all layers except crochet and fabric fused to crochet.

Ribbon

If using velvet fabric, fold long edges of strip in to meet in center and seam (or use light amount of glue) to create double-thick 2" wide ribbon. Center one end of ribbon at sc flap edge with wrong side of ribbon against right side of flap and tuck 1/2" of ribbon between stabilizer and crochet layers; glue. Wrap ribbon snugly around center FPdc sts of purse from sc flap down front, and glue in place for the first 2". Attach bottom half of magnetic snap to velvet 4 1/2" down from sc flap edge, reinforcing back of velvet with 1 1/2" square of stabilizer. Continue gluing velvet to FPdc sts, keeping petals away from velvet as you go around bag to end of buttercup flap. Stop gluing 1/2" before edge of flap and let rem of velvet fall past edge down front of bag again. Feed end of velvet through buckle so that back of buckle hangs directly over snap bottom with purse flaps closed. Glue back of buckle to velvet. Trim velvet to about 7" past buckle so that 1 1/2" extends past buckle, folds back toward edge of flap and extends about 1/2" past flap. Tuck end between velvet and edge of flap and glue.

Attach top half of snap to velvet behind buckle: cut small slits in center of 1 1/2" square of stabilizer and in back of velvet behind center of buckle. Attach snap to back of velvet with stabilizer behind it. Glue all layers of velvet ribbon tog from buckle to edge of flap.

Wrap rem fabric edges around to wrong side of 9" ends of stabilizer and fuse, then fuse or glue rest of layers tog. Glue crochet edge to lining edge all around bag opening.

#7 BE BOP BAG

Designed by Patons Design Staff

SIZE

11 ¹/₂" x 9 ¹/₂" plus shoulder strap

MATERIALS

Sport weight cotton yarn
 3 ¹/₂ oz red

Eyelash yarn
 5 ¹/₄ oz variegated

Note: *Photographed model made with Patons® Grace #60409 Ruby and Patons® Cha Cha #02003 Be Bop*

Size H (5 mm) crochet hook
 (or size required for gauge)

Toggle

GAUGE

12 dc and 7 dc rows = 4" with one strand of each yarn held tog

INSTRUCTIONS

Body

Note: *Body of bag is worked from wrong side throughout.*

With 1 strand of each yarn held tog, ch 22.

Rnd 1: Sc in 2nd ch from hook, sc in each ch across to last ch, 5 sc in last ch; working in rem lps on opposite side of foundation ch: sc in next 19 chs, 4 sc in next ch: 48 sc; join with sl st in first sc.

Rnd 2: Ch 1, 2 sc in same sc as joining, sc in next 19 sc, 2 sc in each of next 5 sc, sc in next 19 sc, 2 sc in each of last 4 sc: 58 sc; join as before.

Rnd 3: Ch 1, 2 sc in same sc as joining, sc in next 20 sc, (2 sc in next sc, sc in next sc) 5 times, sc in next 19 sc, (2 sc in next sc, sc in next sc) 4 times: 68 sc; join.

Rnd 4: Ch 3 (counts as dc), dc in next sc and in each sc around: 68 dc; join with sl st in 3rd ch of beg ch-3.

Rep Rnd 4 until piece measures 9". At end of last rnd, finish off; weave in ends. Turn bag right side out if necessary.

Shoulder Strap

With one strand of each yarn held tog, ch 133.

Row 1 (right side): Dc in 4th ch from hook, dc in next ch and in each ch across; ch 3 (counts as dc on next row now and throughout), turn.

Row 2: Dc in next dc and in each dc across; ch 3, turn.

Rows 3 and 4: Rep Row 2 two times more. Finish off; weave in ends.

Fold strap in half widthwise and sew Rows 1 and 4 tog with eyelash yarn. Sew strap to sides of bag as shown in photograph.

Finishing

With 1 strand of each yarn held tog, ch 20, sl st in each ch across. Finish off. Fold ch in half to form a loop. Center and sew ends of loop to upper edge of Back of bag. Sew toggle to Front of bag to correspond to folded end of loop as shown in photograph.

#71 STRIPED HOBO BAG

Designed by Judi & Co.

SIZE
9" x 10 ¹/₂"

MATERIALS
Rayon raffia
  288 yds tan (MC)
  72 yds orange (A)
  72 yds purple (B)
  72 yds hot pink (C)

Note: *Photographed model made with Judi & Co's raffia tan, orange, purple and hot pink*

One magnetic snap, ³/₄" diameter

Fruit ornament

Stitch marker

Size F (3.75 mm) crochet hook
  (or size required for gauge)

GAUGE
16 sc = 4"

INSTRUCTIONS

Starting at bottom, ch 4; join with a sl st to form a ring.

Rnd 1: 6 sc in ring; do not join, mark beg of rnds.

Rnd 2: 2 sc in each sc around: 12 sts.

Rnd 3: *2 sc in first st, sc in next st; rep from * around: 18 sts.

Rnd 4: *2 sc in first st, sc in next 2 sts; rep from * around: 24 sts.

Rnd 5: *2 sc in first st, sc in next 3 sts; rep from * around: 30 sts.

Continue in this manner, increasing 6 sts on each rnd, until there are 84 sts.

Sides

Rnd 1: Sc in back lp only of each sc around.

Continue to work even in sc in unjoined rnds in following

Color sequence

2 rnds MC

6 rnds A

2 rnds MC

2 rnds B

2 rnds MC

6 rnds C

2 rnds MC

2 rnds B

2 rnds MC

6 rnds A

6 rnds MC

Straps

Dividing Row: With MC, sl st across next 12 sts, sc in next 30 sts; ch 1, turn.

Working now in turned rows on 30 sts, dec one st at each end of row every other row until 8 sts rem. Work even on 8 sts until strap measures 14" from Dividing Row. Finish off.

Working opposite first strap, sc in 30 sts. Working now in turned rows on 30 sts, work same as first strap.

Sew the 2 straps ends tog.

Finishing
Magnetic Snap Stabilizers
(make 2)
Ch 5.

Row 1: Sc in 2nd ch from hook and in each rem ch; ch 1, turn.

Row 2: Sc in each sc; ch 1, turn.

Rep Row 2 until piece is 1" long. Finish off; weave in ends.

Attach one piece of snap to each stablizer, inserting prongs through the stablizer and the metal washer; bend prongs over washer. Sew the two pieces at inside top, centered opposite each other.

Sew fruit ornament on front as shown in photo. With MC, tie a loose bow around ornament.

#72 MINI BAG

Designed by Glenda Winkleman for Coats and Clark

SIZE
5" in diameter x 6 ½" high

MATERIALS
Size 3 cotton crochet thread
200 yds natural

Note: *Photographed model made with J&P Coats® Aunt Lydia's® Cable 3 Crochet Thread #226 Natural*

Size F (3.75 mm) crochet hook (or size required for gauge)

GAUGE
Rnds 1 through 6 = 3 ½"

INSTRUCTIONS

With F hook, ch 4.

Rnd 1: Work 11 dc in 4th ch from hook (3 skipped chs count as dc): 12 dc; join with sl st in first skipped ch.

Rnd 2: Ch 1, 2 sc in same ch as joining, sc in next dc; *2 sc in next dc, sc in next dc; rep from * around: 18 sc; join with sl st in first sc.

Rnd 3: Ch 3 (counts as dc now and throughout), dc in same sc as joining, 2 dc in next sc and in each sc around: 36 dc; join with sl st in 3rd ch of beg ch-3.

Rnd 4: Ch 1, 2 sc in same ch as joining, sc in next 3 dc; *2 sc in next dc, sc in next 3 dc; rep from * around: 45 sc; join with sl st in first sc.

Rnd 5: Ch 3, dc in same sc as joining, dc in next 2 sc; *2 dc in next sc, dc in next 2 sc; rep from * around: 60 dc; join with sl st in 3rd ch of beg ch-3.

Rnd 6: Ch 1, sc in same ch as joining, sc in next dc and in each dc around: 60 sc; join with sl st in first sc.

Rnd 7: Ch 3, dc in next sc and in each sc around: 60 dc; join with sl st in 3rd ch of beg ch-3.

Rnd 8: Rep Rnd 6.

Rnd 9: Ch 1, (sc, ch 2, sc) in same sc as joining, skip next sc; *(sc, ch 2, sc) in next sc, skip next sc; rep from * around: 60 sc and 30 ch-2 sps; do not join. Place marker in first st in each rnd through Rnd 32.

Rnds 10 through 31: (Sc, ch 2, sc) in each ch-2 sp around: 60 sc and 30 ch-2 sps; do not join.

Rnd 32: (Sc, ch 2, sc) in first ch-2 sp, skip next ch-2 sp; *(sc ch 2, sc) in each of next 5 ch-2 sps, skip next ch-2 sp; rep from * around to last 4 ch-2 sps; (sc, ch 2, sc) in each of last 4 ch-2 sps: 50 sc and 25 ch-2 sps; do not join.

Rnd 33: 2 sc in each ch-2 sp around: 50 sc; join with sl st in first sc.

Rnd 34: Ch 4 (counts as dc and ch-1 sp), (dc, ch 1) in each sc around: 50 dc and 50 ch-1 sps; join with sl st in 3rd ch of beg ch-4.

Rnd 35: Ch 1, (sc, ch 2, sc) in first ch-1 sp, skip next ch-1 sp; *(sc, ch 2, sc) in next ch-1 sp, skip next ch-1 sp; rep from * around: 50 sc and 25 ch-2 sps; join with sl st in first sc. Finish off; weave in ends.

Drawstring

Ch 120. Finish off; weave in ends. Weave drawstring in and out of each ch-1 sp on Rnd 34, pull tog and tie in bow.

Right-hand Shoulder Strap

Ch 200, insert hook in ch-2 sp on Rnd 35 in center of right-hand side of handbag, place beg end of strap on inside of handbag at same ch-2 sp, insert hook through first ch of strap, sc through all 3 thicknesses. Finish off; weave in ends.

Left-hand Shoulder Strap

Ch 200, insert hook in ch-2 sp on Rnd 35 in center of left-hand side of handbag, place beg end of strap down through center of right-hand shoulder strap, align beg end of strap on inside of handbag at same ch-2 sp, insert hook through first ch of strap, sc through all 3 thicknesses. Finish off; weave in ends.

#73 FLOWER POWER

Designed by Bernat Design Staff

SIZE

18 1/2" wide x 12 1/2" high

MATERIALS

Worsted weight cotton yarn
  7 oz blue
  3 1/2 oz green
  3 1/2 oz orange
  3 1/2 oz pink
  3 1/2 oz yellow

Note: *Photographed model made with Bernat® Handicrafter® #13742 Hot Blue, #13712 Hot Green, #13628 Hot Orange, #13740 Hot Pink and #56 Yellow*

Size H (5 mm) crochet hook
  (or size required for gauge)

Safety pins or straight pins

GAUGE

Motif Rnds 1 and 2 = 2"

Motif = 6" square

INSTRUCTIONS

Note: Make 12 motifs total, 2 of each of 6 motifs as follows:

Motif 1: Color 1: blue; color 2: green; color 3: pink.

Motif 2: Color 1: yellow; color 2: pink; color 3: orange.

Motif 3: Color 1: green; color 2: yellow; color 3: blue.

Motif 4: Color 1: pink; color 2: yellow; color 3: blue.

Motif 5: Color 1: orange; color 2: blue; color 3: green.

Motif 6: Color 1: blue; color 2: orange; color 3: pink.

Motif

With color 1, ch 2.

Rnd 1 (right side): 6 sc in 2nd ch from hook: 6 sc; join with sl st in first sc.

Rnd 2: Ch 3 (counts as dc now and throughout), 2 dc in same sc as joining, 3 dc in next sc and in each sc around: 18 dc; join with sl st in 3rd ch of beg ch-3. Finish off; weave in ends.

Flower Petals
First Petal

Row 1: With right side facing, join color 2 with sl st in front lp of any dc, ch 3, dc in front lp of same dc as joining, dc in front lp of next dc, 2 dc in front lp of next dc: 5 dc; ch 3 (counts as dc on next row now and throughout), turn.

Row 2: Dc in next dc and in each dc across: 5 dc; ch 3, turn.

Row 3: 3 dc dec in next 3 dc, dc in next dc: 3 dc. Finish off, leaving a long end for sewing.

Second Petal

Row 1: With right side facing, join color 2 with sl st in front lp of next unworked dc on Rnd 2, ch 3, dc in front lp of same dc as joining, dc in front lp of next dc, 2 dc in front lp of next dc: 5 dc; ch 3, turn.

Rows 2 and 3: Rep Rows 2 and 3 on First Petal.

Third through Sixth Petals

Rep Rows 1 through 3 on Second Petal four times more.

Motif (continued)

Rnd 3: With right side facing, join color 3 with sl st in back lp of any dc on Rnd 2, ch 3, dc in back lp of same dc as joining, 2 dc in back lp of next dc on Rnd 2 and in back lp of each dc on Rnd 2 around: 36 dc; join with sl st in 3rd ch of beg ch-3.

Rnd 4: Ch 3, dc in same ch as joining; *dc in next dc, 2 dc in next dc; rep from * to last 5 dc; 2 dc in each of next 4 dc, dc in last dc: 56 sc; join as before.

185

Instructions continue on next page. →

Rnd 5: Ch 1, sc in same ch as joining, sc in next 4 dc; *hdc in next 2 dc, dc in next 2 dc, 5 tr in next dc for corner, dc in next 2 dc, hdc in next 2 dc**, sc in next 5 dc; rep from * two times more, then from * to ** once: 20 sc, 16 hdc, 16 dc and 20 tr; join with sl st in first sc.

Rnd 6: Ch 1, sc in each st around, working 3 sc in middle tr in corners: 80 sc; join as before. Finish off; weave in ends.

Using yarn ends from each petal, sew outer edges of petals to motif.

With right sides facing, sew 6 Motifs together as shown in photograph, or as desired, for Front and 6 for Back.

Side and Bottom Section
With blue, ch 11.

Row 1 (right side): Dc in 4th ch from hook (3 skipped chs count as dc), dc in next ch and in each ch across: 9 dc; drop yarn, do not turn work.

Note: Use green for Rows 2 and 4 and blue for Row 3.

Row 2 (right side): With next color, sc in top of ch-3 and in each dc across, changing to next color in last sc: 9 sc; ch 3 (counts as dc on next row and throughout), turn.

Row 3 (wrong side): Dc in next sc and in each sc across: 9 dc; drop color, do not turn work.

Row 4 (wrong side): Rep Row 2.

Continue in this manner, working 2 rows on right side, then 2 rows on wrong side, changing colors on each row, and following color pattern below until piece meaures about 43" (or length down one side of Bag, across bottom and up other side of Bag). Finish off; weave in ends.

Color pattern: (Orange, pink, orange, pink), (green, blue, green, blue), (pink, orange, pink, orange), (blue, green, blue, green).

With wrong sides together, pin long edges of Side and Bottom Section to side and bottom edges of Front and Back.

Edging
Rnd 1: With right side of Front facing, join blue with sl st in middle sc of 3 sc in top left corner of Front, ch 1, 3 sc in same sc as joining, work sc evenly around entire Front, working 3 sc in corners and working through both layers where Front and Side sections are pinned; join with sl st in first sc.

Rnd 2: Ch 1, work rev sc in each sc around; join as before. Finish off; weave in ends.

Rep edging for Back of Bag.

Handles (make 2)
With blue, ch 50.

Row 1 (right side): Dc in 4th ch from hook (3 skipped chs count as dc), dc in next ch and in each ch across: 48 dc; ch 3 (counts as dc on next row now and throughout), turn.

Row 2: Dc in next dc and in each dc across; ch 3, turn.

Row 3: Dc in next dc and in each dc across; ch 1, turn.

Row 4: Fold Handle in half widthwise with right sides together, sc in each dc on Row 3 and in each free lp of foundation ch together: 48 sc. Finish off.

Sew short ends of handles to top edge of Bag as shown in photograph.

#74 IRISH ROSE

Designed by Nancy Nehring

SIZE
4" wide x 7" high with fringe

MATERIALS
Size 30 cotton crochet thread 567 yds white

Note: *Photographed model made with DMC® Cebelia size 30 White*

Size 11 (1.1 mm) steel crochet hook (or size required for gauge)

10" x 6" jewel tone lining fabric (optional)

3 mm white pearls, 453

Nail polish or cyanoacrylic glue

Sharp sewing needle (optional)

Sewing thread to match lining fabric (optional)

GAUGE
Motif Rnds 1 through 12 = 4" square

SPECIAL STITCHES
Pearl Cluster: Slide pearl up to hook, sl st in first ch from hook, slide pearl up to hook, ch 1, slide pearl up to hook, sl st in same ch as last sl st: pearl cluster made.

Scallop: Work (sc, hdc, 6 dc, hdc, sc) in specified lp: scallop made.

INSTRUCTIONS

Irish Rose Motif (make 2)
Stiffen end of crochet thread with nail polish or cyanoacrylic glue and allow to dry. String 132 pearls onto stiffened thread.

Rose
Ch 8; join with sl st to form a ring.

Rnd 1 (right side): Ch 6 (counts as dc and ch-3 lp); *dc in ring, ch 3; rep from * 6 times more: 8 dc and 8 ch-3 lps; join with sl st in 3rd ch of beg ch-6.

Rnd 2: *Work (sc, hdc, 3 dc, hdc, sc) in next ch-3 lp; rep from * 7 times more: 24 dc, 16 hdc and 16 sc.

187

Instructions continue on next page. →

Rnd 3: Working behind petals on Rnd 2, sc in joining sl st on Rnd 1, ch 5; *sc in next dc on Rnd 1, ch 5; rep from * 6 times more: 8 sc and 8 ch-5 lps; join with sl st in beg sc.

Rnd 4: *Work (sc, hdc, 5 dc, hdc, sc) in next ch-5 lp; rep from * 7 times more: 40 dc, 16 hdc and 16 sc.

Rnd 5: Working behind petals on Rnd 4, sc in joining sl st on Rnd 3, ch 7; *sc in next sc on Rnd 3, ch 7; rep from * 6 times more: 8 sc and 8 ch-7 lps; join with sl st in beg sc.

Rnd 6: *Work (sc, hdc, 7 dc, hdc, sc) in next ch-7 lp; rep from * 7 times more: 56 dc, 16 hdc and 16 sc.

Rnd 7: Working behind petals on Rnd 6, sc in joining sl st on Rnd 5, ch 9; *sc in next sc on Rnd 5, ch 9; rep from * 6 times more: 8 sc and 8 ch-9 lps; join with sl st in beg sc.

Rnd 8: *Work (sc, hdc, 9 dc, hdc, sc) in next ch-9 lp; rep from * 7 times more: 72 dc, 16 hdc and 16 sc.

Background

Rnd 9: Sl st in first 4 sts of first petal; *ch 7, pearl cluster, ch 6, sc in 10th st of same petal; ch 7, pearl cluster, ch 6, sc in 7th st of next petal; ch 7, pearl cluster, ch 6, sc in 4th st of next petal; rep from * 3 times more: 12 pearl clusters.

Rnd 10: Sl st in first 6 chs of beg ch-7 on Rnd 9; ch 1, sl st between 1st and 2nd pearls of first pearl cluster, ch 1 behind pearls, sl st between 2nd and 3rd pearls of same pearl cluster; *ch 7, pearl cluster, ch 6, sl st between 1st and 2nd pearls of next pearl cluster, ch 1 behind pearls, sl st between 2nd and 3rd pearls of same pearl cluster, ch 11, sl st between 1st and 2nd pearls of next cluster,

ch 1, turn; 12 sc in ch-11 lp, sl st in ch-1 behind pearls of previous pearl cluster, ch 1, turn; sc in next 12 sc, turn; ch 6, skip first 3 sc, sc in next sc, (ch 6, skip next 3 sc, sc in next sc) 2 times, turn; **scallop in next ch-6 lp; rep from ** 2 times more; sl st in edge of next 2 sc, sl st between 1st and 2nd pearls of next pearl cluster, ch 1, sl st between 2nd and 3rd pearls of same pearl cluster; ch 7, pearl cluster, ch 6; sl st between 1st and 2nd pearls of next pearl cluster, ch 1, sl st between 2nd and 3rd pearls of same pearl cluster; rep from * 3 times more: 8 pearl clusters and 4 corners.

Rnd 11: Sl st in first 6 chs of beg ch-7 on Rnd 10; sl st between 1st and 2nd pearls of first pearl cluster, ch 1, sl st between 2nd and 3rd pearls of same pearl cluster; *ch 7, pearl cluster, ch 6, sc in 5th st of first scallop; ch 7, pearl cluster, ch 6, sc in first st of second scallop; (ch 7, pearl cluster, ch 6, sc in last st of second scallop) corner made; ch 7, pearl cluster, ch 6, sc in 6th st of third scallop; **ch 7, pearl cluster, ch 6, sl st between 1st and 2nd pearls of next pearl cluster, ch 1, sl st between 2nd and 3rd pearls of same pearl cluster; rep from ** once; rep from * 3 times more: 24 pearl clusters.

Rnd 12: Ch 1, sl st in first 6 chs of beg ch-7 on Rnd 11; sl st between 1st and 2nd pearls of first pearl cluster, ch 1, sl st between 2nd and 3rd pearls of same pearl cluster, ch 7; *sl st between 1st and 2nd pearls of next pearl cluster, ch 1, sl st between 2nd and 3rd pearls of same pearl cluster, ch 7; rep from * around: 24 ch-7 lps; sl st in beg ch-1. Finish off; weave in ends.

Side Seams

Holding motifs with wrong sides together, working through front and back together; **join with sl st in ch-7 lp on Rnd 12 after corner on Rnd 11; ch 1, 12 sc in same ch-7 lp, ch 3; *12 sc in next ch-7 lp, ch 3; rep from * 3 times more; 12 sc in last ch-7 lp before next corner: 72 sc and 5 ch-3 sps. Finish off; weave in ends**. Skip next 6 ch-7 lps; rep from ** to ** for other side.

Bottom Edging

Rnd 1: Working in front motif only; join with sl st in first skipped ch-7 lp on Rnd 12, ch 1, 12 sc in same ch-7 lp, ch 1; *12 sc in next ch-7 lp, ch 1*; rep from * to * 4 times more; rep from * to * 6 times more on back motif: 144 sc and 12 ch-1 sps. Do not finish off.

Row 1: Fold bag bottom in half along side seams. Working through front and back together; sc in each sc across: 72 sc; ch 1, turn.

Row 2: Sc in first sc and in each sc across; turn.

Row 3 (fringe): Sl st in first sc; *(ch 3, slide pearl up to hook, ch 1) 3 times, ch 4, pearl cluster, (ch 3, slide pearl up to hook, ch 1) 3 times, ch 3, sl st in same sc as last sl st; rep from * 2 times more; ** skip next sc, sc in next 9 sc, skip next sc, sl st in next sc; rep from * 5 times more, except work (sc in next 8 sc) on last rep instead of (sc in next 9 sc); rep from * to ** once: 21 ch/pearl lps and 53 sc. Finish off; weave in ends.

Top Edging

Rnd 1: Working along top edge of motifs; join with sl st in top sc of one side seam; *8 sc in next ch-7 lp*; rep from * to * 5 times more; sl st in top sc of other side seam; rep from * to * 6 times more: 96 sc; join with sl st in first sc.

Rnds 2 through 4: Ch 1, sc in same sc as joining, sc in each sc around; join with sl st in first sc.

Rnd 5: *Ch 3, skip next sc, sc in next sc; rep from * around, ending with ch 3, sc in first ch-3 lp: 48 sc and 48 ch-3 lps.

Rnds 6 through 14: *Ch 3, sc in next ch-3 lp; rep from * around. At end of Rnd 14, finish off; weave in ends.

Drawstrings (make 2)

Ch 125, sl st in back bar of 2nd ch from hook and in back bar of each rem ch across: 124 sl sts. Finish off; weave in ends.

Thread one drawstring through ch-3 lps on Rnd 9 of Top Edging and other drawstring through ch-3 lps on Rnd 10 of Top Edging. Tie ends of each drawstring together. Weave in ends.

Lining (optional)

Fold lining fabric in half crosswise with wrong sides together so fabric is 6" x 5". Sew seam with 1/2" seam allowance along each 5" side. Turn lining wrong side out. Sew seam with 3/4" seam allowance along each side so it encases original seam, thus enclosing raw edges. Turn lining right side out. Fold 1/4" of top lining opening to right side. Position top of lining on inside of bag behind Rnd 4 of Top Edging and stitch in place. Tack bottom corners of lining to bottom corners of bag.

#75 FELTED STRIPES

Designed by Jennifer Pace

SIZE AFTER FELTING

12" long x 5 ½" diameter

MATERIALS

Worsted weight 100% wool yarn
  500 yds of a various colors

*Note: Photographed model made
with Patons® Classic Merino Wool
#00202 Aran, #77115 New
Denim, #00029 Natural Mix,
#00222 Sage, #77116 Denim Marl
and Cascade 220 #2409 Palm,
#7804 Shrimp, #7816 Bluebell,
#7802 Cerise, #7809 Violet, #7814
Chartreuse, #8884 Claret, #9444
Orange Sherbet, #9421 Lagoon,
#7824 Turquoise*

Pair of purse handles, 5 ½" wide
  at base

1 ¼" diameter button

24" Size 10 ½ (6.5 mm) circular
  knitting needle (or size
  required for gauge)

Size 10 ½ double-point knitting
  needles

GAUGE BEFORE FELTING

12 sts and 18 rows = 4" in stock
  st (knit 1 row, purl 1 row)

INSTRUCTIONS

Note: Use yarns in random color sequence of your choice.

First Side

With circular needle, CO 100 sts; do not join, work back and forth in rows.

Row 1: Knit.

Row 2: Purl.

Rows 3 through 100: Rep Rows 1 and 2.

Shape End

Rnd 1: Knit; join to work in rnds.

Rnd 2: *K8, K2tog; rep from * around: 90 sts.

Rnd 3 (and all odd-numbered rnds): Knit.

Rnd 4: *K7, K2tog; rep from * around: 80 sts.

Rnd 6: *K6, K2tog; rep from * around: 70 sts.

Rnd 8: *K5, K2tog, rep from * around: 60 sts.

Rnd 10: *K4, K2tog; rep from * around: 50 sts.

Rnd 12: *K3, K2tog; rep from * around: 40 sts.

Note: Change to double point needles when needed.

Rnd 14: *K2, K2tog; rep from * around: 30 sts.

Rnd 16: *K1, K2tog; rep from * around: 20 sts.

Rnd 18: *K2tog; rep from * around: 10 sts.

Rnd 19: Rep Rnd 18: 5 sts. Cut yarn, leaving a 10" yarn end; thread end into a tapestry needle and draw through rem sts, drawing up tightly and securing. Finish off; weave in all yarn ends.

Second Side

Working on opposite side of CO row, pick up 100 sts.

Work same as First side.

Finishing

Leaving a center opening, sew first 25 rows tog at each end. 50 rows will rem on each side. With circular needle, pick up 1 st in end of each row and using I-Cord bind off, BO 25 sts as follows: CO 3 sts. *K2, K2tog (one st is from from the main piece). Place the 3 sts just worked back onto left needle, pull yarn taut across back of work; rep from * until 25 sts are bound off.

For button lp, sl last 3 sts knitted onto one double-point needle and work I-cord (see page 253) for 7 1/2". Sl these 3 sts back onto circular needle and continue I-cord bind off for rem 75 sts. Sew ends of I-cord edging tog.

Felting

Following Felting instructions on page 252, felt bag to desired size.

Assembly

Sew one side of handle, centered, to front and back of bag. Sew button opposite button lp.

#76 TWINKLE, TWINKLE

Designed by Nancy Brown

SIZE

8" wide x 7 1/2" high plus 28" shoulder strap

MATERIALS

Acrylic blend novelty yarn
  164 yds black/multi color

Note: Photographed model made with Dark Horse, LLC #TW42 Twinkle

Size J (6 mm) crochet hook
  (or size required for gauge)

GAUGE

7 sc and 7 sc rows = 2"

SPECIAL STITCHES

Sc decrease (sc dec): (Insert hook in next st and draw up a lp) twice, YO and draw through all 3 lps on hook: sc dec made.

INSTRUCTIONS

Back

Ch 12.

Row 1 (wrong side): Sc in 2nd ch from hook and in next 9 chs, 5 sc in last ch; working in free lps on opposite side of foundation ch, sc in next 10 chs: 25 sc; ch 1, turn.

Note: Work Rows 2 through 14 in back lps only.

Row 2 (right side): Sc in first sc and in each sc across; ch 1, turn.

Row 3: Sc in first 10 sc, 2 sc in each of next 5 sc, sc in next 10 sc: 30 sc; ch 1, turn.

Row 4: Rep Row 2.

Row 5: Sc in first 10 sc, 2 sc in each of next 10 sc, sc in next 10 sc: 40 sc; ch 1, turn.

Rows 6 through 8: Rep Row 2 three times more.

Row 9: Sc in first 10 sc, 2 sc in each of next 20 sc, sc in next 10 sc: 60 sc; ch 1, turn.

Rows 10 through 12: Rep Row 2 three times more.

Row 13: Sc in first 15 sc; *sc in next sc, 2 sc in next sc; rep from * 14 times more; sc in next 15 sc: 75 sc; ch 1, turn.

Row 14: Rep Row 2. Ch 1, do not turn.

Edging

Sc in edge of Row 14; *skip next row, sc in edge of next row; rep from * across top edge, working sc in foundation ch and ending with sc in other edge of Row 14: 15 sc. Finish off; weave in ends.

Front

Work same as Back. Rep Edging, but do not finish off.

Side Seams

Place Front and Back with wrong sides together. Working through back lp of each piece, sl st in each sc on Row 14 across. Do not finish off.

Top Edging

Working across top of Front; *sc in next sc, 3 sc in next sc*; rep from * to * across to last sc on top of Front; sc in last sc; continuing across top of Back; rep from * to * 3 times more; sc in next sc, (sl st, ch 10 for button lp, sl st) in next sc; rep from * to * 3 times more; sc in last sc on top of Back; join with sl st in beg sc. Finish off; weave in ends.

Shoulder Strap

With Front facing, join 2 strands with sl st in top edge of right side seam, ch about 28" or to desired length; join with sl st in top edge of left side seam. Finish off; weave in ends.

Button

Ch 2.

Rnd 1: Work 4 sc in 2nd ch from hook: 4 sc. Do not join.

Rnd 2: Work 2 sc in first sc and in each sc around: 8 sc.

Rnd 3: Sc dec in first 2 sc; *sc dec in next 2 sc; rep from * 2 times more: 4 sc.

Rnd 4: Sc dec in first 2 sc, sc dec in next 2 sc: 2 sc. Finish off.

Finishing

With right side facing, sew button to top center of Front about 3/4" below top edge. Weave in ends.

#77 PRETTY PAIR

Designed by Anne Rubin for Judi & Co.

SIZE

7 3/4" tall

MATERIALS

Rayon ribbon yarn, 1/2" wide
  100 yds black or cream

Satin cord
  144 yds black or cream

Note: *Photographed model made with Judi & Co's 1/2" Rayon Ribbon and Judi & Co's Satin Cordé*

Stitch marker

Size G (4 mm) crochet hook
  (or size required for gauge)

GAUGE

16 hdc = 4"

INSTRUCTIONS

Starting at bottom with cord, ch 4; join with a sl st to form a ring.

Rnd 1: 8 hdc in ring; do not join, mark beg of rnds.

Rnd 2: 2 hdc in each hdc: 16 hdc.

Rnd 3: * Hdc in next hdc, 2 hdc in next hdc; rep from * around: 24 hdc.

Rnd 4: *Hdc in next 2 hdc, 2 hdc in next hdc; rep from * around: 30 hdc.

Rnd 5: *Hdc in next 3 hdc, 2 hdc in next hdc; rep from * around: 36 hdc.

Continue in this manner, increasing 8 sts each rnd, until piece measures 5" in diameter.

Sides

Finish off cord, join ribbon.

Rnds 1 through 3: Sc in each sc. Finish off ribbon, join cord.

Rnd 4: With cord, sc in each sc; finish off cord, join ribbon.

Rnds 5 and 6: With ribbon, sc in each sc; finish off ribbon, join cord.

Rep Rnds 4 through 6 until sides measure about 6" from start of sides, ending by working a Row 6. Finish off ribbon; weave in all ends.

Top Trim

Rnd 1 (eyelet rnd): Join cord in any sc; ch 4 (counts as a dc and ch-1 sp), skip one sc, dc in next sc; * ch 1, skip next sc, dc in next sc; rep from * around.

Rnd 2: Sc in each dc and ch-1 sp.

Rnd 3: Sc in each sc.

Rnd 4: Ch 1; *work reverse sc in each sc around; join in beg sc, finish off. Weave in all ends.

Twisted Cords

Following Twisted Cord instructions on page 253, with satin cord make two 36" lengths of twisted cord. Weave each length through eyelet rnd, alternating placement, then tie ends in knots.

#78 PLAYING CHECKERS

Designed by Patons Design Staff

SIZE AFTER FELTING
11" x 5 1/2"

MATERIALS
Worsted weight 100% wool yarn
  3 1/2 oz red (A)
  7 oz black (MC)
  7 oz grey (B)

Note: Photographed model made with Patons® Classic Merino Wool, #230 Bright Red (A), #226 Black (MC) and #224 Grey Mix (B)

1 toggle fastener

Stitch marker

Sewing pins

Sharp scissors

Size 7 (4.5 mm) straight knitting needles (or size required for gauge)

Set of four Size 7 (4.5 mm) double-point knitting needles

GAUGE BEFORE FELTING
20 sts and 26 rows = 4" in stock st (knit 1 row, purl 1 row)

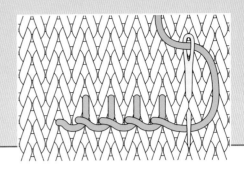

Blanket stitch

INSTRUCTIONS

With MC, CO144 sts.

Row 1 (right side): *With MC, K12. With B, K12; rep from * across.

Row 2: *With B, P12, with MC, P12; rep from * across.

Rows 3 to 20: Rep Rows 1 and 2.

Row 21: *With B, K12, with A, K12; rep from * across.

Row 22: *With A, P12, with B, P12; rep from * across.

Rows 23 to 40: Rep Rows 21 and 22.

Rows 41 to 120: Rep Rows 1 through 40 twice more. BO in patt.

Handle (make 2)
With MC, CO 11 sts on one double-point needle.

Divide sts evenly on 3 needles and place marker to indicate beg of rnds. Knit in rnds until work from beg measures 16". BO.

Toggle Loop
With MC, CO 4 sts; following I-Cord instructions on page 253, make 13" of I-Cord.

Finishing
Felt all pieces following felting instructions on page 252. Main section felted piece should measure about 13 ¾" wide x 24 ½" long.

Following Cutting Diagram, cut Main Section 11" wide x 17 ¼" long. Cut 2 round pieces each 5 ½" diameter.

Pin round sides to Main Section. With wrong sides tog, join sides to Main Section, using MC and blanket stitch. With MC, sew top opening with blanket stitch.

Trim handles to measure 12". Trim toggle lp to measure 9". Sew handles, toggle lp and toggle in position as shown in photo.

Cutting Diagram

Sides of Bag

Felted Piece

5½"

Main Section

17½"

11"

#79 DAISY CLUTCH

Designed by Nancy Nehring

SIZE

12" wide x 8" high

MATERIALS

Double strand size 3 cotton crochet thread
  300 yds yellow/orange

Size 10 cotton crochet thread
  450 yds white

Note: Photographed model made with Aunt Lydia's® Double Strand #460 Golden Yellow/Pumpkin and J&P Coats® Knit-Cro-Sheen #1 White

12" white zipper

Daisy buttons or other buttons as desired

Sewing needle

Yellow quilting thread

Size 0 (3.25 mm) steel crochet hook (or size required for gauge)

GAUGE

12 sc in back lp only = 2"

15 sc over padding cord = 2"

INSTRUCTIONS

Note: Use 2 strands of white thread (1 strand from each of two balls) held together throughout unless stated otherwise.

Bag Bottom

Back

With white, ch 31.

Row 1 (right side): Sc in 2nd ch from hook and in each rem ch: 30 sc; ch 1, turn.

Rows 2 and 3: Sc in back lp of first sc and in back lp of each sc across; ch 1, turn. At end of Row 3, do not ch 1. Finish off; weave in ends. Do not turn.

Front

With white, ch 31.

Rows 1 through 3: Rep Rows 1 through 3 of Back. At end of Row 3, ch 6. Do not finish off. With right side facing, join with sl st in first sc on Row 3 of Back. Finish off; weave in ends.

Front and Back

Row 4: With wrong side facing, join white with sc in back lp of first sc on Row 3 of Back, sc in back lp of next sc and in back lp of each sc across to chs, sc in each of next 6 chs, sc in back lp of next sc on Row 3 of Front and in back lp of each sc across: 66 sc; ch 1, turn.

Row 5: Sc in back lp of first sc and in back lp of each sc across, turn. Finish off; weave in ends.

Row 6: With wrong side facing, join yellow/orange with sc in back lp of first sc, sc in back lp of next sc and in back lp of each sc across: 66 sc; ch 1, turn.

Rows 7 through 10: Sc in back lp of first sc and in back lp of each sc across; ch 1, turn. At end of last row, do not ch 1. Finish off; weave in ends.

Row 11: With right side facing, join white with sc in back lp of first sc, sc in back lp of next sc and in back lp of each sc across: 66 sc; ch 1, turn.

Rows 12 through 15: Rep Rows 7 through 10.

Rows 16 through 85: Rep Rows 6 through 15 seven times more.

Rows 86 through 90: Rep Rows 6 through 10.

Rows 91 and 92: Rep Rows 11 and 12.

Front

Row 93: Sc in back lp of first 30 sc: 30 sc; ch 1, turn, leaving rem 36 sc unworked.

Rows 94 and 95: Sc in back lp of first sc and in back lp of each sc across; ch 1, turn. At end of Row 95, do not ch 1. Finish off; weave in ends.

Back

Row 93: With right side facing, skip next 6 unworked sc on Row 92, join white with sc in back lp of next sc, sc in back lp of next sc and in back lp of each rem sc across: 30 sc; ch 1, turn.

199

Instructions continue on next page. →

Rows 94 and 95: Rep Rows 94 and 95 on Front.

Fold bag in half lengthwise with wrong sides together so beg chs on Row 1 of Front line up with beg chs on Row 1 of Back. With one strand of white, sc beg chs of Front and Back tog. With one strand of white, sc Front and Back of Rows 95 tog. There is a small hole remaining near bottom at fold line where 6 chs were added at beg and 6 sc were skipped at end. Fold hole in half at 90 degrees to seam just made. With one strand of white, sc two sides of this fold together. Rep for other end of bag. Two seams just made should look like a "T".

Bag Top

Remove 12 yds of yellow/orange from ball to be used as a padding cord for bag top. Hold this thread at top of previous row and work sc over this thread and into top of sts of previous row as you normally would.

First rnd of bag top is worked with one sc in edge of each row of bag bottom. All sts are worked through both top lps of row below. All sts are worked over padding cord. Work in a spiral, do not join rnds. Pull up on padding cord as needed to keep it snug under sc but not so tight that you gather top sts. If you have trouble keeping tension of padding cord even, measure off every 11 3/4" on padding cord and mark. Each 11 3/4" is for one side of bag top.

Rnd 1: With right side facing, join yellow/orange with sc in edge of Row 5 on Back, position padding cord along edges of rows on Front and Back of Bag Bottom as you work, sc in edge of next row of Bag Bottom and in edge of each row around, working all sc over padding cord: 190 sc; do not join.

Rnds 2 through 15: Sc in next st and in each st around, working all sc over padding cord. At end of Rnd 15, drop padding cord, sl st in last two sts. Finish off; weave in ends.

Finishing

With needle and thread, sew zipper into place along top edge of bag, aligning outer edges of zipper tape with bottom of Rnd 14. Sew buttons into place on Bag Top as desired. Knot five 4" lengths of yellow/orange through eye of zipper pull for a decorative zipper pull.

#80 FLOWER TOTE

Designed by Bernat Design Staff

SIZE
7" x 11"

MATERIALS
Worsted weight cotton yarn
   3 oz bright blue (MC)
   1 ³/4 oz bright green (CC 1)
   1 ³/4 oz bright orange(CC 2)
   1 ³/4 oz bright pink (CC 3)

Note: *Photographed model made with Bernat® Handicrafter® Cotton #13742 Hot Blue, #13712 Hot Green, #13628 Hot Orange, #13700 Hot Pink*

Size H (5 mm) crochet hook
   (or size required for gauge)

GAUGE
14 sc = 4"

STITCH GUIDE
Reverse single crochet (rev sc): Ch 1; * insert hook in first st to the right, turn hook downward to catch yarn and draw up a lp. YO, pull yarn through both lps; rep from * for rev sc.

Sc2tog: Insert hook in sc, YO, pull up lp, insert hook in next sc, YO, pull up lp, YO, pull yarn through all 3 lps on hook: sc2tog decrease made.

INSTRUCTIONS

Note: *To change colors, work to last 2 lps on hook of st, drop first color, YO with second color and pull through all 2 lps.*

Note: *First ch-3 of rnd or row counts as 1 dc throughout pattern.*

Base
With MC, ch 2.

Rnd 1: 6 sc in 2nd ch from hook; join with sl st to first sc: 6 sc; ch 3 (counts as a dc throughout pattern), turn.

201

Instructions continue on next page. →

Rnd 2: 2 dc in base of ch, 3 dc in each sc around; join with sl st in 3rd ch of ch-3: 18 dc; ch 3, turn.

Rnd 3: Dc in base of ch; *dc in next dc, 2 dc in next dc; rep from * around to last dc, dc in last dc: 27 dc; join, ch 3, turn.

Rnd 4: Dc in base of ch; *2 dc in next dc; rep from * around, join: 54 dc; ch 3, turn.

Rnd 5: Dc in base of ch; *dc in next 3 dc, 2 dc in next dc; rep from * to last dc, dc in last dc, join: 68 dc; ch 3, turn.

Rnd 6: Dc in base of ch; *dc in next 4 dc, 2 dc in next dc; rep from * to last 2 dc, dc in last 2 dc: 82 dc. Finish off; weave in ends.

Body

With MC, ch 33.

Row 1 (right side): Dc in 4th ch from hook and in each rem ch; change to CC 1 in last st, ch 1, turn: 31 dc.

Row 2: Sc in each dc, join MC in last sc, ch 3, turn.

Row 3: *Dc in next sc; rep from * across, join CC 1 in last sc, ch 1; turn.

Row 4: Sc in each dc, join CC 2 in last sc, ch 3; turn.

Row 5: *Dc in next sc; rep from * across, join CC 3 in last dc, ch 1; turn.

Row 6: Rep Row 4.

Row 7: Rep Row 5.

Row 8: Sc in each dc, join CC 1 in last sc, ch 3; turn.

Row 9: *Dc in next sc; rep from * across, join MC in last dc, ch 1; turn.

Row 10: Sc in each dc, join CC 1 in last sc, ch 3: turn.

Row 11: Rep Row 9.

Row 12: Sc in each dc, join CC 3 in last sc, ch 3; turn.

Row 13: *Dc in next sc; rep from * across, join CC 2 in last dc, ch 1; turn.

Row 14: Rep Row 12.

Row 15: Rep Row 13.

Row 16: Rep Row 2.

Row 17: Rep Row 1.

Rep Rows 2 through 17 for pattern until piece measures about 22" from beg, ending by working a Row 16. Finish off; weave in ends.

Sew first and last rows tog (center back seam).

Top Edging

Rnd 1: With right side facing you, join MC in center back seam with sl st, work 72 sc evenly around edge, join in first sc with sl st: 72 sc.

Rnd 2 (eyelet rnd): Ch 3, dc in next sc; *ch 1, skip next sc, dc in next 2 sc; rep from * to last sc, ch 1, skip last sc, join with sl st in top of ch 3: 48 dc, 24 ch-1 sps.

Rnd 3: Ch 3, dc in next dc; *dc in ch-1 sp, dc in next 2 dc: rep from * to last ch-1 sp, dc in ch-1 sp, join with sl st in top of beg ch 3: 72 dc.

Rnd 4: Work rev sc around, join. Finish off; weave in ends.

Straps (make 2)

With MC, ch 72.

Row 1 (right side): Sc in 2nd ch from hook and in each rem ch: 71 sc; ch 1, turn.

Rows 2 and 3: Sc across, ch 1; turn.

Row 4: Sc across, ch 1; do not turn.

Edging: Work rev sc across. Finish off; weave in ends

Opposite Edging: With right side facing, join MC with sl st in left side lp of foundation ch, ch 1; work rev sc across. Finish off; weave in ends.

Drawstring

With MC, crochet a chain 42" long, turn chain sideways, sl st in each back bump of ch. Finish off.

Assembly

Pin bottom of bag to base. With right side facing, join MC in center back seam with sl st.

Rnd 1: Work sc evenly around, joining base and bag together. Join in first sc with sl st, ch 1; do not turn.

Rnd 2: Work rev sc around, join. Finish off.

Sew end of one strap on one side of back seam at top of bag, under the edging. Sew other end of strap 3" from same side of back seam at the base. Rep on other side of seam for the 2nd strap.

Weave drawstring through eyelet round of top edging. Ends should meet at center front. Knot ends.

Applique Flowers

Flower A (make 1)

With MC, ch 2.

Rnd 1: 6 sc in 2nd ch from hook, join in first sc with sl st: 6 sc.

Rnd 2: Ch 1; 2 sc in each sc, join in first sc with sl st: 12 sc.

Finish off; weave in ends.

First Petal

Row 1: Join CC 1 with sl st in front lp of any sc, *ch 1; 2 sc in same sp, 2 sc in front lp of next sc, ch 1; turn: 4 sc.

Row 2 through Row 4: Sc in each sc, ch 1; turn.

Row 5: (Sc2tog) twice. Finish off.*

Petals 2 through 6

Join CC 1 with sl st in front lp of next unworked sc of Rnd 2; rep from * to *.

Flower B (make 1)

Rep instructions for Flower A, substituting CC 3 for MC and CC 2 for CC 1.

Flower C (make 1)

Rep instructions for Flower A, substituting CC 1 for MC and MC for CC 1.

Flower D (make 1)

Rep instructions for Flower A, substituting CC 2 for MC and CC 3 for CC 1.

Pin flowers randomly around bag, sew to bag.

#81 GRANNY BAG

Designed by Judi & Co.

SIZE
9 ¹/₂" x 10 ¹/₂"

MATERIALS
Rayon Raffia yarn
  144 yds black
  144 yds off-white
  144 yds brown

Note: *Photographed model made with Judi & Co's Satin Cord Black, Eggshell and Brown*

Two ³/₄" diameter brown
  plastic rings

Size I (5.5 mm) crochet hook
  (or size required for gauge)

GAUGE
8 sc = 2"

First 3 rnds of granny square =
  3 ¹/₂"

INSTRUCTIONS

Granny Square (make 8)

With off-white, ch 4, join with a sl st to form a ring.

Rnd 1: Ch 3 (counts as a dc), 2 dc in ring; (ch 3, 3 dc in ring) 3 times, ch 3, join with sl st in 3rd ch of beg ch-3. Finish off-white.

Rnd 2: Join brown with a sl st in any ch-3 corner sp; ch 3, (2 dc, ch 3, 3 dc) in same sp; *ch 2, in next ch-3 corner sp work (3 dc, ch 3, 3 dc); rep from * two times more, ch 2, join with sl st in beg ch-3.

Rnd 3: Sl st across next 2 dc and into ch-3 sp; (ch 3, 2 dc, ch 3, 3 dc) in same sp; ch 2, 3 dc between next two 3-dc groups, ch 2; *in next ch-3 corner sp work (3 dc, ch 3, 3 dc); ch 2, 3 dc between next two 3-dc groups, ch 2; rep from * two times more, join with sl st in beg ch-3. Finish off brown.

Rnd 4: Join black with a sl st in any ch-3 corner sp; ch 1, 5 sc in same sp; *3 sc in each of next 2 ch-2 sps, 5 dc in next ch-3 sp; rep from * two times more, 3 sc in each of last 2 ch-2 sps; join with sl st in beg sl st. Finish off black; weave in all ends.

Front Assembly

Hold two granny squares with wrong sides tog; with black, join with sc across one pair of side edges. Rep with two more squares. Hold the two pairs of squares with wrong sides tog and join with sc along one long edge, forming one 4-square unit. Measure one outside edge of the unit, which will determine length of gusset.

Back Assembly

Work same as front assembly.

Gusset

With black, ch 8.

Row 1: Sc in 2nd ch from hook and in each rem ch: 7 sc; ch 1, turn.

Row 2: Sc in each sc, ch 1, turn.

Rep Row 2 until piece measures 3 times the outside edge of the square unit, as measured in Front Assembly instructions. Do not finish off. Pin gusset around 3 sides of one square unit to determine correct length. Add or subtract rows as necessary to fit correctly. Finish off; weave in ends.

Working through back lps only of squares, with wrong sides tog, sew opposite edge of gusset around 3 sides of Front. Then sew gusset around 3 sides of Back

Top Border

Hold piece with right side facing and opening at top. Join black with a sl st in a gusset seam.

Rnd 1: Ch 1, sc in seam; work sc around top edge of front and back pieces and gusset; join in beg sc.

Rnds 2 and 3: Ch 1, sc in each sc around.

Rnd 4: Working from left to right, work one rnd of reverse sc; join, finish off, weave in all ends.

Handle

With black, ch 6.

Row 1: Sc in 2nd ch and in each rem ch: 5 sc; ch 1, turn.

Row 2: Sc in each sc, ch 1, turn.

Rep Row 2 until handle measures 27". Finish off. Sew one end of handle to each gusset top.

Drawstring

With black, make a ch 36" long.

Row 1: Sl st in 2nd ch from hook and in each rem ch; finish off.

Run drawstring through top row of granny squares and across each gusset top. Then insert each drawstring end into a plastic circle; turn drawstsring ends up about $1/2$" and sew in place to secure rings.

#82 SPRINGTIME

Designed by Brenda A. Lewis for Coats & Clark

SIZE

7" x 8"

MATERIALS

Nylon yarn
  150 yds lt green

Note: *Photographed model made with J&P Coats® Crochet Nylon #51 Light Green*

9" x 15" piece cotton lining fabric (optional)

64 oval pearl beads, 3 mm

1 round pearl bead, 8 mm

Sewing needle and thread

One ³/₄" diameter pearl shank button

Yarn needle

Size 2 (2.75 mm) straight knitting needles

Size 6 (4 mm) straight knitting needles (or size required for gauge)

2 Size 6 (4 mm) double point knitting needles

GAUGE

16 sts = 4" in stock st (knit 1 row, purl 1 row)

INSTRUCTIONS

With larger needles, CO 35 sts.

Rows 1 through 5: Knit.

Row 6 (wrong side): K5, P25, K5.

Row 7: Knit

Rep Rows 6 and 7 until purse measures 14 1/4", ending by working a Row 6.

Flap

Row 1: K5, K2tog, knit to last 7 sts, SSK, K5: 33 sts.

Row 2: Knit.

Rows 3 through 24: Rep Rows 1 and 2: 11 sts at end of Row 24.

Row 25: K4, sl 1, K2tog, PSSO, K4.

Row 26: Knit.

Row 27: K3, sl 1, K2tog, PSSO, K3.

Row 28: Knit.

Row 29: K2, sl 1, K2tog, PSSO, K2.

Row 30: Knit.

BO, leaving a 10" yarn end. Thread end through yarn needle and make a st in the first st of Row 30, making a lp for button. Weave in yarn ends.

Finishing

Place piece on a flat surface with right side up. Fold 7 inches from bottom towards top, sew side seams. Turn right side out.

Lining (optional)

Fold cotton fabric in half and lengthwise and sew side seams so lining fits in purse. Press lining under around top edge, in purse. Fold flap over and sew button centered on Front 4 1/2" down from CO row.

Cord Handle

With double point needles, CO 3 sts, leaving a 10" yarn end. Following instructions on page 253, make 36" of I-cord. BO, leaving a 10" yarn end. Sew strap at top side edge on each side of purse.

Beaded Flower

To center flower on flap, measure up 2" from start of stock st point and in 3" from each side.

String 8 oval beads on thread, fold to form a lp and knot securely. Make 8 lps of 8 beads each. Sew lps securely around center, spreading to form a flower as shown in photo. Sew outer petal in place with a st between 4th and 5th beads. Sew each petal to the next by placing a st between 2nd and 3rd bead on each of 2 adjoining petals. Sew 8 mm bead in center of flower.

#83 DANCE WITH ME

Designed by Patons Design Staff

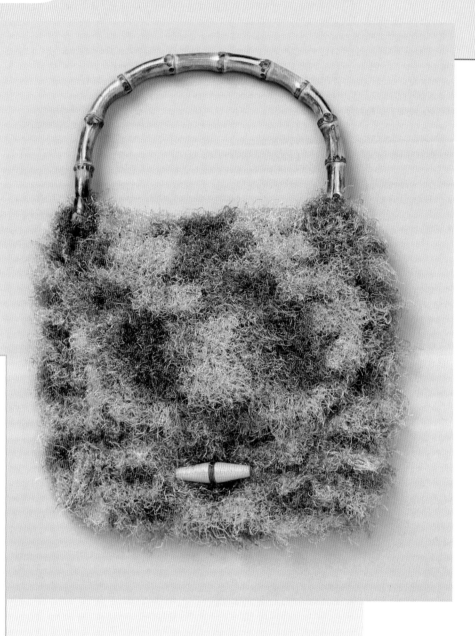

SIZE
11 ¹/₂" x 9 ¹/₂" plus handle

MATERIALS
Sport weight cotton yarn
    3 ¹/₂ oz rose

Eyelash yarn
    5 ¹/₄ oz variegated

Note: Photographed model made with Patons® Grace #60437 Rose and Patons® Cha Cha #02004 Salsa

Size H (5 mm) crochet hook (or
    size required for gauge)

8" Bamboo handle

Toggle

Stitch markers

GAUGE
12 dc and 7 dc rows = 4" with one
    strand of each yarn held tog

INSTRUCTIONS

Body

Note: *Body of bag is worked from wrong side throughout.*

With 1 strand of each yarn held tog, ch 22.

Rnd 1 (wrong side): Sc in 2nd ch from hook, sc in each ch across to last ch, 5 sc in last ch; working in rem lps on opposite side of foundation ch: sc in next 19 chs, 4 sc in next ch: 48 sc; join with sl st in first sc.

Rnd 2: Ch 1, 2 sc in same sc as joining, sc in next 19 sc, 2 sc in each of next 5 sc, sc in next 19 sc, 2 sc in each of last 4 sc: 58 sc; join as before.

Rnd 3: Ch 1, 2 sc in same sc as joining, sc in next 20 sc, (2 sc in next sc, sc in next sc) 5 times, sc in next 19 sc, (2 sc in next sc, sc in next sc) 4 times: 68 sc; join.

Rnd 4: Ch 3 (counts as dc), dc in next sc and in each sc around: 68 dc; join with sl st in 3rd ch of beg ch-3.

Rep Rnd 4 until piece measures 9". At end of last rnd, finish off; weave in ends. Turn bag right side out if necessary.

Flap

With bag lying flat, center handle on Back and place markers in last rnd one st in from handles for Flap. With right side of Back facing, join 1 strand of each yarn held tog with sl st in marked st on right.

Row 1 (right side): Ch 3 (counts as dc), dc in next dc and in each dc to last marker; ch 3 (counts as dc on next row now and throughout), turn, leaving rem sts unworked.

Row 2 (wrong side): Dc in next dc and in each dc across; ch 3, turn.

Rep Row 2 until flap measures about 4", ending by working a wrong side row.

Next row: Dc dec in next 2 dc, dc in each dc across to last 3 dc, dc dec in next 2 dc, dc in last dc; ch 3, turn.

Rep last row once more. At end of row, do not ch 3. Finish off; weave in ends.

Finishing

With 1 strand of each yarn held tog, ch 20, sl st in each ch across. Finish off. Fold chain in half to form a loop. Center and sew ends of loop to lower edge of flap. Fold flap down. Center and sew toggle to Front of bag to correspond to folded end of loop. Sew handle in position as shown in photograph.

#84 ROMANTIC RONDELLE

Designed by Mickie Akins for Coats & Clark

SIZE

6 ¹/₂" diameter

MATERIALS

Size 5 nylon yarn
   150 yds lt beige (A)
   20 yds pink (B)
   5 yds lt brown (C)

Note: Photographed model made with J&P Coats® Crochet Nylon #16 Neutral (A), #52 Pink (B) and #13 Beige (C)

7" off-white zipper

Sewing needle

Matching thread

Stitch markers

Size E (3.5 mm) crochet hook
   (or size required for gauge)

GAUGE

Rnds 1 through 4 = 2 ³/₄"

16 hdc = 4"

INSTRUCTIONS

Side (make 2)

With C, ch 2.

Rnd 1 (right side): 10 sc in 2nd ch from hook: 10 sc; join with sl st in first sc. Finish off; weave in ends.

Rnd 2: With right side facing, join B with sc in any st, ch 3, 4 dc in next st; *sc in next st, 5 dc in next st; rep from * 3 times more: 30 sts; join with sl st in 3rd ch of beg ch-3. Finish off; weave in ends.

Rnd 3: With right side facing, join A with sl st in any sc between 5-dc groups, ch 3, 4 dc in same sc; *sc in back lp of middle dc in next 5-dc group, 5 dc in next sc; rep from * around, ending with sc in back lp of middle dc of last 5-dc group: 30 sts; do not join.

Note: Place marker to indicate first st of each rnd.

Rnd 4: Sc in first st; *2 sc in next st, sc in next 3 sts; rep from * 6 times more; sc in last st: 37 sts.

Rnd 5: (Sc, 2 hdc) in next st; *hdc in next 3 sts, 2 hdc in next st; rep from * 8 times more: 48 sts.

Rnd 6: Hdc in next st and in each st around.

Rnd 7: Hdc in next 3 sts; *2 hdc in next st, hdc in next 4 sts; rep from * 8 times more: 57 sts.

Rnd 8: *2 hdc in next st, hdc in next 5 sts; rep from * 8 times more; hdc in last 3 sts: 66 sts.

Rnd 9: *2 hdc in next st, hdc in next 5 sts; rep from * 10 times more: 77 sts.

Rnd 10: Hdc in next st and in each st around, sc in first st, sl st in next st. Finish off; weave in ends.

Gussett

With A, ch 77, join with sl st to form ring, being careful not to twist ch.

Rnd 1 (right side): Ch 2 (counts as hdc now and throughout); hdc in each ch around: 77 hdc; join with sl st in 2nd ch of beg ch-2.

Rnd 2: Ch 2, hdc in next st and in each st around; join as before.

Rnd 3: Ch 32 (counts as hdc and 30 chs), skip next 30 sts (this forms opening for zipper), hdc in next st and in each rem st: 47 hdc and 30 chs; join with sl st in 2nd ch of beg ch-32.

Rnd 4: Ch 2; hdc in next 30 chs, hdc in next hdc and in each rem st: 77 hdc; join with sl st in 2nd ch of beg ch-2.

Rnd 5: Rep Rnd 2. Finish off; weave in ends.

Joining

Holding gusset and one side with wrong sides tog, working through inside lps on edge of both pieces, join B with sc at bottom of gusset opposite zipper opening, sc pieces tog around, join with sl st in first sc. Finish off; weave in ends. Rep with other side and opposite edge of gusset.

Zipper

Insert zipper in opening left in gusset and sew in place.

Strap

With A, ch 70 for strap.

Row 1 (right side): Hdc in 3rd ch from hook and in each rem ch: 69 hdc; ch 2 (counts as hdc on next row throughout), turn.

Row 2: Hdc in next st and in each st across; ch 2, turn.

Row 3: Hdc in next st and in each st across. Finish off; weave in ends.

Strap Ends

With right side facing and working in edges of last 3 rows, join B with sc in third row, 5 dc across strap on next row, sc in last row of strap. Finish off; weave in ends. Rep on other end of strap.

Sew ends of strap to gusset just below ends of zipper.

#85 RUFFLES AND FLOURISHES

Designed by Mary Jane Ward

SIZE

9" x 9" without handle

MATERIALS

Worsted weight yarn
  5 oz black
  4 oz hot pink

Note: Photographed model made with Lion Brand® Lion Cotton #153 Black and TLC® Cotton Plus™ #3752 Hot Pink

One 1/2" diameter snap

Black sewing thread and sewing needle

Size F (3.75 mm) crochet hook

Size G (4 mm) crochet hook (or size required for gauge)

GAUGE

15 sts and 14 rows = 4" in sc with larger hook

INSTRUCTIONS

With black and larger hook, ch 34.

Rnd 1: Sc in 2nd ch from hook and in each rem ch; sc in end of ch; turn ch and sc in unused lps of each ch across, sc in end of ch: 68 sc; join with sl st in beg sc, ch 1.

Rnd 2: Sc in each sc; join, ch 1.

Rnd 3: Working in back lps only, sc in each st; join, ch 1.

Rnd 4: Hdc in each st; join, ch 1.

Rnd 5: Sc in each st; join, ch 1.

Rnds 6 and 7: Rep Rnds 4 and 5.

Rnd 8: Rep Rnd 4.

Rnd 9: Working in back lps only, *sc2tog, sc in next 32 sts; rep from * across; join, ch 1: 66 sts.

Rnds 10 through 14: Rep Rnds 4 through 8.

Rnd 15: Working in back lps only, * sc2tog, sc in next 31 sts; rep from * across; join, ch 1: 64 sts

Rnds 16 through 20: Rep Rnds 4 through 8.

Rnd 21: Rep Rnd 15: 62 sts.

Rnds 22 through 25: Rep Rnds 4 and 5 twice

Rnd 26: Work (hdc2tog) twice, hdc in each st to last 4 sts, (hdc2tog) twice: 58 sts; join, ch 1.

Rnd 27: Working in back lps only, (sc2tog) twice, sc to last 4 sts, (sc2tog) twice: 54 sts; join, ch 1.

Rnds 28 and 29: Sc in each st, join, ch 1.

Rnd 30: Working in back lps only, sc2tog, sc to last 2 sts, sc2tog: 52 sts; join, ch 1.

Rnd 31: Working in back lps only, sc in each st. Finish off; weave in ends.

Ruffles

Hold purse with bottom at top.

With larger hook, join pink in any unused lp of Rnd 9.

Rnd 1: Ch 5, Edtr in same lp; *2 Edtr in next lp; rep from * around, join in top of beg ch-5; ch 1.

Rnd 2: Sc in top of ch-5 and in each Edtr around; join, finish off.

Working in unused lps of Rnds 15, 21 and 27 of purse, work ruffles in same manner. Finish off; weave in ends.

Edgings

Hold purse with bottom at top. With smaller hook and pink, join yarn in any unused lp of Rnd 3; sl st in each lp around; join. Finish off.

Hold purse with top at top. With smaller hook and pink, join yarn in any unused lp of Rnd 30; sl st in each lp around, join. Finish off. Rep in Rnd 31. Finish off; weave in ends.

Handle

Note: Handle is worked as a spiral tube.

Rnd 1: With larger hook and black, ch 2, 6 sc in 2nd ch from hook; do not join.

Rnd 2: Sl st loosely in back lp only of each st.

Repeat Row 2 until handle measures 38" or desired length.

Embellishment Stripe

With pink and smaller hook, join yarn with sl st at one end of handle in any unused lp of Rnd 1. You are going to work sl sts in a spiral around the handle, working in the unused lps. Sl st in next lp one row up and one lp to the left; continue to work sl sts in this manner to opposite end of handle. Finish off; weave in ends.

Sew handle ends to inside of purse at sides. Sew one side of snap centered on each side of purse on inside.

#86 FELTED MITERED BAGS

Designed by Christine L. Walter
For the advanced knitter

SIZE BEFORE FELTING
11 1/2" x 16" from point to point

SIZE AFTER FELTING
10 3/4" x 14" from point to point.

MATERIALS
Worsted weight wool yarn
  150 g (5 1/2 oz)
  pink/green/orange blend (A)
  150 g (5 1/2 oz) or
  brown/grey/black blend (B)

Note: *Photographed models made with Noro Kureyon #154 (A) and #055 (B)*

1" diameter button (or size to fit buttonhole)

Stitch Holder

32" Size 9 (5.5 mm) circular knitting needle (or size required for gauge)

Two Size 10 1/2 (6.5 mm) double-point knitting needle (dpn)

GAUGE
17 sts and 32 rows = 4" with smaller needles in garter stitch (knit every row)

INSTRUCTIONS

Body

CO 77 sts.

Row 1: K1b, K36, K3togb, K36, yif, sl 1P.

Row 2 (right side): K1b, knit to last st, yif, sl 1P.

Row 3: K1b, K35, k3togb, K35, yif, sl 1P.

Row 4: K1b, knit to last st, yif, sl 1P.

Row 5: K1b, K34, K3togb, K34, yif, sl 1P.

Row 6: K1b, knit to last st, yif, sl 1P.

Row 7: K1b, yif, P33, P3tog, P33, sl 1P.

Row 8: K1b, knit to last st, yif, sl 1P.

Rep Rows 1 through 8 four more times, decreasing two more stitches on every wrong-side row, then rep Rows 1 through 6 once more. Sl rem 31sts to stitch holder.

Shape Bottom

With right side facing, pick up and knit 22 sts along left edge of mitered square (one for each selvage stitch), then pick up 77sts along CO edge, and 22 sts along right edge: 121 sts. Knit 5 rows, end by working a wrong-side row (3 ridges on right side of work).

Begin Short Rows

Row 1: K114, W&T (see Stitch Guide).

Row 2: K107, W&T.

Row 3: K100, W&T.

Row 4: K93, W&T.

Row 5: K85, W&T.

Row 6: K77, W&T.

Row 7: Knit: 100 sts.

Row 8: Knit all stitches: 121 sts.

Row 9: K100, W&T.

Row 10: K79, W&T.

Row 11: K87, W&T.

Row 12: K93, W&T.

Row 13: K100, W&T.

Row 14: K107, W&T.

Row 15: K114.

Row 16: K121.

Rows 17 through 20: Knit.

Second Mitered Square
(Bag Back)

Row 1 (right side): K98, yif, P2tog, turn.

Row 2: Sl 1K, K36, K3togb, K36, K2togb, turn.

Row 3: Sl 1P, yib, K73, yif, P2tog, turn.

Row 4: Sl 1K, K35, K3togb, K35, K2togb, turn.

Row 5: Sl 1P, yib, K71, P2tog, turn.

Row 6: Sl 1K, K34, K3togb, K34, K2togb, turn.

Row 7: Sl 1P, yib, K69, P2tog, turn.

Row 8: Sl 1K, P33, P3tog, P33, yib, K2togb, turn.

Row 9: Sl 1P, yib, K67, yif, P2tog, turn.

Row 10: Sl 1K, K32, K3togb, K32, K2togb, turn.

Row 11: Sl 1P, yib, K65, yif, P2tog, turn.

Row 12: Sl 1K, K31, K3togb, K31, K2togb, turn.

Row 13: Sl 1P, yib, K63, yif, P2tog, turn.

Row 14: Sl 1K, K30, K3togb, K30, yif, K2togb, turn.

Row 15: Sl 1P, yib, K61, yif, P2tog, turn.

Row 16: Sl 1K, P29, P3tog, P29, yib, K2togb, turn.

Row 17: Sl 1P, yib, K59, yif, P2tog, turn.

Row 18: Sl 1K, K28, K3togb, K28, K2togb, turn.

Row 19: Sl 1P, yib, K57, yif, P2tog, turn.

Row 20: Sl 1K, K27, K3togb, K27, K2togb, turn.

Row 21: Sl 1P, yib, K55, yif, P2tog, turn.

Row 22: Sl 1K, K26, K3togb, K26, K2togb, turn.

Row 23: Sl 1P, yib, K53, yif, P2tog, turn.

Row 24: Sl 1K, P25, P3tog, P25, K2togb, turn.

Row 25: Sl 1P, yib, K51, yif, P2tog, turn.

Row 26: Sl 1K, K24, K3togb, K24, K2togb, turn.

Row 27: Sl 1P, yib, K49, yif, P2tog, turn.

Row 28: Sl 1K, K23, K3togb, K23, K2togb, turn.

Row 29: Sl 1P, yib, K47, yif, P2tog, turn.

Row 30: Sl 1K, K22, K3togb, K22, K2togb, turn.

Row 31: Sl 1P, yib, K45, yif, P2tog, turn.

Row 32: Sl 1K, P21, P3tog, P21, K2togb, turn.

Row 33: Sl 1P, yib, K43, yif, P2tog, turn.

Row 34: Sl 1K, K20, K3togb, K20, K2togb, turn.

Row 35: Sl 1P, yib, K41, yif, P2tog, turn.

Row 36: Sl 1K, K19, K3togb, K19, K2togb, turn.

Row 37: Sl 1P, yib, K39, yif, P2tog, turn.

Row 38: Sl 1K, K18, K3togb, K18, K2togb, turn.

Row 39: Sl 1P, yib, K37, yif, P2tog, turn.

Row 40: Sl 1K, P17, P3tog, P17, K2togb, turn.

Row 41: Sl 1P, yib, K35, yif, P2tog, turn.

Row 42: Sl 1K, K16, K3togb, K16, K2togb, turn.

Row 43: Sl 1P, yib, K33, yif, P2tog, turn.

Row 44: Sl 1K, K15, K3togb, K15, K2togb, turn.

Shape Flap

Row 45: K1b, K31, yif, sl 1P.

Row 46: K1b, K14, K3togb, K14, sl 1P.

Row 47: K1b, K29, yif, sl 1P.

Row 48: K1b, K13, K3togb, K13, sl 1P.

Row 49: K1b, K27, yif, sl 1P.

Row 50: K1b, K12, K3togb, K12, sl 1P.

Row 51: K1b, K25, yif, sl 1P.

Row 52: K1b, K11, K3togb, K11, sl 1P.

Row 53: K1b, K23, yif, sl 1P.

Row 54: K1b, K10, K3togb, K10, sl 1P.

Row 55: K1b, K21, yif, sl 1P.

Row 56: K1b, K9, K3togb, K9, sl 1P.

Row 57: K1b, K19, yif, sl 1P.

Row 58: K1b, K8, K3togb, K8, sl 1P.

Row 59: K1b, K17, yif, sl 1P.

Row 60: K1b, K7, K3togb, K7, sl 1P.

Row 61: K1b, K15, yif, sl 1P.

Row 62: K1b, K6, K3togb, K6, sl 1P.

Row 63: K1b, K13, yif, sl 1P.

Row 64: K1b, K5, K3togb, K5, sl 1P.

Row 65: K1b, K11, yif, sl 1P.

Row 66: K1b, K4, K3togb, K4, sl 1P.

Row 67: K1b, K9, yif, sl 1P.

Row 68: K1b, K3, K3togb, K3, sl 1P.

Buttonhole

Row 1: K1b, K1; with yarn in front, sl next st from left to right needle as to purl. Take yarn to back of work and leave it there. *Sl next st from left to right needle as to purl, and pass the first slipped st over it;

Rep from * 4 times more. Sl last bound-off st back to left needle, turn. With yarn at back, CO 6 sts, turn. With yarn at back, sl first st from left to right needle as to purl; pass last CO st over the slipped st: buttonhole made; sl 1P.

Row 2: K1b, K7, sl 1P.

Row 3: K1b, K8.

Edging

Pick up and knit 14 sts along left edge of flap and 7 sts along side edge; knit across 21 sts on holder, pick up and knit 7 sts along side edge, and 14 sts along right edge: total 82 sts. Cut yarn, leaving stitches on needle.

Applied I-cord

With dpn, cast on 3 sts; transfer them to left needle: 85 sts. *K2, sl 1 st knitwise, K1 of the picked-up sts, PSSO. Place the 3 sts back onto left needle; rep from * to beg, then graft or sew live stitches to CO edge of I-cord. Weave in all ends.

I-Cord Handles (make 2)

With dpns, CO 3 sts; following I-cord instructions on page 253, make an I-cord 6' long. BO; weave in ends.

Felting

Place the bag and two I-Cord handles in a zippered pillowcase and felt, following Basic Felting Instructions on page 252. Felt to desired degree; photographed models were lightly felted so that some stitch definition remains. Once desired felting is achieved, block the bag and let dry completely.

Finishing

Attach handles: Pinch in edges of bag and insert double-point needle just below applied I-Cord at top edge of back on each side. Use the dpn (or ice pick or stiletto) to pierce a hole through both layers. Insert ends of cords in holes and sew securely in place.

Sew button to front opposite buttonhole.

#87 BLOOMING CLUTCH

Designed by Rona Feldman for Judi & Co.

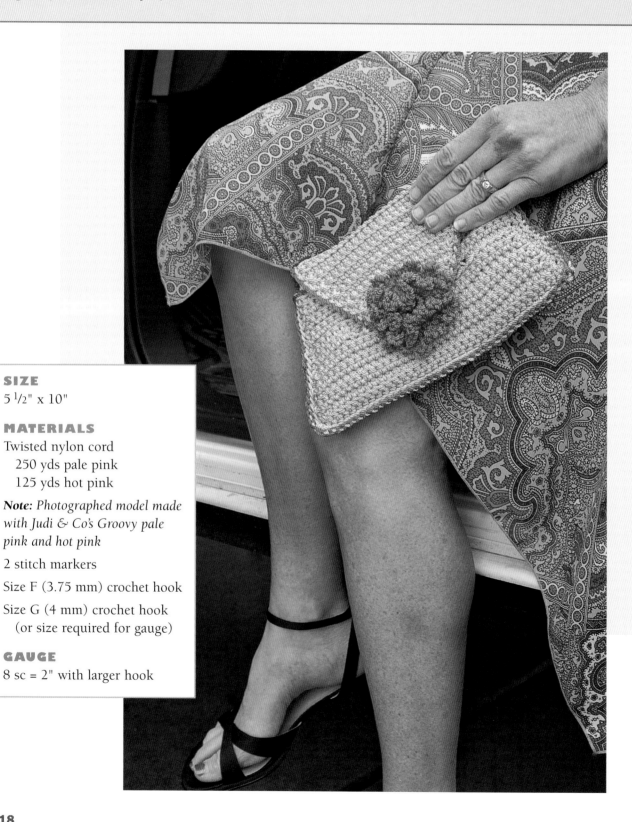

SIZE
5 ¹/₂" x 10"

MATERIALS
Twisted nylon cord
  250 yds pale pink
  125 yds hot pink

Note: *Photographed model made with Judi & Co's Groovy pale pink and hot pink*

2 stitch markers

Size F (3.75 mm) crochet hook

Size G (4 mm) crochet hook
  (or size required for gauge)

GAUGE
8 sc = 2" with larger hook

INSTRUCTIONS

Back and Flap

Note: Work all wrong-side rows in back lps only unless otherwise specified.

Starting at bottom with larger hook and pale pink, ch 39.

Row 1 (right side): Sc in 2nd ch from hook and in each rem ch: 38 sc; ch 1, turn.

Row 2 (decrease row): Sc in first sc, dec over next 2 sc; sc in each sc to last 3 sts, dec over next 2 sc, sc in last sc: 36 sc; ch 1, turn.

Row 3: Sc across; ch 1, turn.

Rows 4, 6, 8, 10 and 12: Rep Row 2: 26 sc at end of Row 12.

Rows 5, 7, 9, 11 and 13: Rep Row 3.

Rows 14 through 20: Rep Row 3.

Mark each end of Row 20 for start of flap.

Flap

Rep Rows 2 and 3 until 10 sts rem; finish off, leaving a long end. Thread end into a tapestry needle and draw through last 10 sts; draw up tightly and finish off securely.

Front

Rep instructions for back through Row 20. At end of Row 20, change to hot pink.

Row 21 (right side): Sc in each sc across. Finish off; weave in ends.

Finishing

Place front on corresponding part of back with wrong sides tog; with smaller hook and hot pink cord, sc Front and Back tog along 3 sides, working 3 sc in corners and leaving top edge of front open. Finish off.

With right side facing, work 1 row sc around outer edges of flap, working 3 sc at center point.

Flower Ornament

With hot pink and smaller hook ch 8; join with a sl st to form a ring.

Rnd 1: Ch 1, 14 sc in ring; join,

Rnd 2: Working in front lps only of Rnd 1, in each st work (sc, ch 6, sc); do not join.

Rnd 3: Working in back lps only of Rnd 1, in each st work (sc, ch 8, sc); join. Finish off; weave in ends.

Lightly steam lps to separate. Sew flower at center point of flap as shown in photo.

#88 TAPESTRY BUCKET

Designed by Marty Miller

SIZE

14" high x 11 ¹/₂" diameter
  plus 50" strap

MATERIALS

Worsted weight cotton yarn
  280 yds Natural
  280 yds Taupe
  140 yds Blue

Note: *Photographed model
made with Plymouth Fantasy
Naturale #8176 Natural #7360
Taupe and #9318 Blue*

Size H (5 mm) crochet hook
  (or size required for gauge)

GAUGE

First 4 rnds = 2" diameter

INSTRUCTIONS

With Taupe, ch 2.

Rnd 1 (right side): 6 sc in 2nd ch from hook: 6 sc; join with sl st in first sc.

Rnd 2: Ch 1, 2 sc in first sc and in each sc around: 12 sc; join as before.

Rnd 3: Ch 1, 2 sc in first sc, sc in next sc; *2 sc in next sc, sc in next sc; rep from * 4 times more: 18 sc; join.

Rnd 4: Ch 1, 2 sc in first sc, sc in next 2 sc; *2 sc in next sc, sc in next 2 sc; rep from * 4 times more: 24 sc; join.

Rnds 5 through 17: Rep Rnd 4 thirteen times more, increasing between increases by one more in each rnd: 6 sc more in each rnd than in rnd before. At end of Rnd 17: 102 sc.

Rnd 18: Ch 1, sc in first sc and in each sc around: 102 sc; join.

Rnds 19 through 32: Rep Rnd 18 fourteen times more. At end of Rnd 32, change to Blue in joining sl st. Finish off Taupe; weave in ends.

Rnds 33 through 37: With Blue, rep Rnd 18 five times more. At end of Rnd 37, change to Natural in joining sl st and work over one strand of Taupe. Finish off Blue; weave in ends.

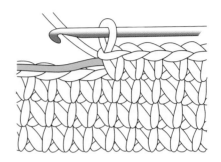

Tapestry crochet

Note: Carry unused color (Taupe or Natural) on top of sts and work sc over carried color throughout Rows 38 through 42 until color is changed and becomes working color (see diagram).

Rnd 38: With Natural, ch 1, sc in same sc as joining and in next 4 sc, changing to Taupe in last sc; with Taupe, sc in next sc, changing to Natural; *with Natural, sc in next 5 sc, changing to Taupe in last sc; with Taupe, sc in next sc, changing to Natural; rep from * around, but do not change to Natural in last Taupe sc; join.

Rnd 39: With Taupe, ch 1, sc in same sc as joining, changing to Natural; *with Natural, sc in next 4 sc, changing to Taupe in last sc; with Taupe, sc in next 2 sc, changing to Natural in last sc; rep from * around, ending by working 1 sc with Taupe instead of 2 sc and do not change to Natural in last Taupe sc; join.

Instructions continue on next page. →

Rnd 40: With Taupe, ch 1, sc in same sc as joining and in next sc, changing to Natural in last sc; *with Natural, sc in next 3 sc, changing to Taupe in last sc; with Taupe, sc in next 3 sc, changing to Natural in last sc; rep from * around, ending by working 1 sc with Taupe instead of 3 sc and do not change to Natural in last Taupe sc; join.

Rnd 41: With Taupe, ch 1, sc in same sc as joining and in next 2 sc, changing to Natural in last sc; *with Natural, sc in next 2 sc, changing to Taupe in last sc; with Taupe, sc in next 4 sc, changing to Natural in last sc; rep from * around, ending by working 1 sc with Taupe instead of 4 sc and do not change to Natural in last Taupe sc; join.

Rnd 42: With Taupe, ch 1, sc in same sc as joining and in next 3 sc, changing to Natural in last sc; *with Natural, sc in next sc, changing to Taupe; with Taupe, sc in next 5 sc, changing to Natural in last sc; rep from * around, ending by working 1 sc with Taupe instead of 5 sc and changing to Blue in last sc. Finish off Taupe and Natural; weave in ends.

Rnds 43 through 47: With Blue, rep Rnd 18 five times more. At end of Rnd 47, change to Natural in joining sl st. Finish off Blue; weave in ends.

Rnds 48 through 62: With Natural, rep Rnd 18 fifteen times more.

Rnd 63: Ch 1, sc in first 49 sc, ch 4, skip next 4 sc, sc in last 49 sc: 98 sc and one ch-4 sp; join.

Rnd 64: Ch 1, sc in first 49 sc, sc in next 4 chs, sc in last 49 sc: 102 sc; join.

Rnds 65 and 66: Rep Rnd 18 two times more. At end of Rnd 66, finish off; weave in ends.

Strap

With Taupe, ch 151, or to desired length, leaving 24" length at beg of ch for braid.

Row 1 (right side): Sc in 2nd ch from hook and in each ch across: 150 sc. Finish off Taupe, leaving 24" end. Turn.

Row 2 (wrong side): With wrong side facing, leaving 24" end, join Blue with sc in first sc, sc in next sc and in each sc across: 150 sc; ch 1, turn.

Row 3: Sc in first sc and in each sc across. Finish off Blue, leaving 24" end. Turn.

Rows 4 and 5: With Natural, rep Rows 2 and 3. At end of Row 5, finish off Natural, leaving 24" end. Turn.

Rows 6 and 7: With Taupe, rep Rows 2 and 3. At end of Row 7, finish off Taupe, leaving 24" end.

With right side of strap facing, leaving 24" end, join Taupe with sc in unused lp of first ch of foundation ch, sc in unused lp of next ch and unused lp of each ch across: 150 sc. DO NOT FINISH OFF.

Finishing

Place right sides of strap and side of bag together, centering unfringed end of strap over joining on Rnd 66 of bag. With Taupe, sc strap to bag through top edge of Rnd 66 and unfringed edge of strap. Finish off; weave in ends.

Make 12" braid with fringes at other end of strap. Thread braided end of strap through ch-4 sp on Rnd 63 of bag and tie strap in a knot.

#89 GINGHAM TOTE

Designed by Bernat Design Staff

SIZE
15" wide x 13" high

MATERIALS
Worsted weight cotton yarn
  10 ½ oz blue (MC)
  3 ½ oz white A
  1.5 oz red ombre
  1.75 oz sage green

Note: *Photographed tote made with Bernat® Handicrafter® #0083 Cornflower (MC), #01 White A, #84 Sage Green and #21 Cherry Swirl*

Size H (5 mm) crochet hook
  (or size required for gauge)

GAUGE
14 dc = 4"

STITCH GUIDE
Reverse Single Crochet (rev sc): Ch 1;
* Insert hook in next st to the right, turn hook downward to catch yarn and draw up a lp. YO, pull yarn through both lps. rep from * for rev sc.

INSTRUCTIONS

Note: *To change colors: Work last st with first color to last step; drop drop first color; complete st with new color. When color is not in use, work over it.*

Front and Back Panels (make 2)

With MC, ch 54.

Row 1 (right side): Dc in 4th ch from hook and in each rem ch: 52 dc; ch 1, turn.

Row 2: Sc in each dc across; ch 3; turn. Note: Turning ch 3 counts as first dc of following row throughout pattern.

Row 3: Dc across; ch 1, turn.

Rep Rows 2 and 3 until piece measures 13", ending by working a Row 3. Finish off; weave in ends.

Sides and Bottom (1 strip)

With MC, ch 7.

Row 1 (right side): Dc in 4th ch from hook and in each ch across; ch 1; turn: 5 dc.

Row 2: Sc in each dc, ch 3, turn.

Row 3: Dc across; ch 1, turn.

Rep Rows 2 and 3 until strip length is equal to the sum of the length of both sides and the width of the Front piece, about 40". Finish off; weave in ends.

Pocket

With MC, ch 29.

Row 1 (right side): Dc in 4th ch from hook, dc in next ch; *change to A, dc in each of next 3 chs, change to MC, dc in each of next 3 chs; rep from * to end of ch, change to A in last dc. ch 3, turn: 27 dc.

Row 2: Dc in each of next 2 dc; *change to MC, dc in each of next 3 dc, change to A, dc in each of next 3 dc; rep from * to end of row, change to MC in last dc; ch 3, turn.

Row 3: Dc in each of next 2 dc; *change to A, dc in each of next 3 dc, change to MC, dc in each of next 3 dc; rep from * to end of row, change to A in last dc; ch 3, turn.

Rows 4 through 14: Rep Rows 2 and 3.

Row 15: Rep Row 2.

Row 16: Dc in each of next 2 dc; *change to A, dc in each of next 3 dc, change to MC, dc in each of next 3 dc; rep from * to end of row; ch 1, turn.

Row 17: Sc in each dc across; ch 1. Do not turn.

Row 18: Work rev sc in each sc across. Finish off; weave in ends.

Strap (make 2)

Note: Strap is worked sideways.

With MC, ch 156.

Row 1 (right side): Sc in 2nd ch from hook and in each rem ch; ch 1, turn: 155 sc.

Row 2: Sc in each sc; ch 1, turn.

Rows 3 through 5: Rep Row 2. Finish off. Weave in ends.

Rose (make 2)

With red ombre, ch 16.

Row 1 (right side): 2 dc in 4th ch from hook, 3 dc in each rem ch. Finish off; weave in ends.

Leaf (make 4)

With sage green, ch 8.

Row 1: Sc in 2nd ch from hook, hdc in next ch, dc in next 3 ch, hdc in next ch, sc in last ch. Finish off. Weave in ends.

Finishing

Center pocket on front panel, sew sides of pocket to panel. Pin one strap to each side of pocket as shown in photographed piece, sew in place. Pin other strap to back panel in same position as strap on front panel; sew in place. Pin the strip for sides and bottom to Front and Back panel.

Front Edging

Row 1: With right side facing, join MC to front panel and strip in any top corner, work one row of sc evenly down one side, across the bottom and up the other side, making sure to work into pocket and straps on bottom row. Do not turn.

Row 2: Work rev sc around. Finish off. Weave in ends.

Back Edging

Row 1: With right side facing, join MC to back panel and strip in any top corner, ch 1; work one row of sc evenly down one side, across the bottom and up the other side, making sure to work into straps on bottom row; do not turn.

Row 2: Work rev sc in each st around. Finish off; weave in ends.

Top Edging

Join MC with sl st in any seam on top edge. Work rev sc around top edge, join with sl st in first sc. Finish off; weave in ends.

Fold unattached portion of each strap in half, sl st edges together.

Coil rose to form a rosebud and sew to Front of Bag as illustrated.

Sew one leaf to each side of rose as shown in photo.

#90 SHINY SHELLS

Designed by Mickie Akins for Coats & Clark

SIZE

7" wide x 5" high plus 17" or 28" strap

MATERIALS

Nylon yarn
  150 yds pink
  100 yds white

Note: *Photographed model made with J&P Coats® Crochet Nylon #52 Pink and #1 White*

Size E (3.5 mm) crochet hook (or size required for gauge)

¹/₄ yd pink fabric for lining (optional)

Needle and sewing thread to match lining fabric (optional)

7" pink zipper

GAUGE

17 sc and 16 sc rows = 4"

INSTRUCTIONS

Side (make 2)

Starting at bottom, with pink, ch 27.

Row 1 (wrong side): Sc in 2nd ch from hook; *skip next ch, shell in next ch, skip next 2 chs, sc in next ch; rep from * across, changing to white in last sc: 5 shells and 6 sc; ch 3 (counts as dc on next row now and throughout), turn.

Row 2 (right side): Work 2 dc in first sc; *skip next 2 dc, sc in next dc, skip next 2 dc, shell in next sc; rep from * 3 times more; skip next 2 dc, sc in next dc, skip next 2 dc, 3 dc in last sc, changing to pink in last dc: 4 shells, 6 dc and 5 sc; ch 1, turn.

Row 3: Sc in first dc; *skip next 2 dc, shell in next sc, skip next 2 dc, sc in next dc; rep from * across, changing to white in last sc: 5 shells and 6 sc; ch 3, turn.

Rows 4 through 11: Rep Rows 2 and 3 four times more. At end of Row 11, ch 1 instead of ch 3.

Row 12: With right side facing, (sc, 2 hdc) in first st, hdc in next st, sc in next 3 sts; *hdc in next 3 sts, sc in next 3 sts; rep from * 3 times more; hdc in next st, (2 hdc, sc) in last st; working in left edge of rows, evenly space 19 sc across left side down to Row 1, 3 sc in first st on Row 1, evenly space 29 sc across Row 1, 3 sc in last st; working in right edge of rows, evenly space 19 sc across right side up to Row 11: 90 sc and 18 hdc; join with sl st in first sc. Finish off; weave in ends.

Gusset

With pink, ch 74.

Row 1 (wrong side): Working in back bar of chs, sc in 2nd ch from hook, sc in next ch and in each ch across: 73 sc; ch 2, turn.

Row 2 (right side): Hdc in first st and in each st across: 73 hdc; ch 2, turn.

Row 3: Hdc in first st and in each st across; ch 1, turn.

Row 4: Sc in first st and in each st across: 73 sc. Finish off; weave in ends.

Lining (optional)

Using crochet pieces as patterns and adding ½" extra on all edges for seams, cut 2 Side pieces and 1 Gusset piece from lining fabric.

Joining

With wrong sides together, matching sts on sides and bottom of one Side to chs on foundation ch of Gusset, working through both layers, join pink with sc in first sc at top left corner of Side, sc Side and Gusset together across sides and bottom to last sc at top right corner of Side. Finish off; weave in ends. Rep with other Side and sts on Row 4 of Gusset. With right side of zipper facing wrong side of top edges of Sides, sew long edge of zipper in place along Sides; fold each end of zipper ¼" to wrong side and sew to Gusset.

Lining Continued (optional)

With right sides of lining together, sew lining pieces together in same manner as crochet Sides and Gusset with ½" seams. Press top edges of lining ½" to wrong side. With wrong side of lining facing outward, insert lining into assembled handbag; sew top edges of lining to wrong side of zipper along previous zipper seam.

Strap

With pink, ch 112 for shoulder strap or 70 for arm strap.

Row 1: Working in back bar of chs, sc in 2nd ch from hook, sc in next ch and in each ch across: 111 or 69 sc; ch 1, turn.

Rows 2 through 4: Sc in first st and in each st across; ch 1, turn. At end of Row 4, do not ch 1. Finish off; weave in ends.

Sew edges of rows on Strap to top edges of Gusset.

#91 WATCH YOUR BACK

Designed by Patons Design Staff

SIZE

11 1/4" x 12 1/2" after felting

MATERIALS

Worsted weight wool yarn
17 1/2 oz dark grey
3 1/2 oz red

Note: Photographed model made with Patons® Classic Merino Wool #225 Dark Grey Mix and #207 Rich Red

One toggle closure

Small hole punch (or ice pick)

Size 7 (4.5 mm) 16" circular knitting needle (or size required for gauge)

Size 7 (4.5 mm) double-point knitting needles

GAUGE

20 sts and 26 rows = 4" in stock st (knit 1 row, purl 1 row) before felting

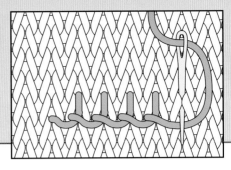

Blanket stitch

INSTRUCTIONS

Main Section

With circular needle and grey, CO 156 sts, join; place marker to indicate beg of rnds. Knit for 15". BO.

Base and Flap (make alike)

With grey and circular needle, CO 48 sts. Do not join; work back and forth in stock st for 17", ending by working a purl row. BO.

Strap (make 2)

With grey and 2 double-point needles, CO 11 sts.

Row 1 (right side): * K1, P1; rep from * across, end K1.

Rep Row 1 for 27". BO.

Toggle Loop

With grey and 2 double-point needles, CO 4 sts. Work I-cord (see page 253) for 15". BO.

Finishing

Felt all pieces (see page 252).

After felting, pieces should measure:

Straps: 1 1/2" x 23"

Main Section: 11 1/4" high and 25" around.

Base and Flap: 9" x 7 1/2"

Cut base to an oval shape 10" x 5". Pin base to bottom of main section and with red, sew it to main section with blanket stitch. Punch 8 small holes around top edge of bag for drawstring 1 1/4" down from top edge and spaced about 3 1/4" apart.

Cut flap 9" x 7 1/2" , with oval shape at front and straight edge at back. With red, blanket st around Flap. Sew Flap to back of main section under row of drawstring holes.

Trim Straps to 24". With red, blanket st sides of straps. Mark center st at top and at base of main section (center back). Sew ends of straps on either side of marked st at top of main section, under row of drawstring holes. Sew other ends of Straps 4" either side of marked st at base.

Trim toggle lp to 11" and sew to flap as shown in photo. Sew toggle to correspond to lp.

Twisted Cord

With 4 strands of grey cut 95" long, make Twisted Cord (see page 253). Weave cord through drawstring holes with cord ends meeting at center front.

#92 FLOWER BASKET

Designed by Nancy Nehring

SIZE
About 8" high x 10" wide

MATERIALS
Bulky weight suede finish yarn
  6 oz taupe

Sport weight microfiber yarn
  2 1/2 oz yellow
  2 1/2 oz orange

Bulky weight novelty yarn
  1 3/4 oz red/orange/yellow
  1 3/4 oz red

Worsted weight yarn
  6 oz red

Size 5 perle cotton
  2 yds taupe

Note: Photographed model made with Lion Brand® Lion Suede #123 Taupe, Lion Brand® Microspun #158 Buttercup and #186 Mango, Bernat® Boa, #81605 Tweety Bird, Bernat® Frenzy, #55530 Racy Red and TLC® Amoré™ #3907 Red Velvet

Size H (5 mm) crochet hook
  (or size required for gauge)

6" Bamboo handles (Darice #1977-59)

Tapestry needle

2 stitch markers

GAUGE
7 sc and 7 ch-1 sps = 4"

INSTRUCTIONS

Body

Starting at bottom, with taupe bulky yarn, ch 19, sl st in back bar of 2nd ch from hook, sl st in back bar of next 17 chs: 18 sl sts.

Note: Work bag in a spiral; do not join.

Rnd 1: 3 sc in same sp as last sl st, place marker in 2nd sc of 3 sc just made, sc in both lps of next 17 chs of foundation ch, 3 sc in first sl st, place marker in 2nd sc of 3 sc just made, sc in next 17 sl sts, sc in first sc: 40 sc. Move markers up to same positions in Rnds 2 through 4.

Rnd 2: 3 sc in marked st, sc in next 19 sts, 3 sc in marked st, sc in next 20 sts: 44 sc.

Rnd 3: 3 sc in marked st, sc in next 21 sts, 3 sc in marked st, sc in next 22 sts: 48 sc.

Rnd 4: *3 sc in marked st, sc in next 23 sts; rep from * once; sl st in next st: 52 sc.

Note: Leave markers in place. Begin sides.

Rnd 5: Sc in back lp of next st and in back lp of each st around: 52 sc.

Rnd 6: *Ch 1, skip next st, sc in next st; rep from * around: 26 sc and 26 ch-1 sps.

Rnd 7: (Sc, ch 1, sc) in ch-1 sp above first marked st; *ch 1, skip next sc, sc in next ch-1 sp*; rep from * to * across to ch-1 sp above second marked st; (ch 1, sc) 2 times in next ch-1 sp above second marked st; rep from * to * across to beg st above first marked st: 28 sc and 28 ch-1 sps.

Rnd 8: *Ch 1, skip next sc, sc in next ch-1 sp; rep from * around: 28 sc and 28 ch-1 sps.

Rnds 9 through 26: Rep Rnds 7 and 8 nine times more: 2 more sc and 2 more ch-1 sps in every 2 rnds than in previous 2 rnds. At end of Rnds 25 and 26: 46 sc and 46 ch-1 sps.

Rnds 27 through 32: Rep Rnd 8 six times more: 46 sc and 46 ch-1 sps. At end of Rnd 32, sl st in next 2 sts. Finish off; weave in ends.

Flowers

(Make 12 total: 4 each of 3 different types of yarn)

Center (make 12)

With yellow sport weight microfiber yarn, ch 12; join with sl st to form a ring.

Rnd 1: Sc in back lp of each ch around: 12 sc. Do not join.

Rnd 2: Sc in back lp of next st and in back lp of each st around.

Rnds 3 through 7: Rep Rnd 2 five times more. At end of Rnd 7, finish off.

Instructions continue on next page. →

Weave end tail through Rnd 7 and pull tight to gather. Finish off; weave in end. This becomes base of center. Weave beg tail through Rnd 3 and pull tight to gather. Finish off; weave in end. Rnd 1 becomes top of center.

Petals

(Make 4 with red/orange/yellow bulky weight novelty yarn, 4 with red worsted weight yarn, and 4 with one strand red bulky weight novelty yarn held together with one strand sport weight microfiber orange yarn)

Work sts loosely. Join appropriate yarn with sl st in front lp of any sc on Rnd 5 of center; working in front lp of each sc on Rnd 5; (ch 1, hdc, dc) in same sc, 3 tr in next sc; (dc, hdc, sc) in next sc; *(sc, hdc, dc) in next sc, 3 tr in next sc; (dc, hdc, sc) in next sc; rep from * 2 times more: 4 petals; join with sl st in beg ch. Finish off, leaving 12" end; weave in beg end.

Assembly

Sew handles in place on top edge of bag with tapestry needle and perle cotton. Sew flowers in place with end of yarn, stitching between petals and into bag.

#9B HOBO WAVE

Designed by Cynthia G. Grosch

SIZE

28" circumference x 11"

MATERIALS

DK weight cotton yarn

- 3 ¹/₂ oz taupe
- 1 ³/₄ oz orange
- 1 ³/₄ oz lt green

Note: *Photographed model made with Patons® Grace #60012 Taupe, #60604 Terracotta and #60027 Ginger*

Stitch marker

Size G (4 mm) crochet hook (or size required for gauge)

Size C (2.75 mm) crochet hook

GAUGE

22 sc = 4" with larger hook

STITCH GUIDE

Sc decrease (sc dec): *Insert hook in next specified st and draw up a lp; rep from * once; YO and draw through all 3 lps on hook: dec made.

Instructions continue on next page. →

INSTRUCTIONS

Starting at bottom with G hook and taupe, ch 270; join with sl st in first ch to form a ring, being careful not to twist ch. Place marker in first st to indicate beg of rnd and move marker up to first st in each rnd.

Rnd 1 (right side): Ch 1, 2 sc in same ch as joining; *sc in next 21 chs, skip next 2 chs, sc in next 21 chs**; 3 sc in next ch; rep from * 4 times more; rep from * to ** once; sc in same ch as joining: 270 sc; join with sl st in first sc.

Rnd 2: Ch 1, 2 sc in same sc as joining; *sc in next 21 sc, skip next 2 sc, sc in next 21 sc**; 3 sc in next sc; rep from * 4 times more; rep from * to ** once; sc in same sc as joining: 270 sc; join as before.

Rnds 3 through 10: Rep Rnd 2 eight times more.

Rnd 11: Ch 1, 2 sc in same sc as joining; *sc in next 19 sc, sc dec in next 2 sc, skip next 2 sc, sc dec in next 2 sc, sc in next 19 sc**; 3 sc in next sc; rep from * 4 times more; rep from * to ** once; sc in same sc as joining: 258 sc; join.

Rnds 12 through 14: Rep Rnd 11 three times more, decreasing underlined numbers by one in each rnd. At end of Rnd 12: 246 sc. At end of Rnd 13: 234 sc. At end of Rnd 14: 222 sc. Finish off; weave in ends.

Rnd 15: With right side facing, join orange with sl st in first sc, ch 1, 2 sc in same sc as joining; *sc in next 15 sc, sc dec in next 2 sc, skip next 2 sc, sc dec in next 2 sc, sc in next 15 sc**; 3 sc in next sc; rep from * 4 times more; rep from * to ** once; sc in same sc as joining: 210 sc; join.

Rnds 16 through 19: Rep Rnd 15 four times more, decreasing underlined numbers by one in each rnd. At end of Rnd 16: 198 sc. At end of Rnd 17: 186 sc. At end of Rnd 18: 174 sc. At end of Rnd 19: 162 sc.

Rnd 20: Ch 1, 2 sc in same sc as joining; *sc in next 12 sc, skip next 2 sc, sc in next 12 sc**; 3 sc in next sc; rep from * 4 times more; rep from * to ** once; sc in same sc as joining: 162 sc; join.

Rnds 21 and 22: Rep Rnd 20 two times more. At end of Rnd 22, finish off; weave in ends.

Rnd 23: With right side facing, join lt green with sl st in first sc, rep Rnd 20.

Rnds 24 and 25: Rep Rnd 20 two times more. At end of Rnd 25, finish off; weave in ends.

Rnd 26: With right side facing, join taupe with sl st in first sc, rep Rnd 20.

Rnds 27 through 31: Rep Rnd 20 five times more. At end of Rnd 31, finish off; weave in ends.

Rnd 32: With right side facing, join orange with sl st in first sc, rep Rnd 20.

Rnds 33 and 34: Rep Rnd 20 two times more. At end of Rnd 34, finish off; weave in ends.

Rnd 35: With right side facing, join lt green with sl st in first sc, rep Rnd 20.

Rnds 36 through 39: Rep Rnd 20 four times more. At end of Rnd 39, finish off; weave in ends.

Rnd 40: With right side facing, join taupe with sl st in first sc, rep Rnd 20.

Rnd 41: Rep Rnd 20. Do not join. Do not finish off.

Rnd 42: *Ch 4 for eyelet, skip next sc, sc in next 12 sc, skip next 2 sc, sc in next 12 sc; rep from * 5 times more: 144 sc and 6 ch-4 sps. Do not join.

Rnd 43: *5 sc in next ch-4 sp, sc in next 11 sc, skip next 2 sc; **sc in next 11 sc; rep from * 5 times more: 162 sc. Do not join.

Rnd 44: Sc in next 2 sc; *3 sc in next sc, sc in next 12 sc; skip next 2 sc; sc in next 12 sc; rep from * 5 times more: 164 sc; join with sl st in next sc. Finish off; weave in ends.

With tapestry needle and taupe, whipstitch free lps of foundation ch together with bottom points meeting in center.

Spiral Cord

With C hook and orange, ch 5; join with sl st to form a ring.

Rnd 1: Ch 1, 6 sc in ring. Do not join.

Working in a spiral, sc in each sc around until cord measures about 44", or to desired length. Finish off; weave in ends.

Weave cord through eyelets on Rnd 42 and draw up to close. Knot ends of cord as shown in photo.

#94 SHIMMERY BEADS

Designed by Brenda Lewis for Coats & Clark

SIZE
6" x 9"

MATERIALS
Sport weight yarn
  4 oz white
  4 oz blue

Note: *Photographed model made with Aunt Lydia's® Shimmer, #1001 White and #9559 Light Blue.*

106 pearl beads, 1/8" diameter

9" white zipper

White sewing thread and needle

Size 7 (4.5 mm) knitting needles
  (or size required for gauge)

Size 7 double-point knitting needles

Size H (5 mm) crochet hook

GAUGE
17 sts and 32 rows = 4" with 2
  strands held tog in pattern stitch

INSTRUCTIONS

Notes: *(1) Work with 2 strands of each color throughout unless otherwise specified. (2) Slip all sts as to purl.*

With 2 strands of white held tog, CO 39 sts. Purl one row.

Row 1: With 2 strands of blue held tog, K2, *wyif sl next 5 sts, K1; rep from * to last st, K1.

Row 2: With blue, P2, *wyib sl 5 sts, P1; rep from * to last st, P1.

Row 3: With white, knit.

Row 4: With white, purl.

Row 5: With white, K4; * insert right needle under loose strands of blue, K1, catching strands of blue behind the st, K5; rep from * across, ending last rep with K4.

Row 6: With white, purl.

Row 7: With blue, K1, wyif sl 3, K1; *wyif sl 5, K1, rep from * to last 4 sts, wyif sl 3, K1.

Row 8: With blue, P1, wyib sl 3 as, P1; * wyib sl 5, P1; rep from * to last 4 sts, wyib sl 3.

Row 9: With white, knit.

Row 10: With white, purl.

Row 11: With white, K1; *insert right needle under loose strands of blue and K1 catching loose strands of blue behind the st, K5; rep from * across, ending last rep with K1.

Row 12: With white, purl.

Rep Rows 1 through 12, seven times more. BO.

Finishing

With crochet hook and 2 strands of blue, sc in each st across top and bottom edges. With sewing thread and needle, sew one pearl bead at each point where blue and white yarns come tog, as shown in photo. Fold purse in half with wrong sides tog and sew sides tog. Turn purse right side out.

Zipper

Sew zipper to inside of purse just below sc sts at top. If the zipper is a little long let the end go down into the purse, do not stretch the top of purse.

Strap

With double-point needles and one strand of white, work I-cord (see page 253) for 36". BO. Sew ends of cord to opposite sides of purse at top.

#95 FURRY LITTLE BAG

SIZE
About 7" wide x 6" high

MATERIALS
Ribbon yarn
  1 3/4 oz blue

Eyelash yarn
  1 3/4 oz blue

Note: Photographed model made with Lion Brand® Incredible #202 Blue Shades and Lion Brand Fun Fur #109 Sapphire

Size K (6.5 mm) crochet hook (or size required for gauge)

Sewing needle and thread to match

GAUGE
10 sc and 12 sc rows = 4" with 1 strand of each yarn held tog

INSTRUCTIONS

Front
With 1 strand of each yarn held tog, ch 19.

Row 1 (wrong side): Sc in 2nd ch from hook and in each ch across: 18 sc; ch 1, turn.

Row 2 (right side): Sc in first sc and in each sc across: 18 sc; ch 1, turn.

Rows 3 through 18: Rep Row 2 sixteen times more. At end of Row 18, do not ch 1. Finish off; weave in ends.

Back
Work same as Front.

Finishing
Place Front and Back with right sides tog. With eyelash yarn only, sl st sides and bottom of Front and Back tog, matching rows and chs on foundation ch. Finish off; weave in ends. Turn right side out.

Handles (make 2)
With ribbon yarn only, ch 4.

Row 1: Keeping all lps on hook, insert hook and draw up a lp in 2nd, 3rd, and 4th chs from hook (4 lps on hook); YO and draw through one lp on hook, (YO and draw through 2 lps on hook) 3 times (1 lp rem on hook).

Row 2: Skip first vertical bar, insert hook and draw up a lp in 2nd, 3rd and 4th vertical bars (4 lps on hook); YO and draw through one lp on hook, (YO and draw through 2 lps on hook) 3 times (1 lp rem on hook).

Rep Row 2 until Handle measures 13". Sl st in 2nd, 3rd and 4th vertical bars. Finish off; weave in ends.

With sewing needle and thread on each handle, sew long edges together to form a long tube. Sew ends of each tube to inside of Front and Back as shown in photograph. Cut two 7" lengths of ribbon yarn. Sew to inside of center top edges for ties. Tie in a bow to close Bag.

#96 POTHOLDER

SIZE
8" wide x 7" high

MATERIALS
Super bulky weight yarn
  5 oz multi-color

Note: Photographed model made with Lion Brand® Jiffy® Thick & Quick® #208 Rocky Mountains

Size N (9 mm) crochet hook
  (or size required for gauge)

Sewing needle and thread to
  match

One 7/8" diameter snap

GAUGE
7 sc and 8 sc rows = 4"

INSTRUCTIONS

Front
Ch 15.

Row 1 (right side): Sc in 2nd ch from hook and in each ch across: 14 sc; ch 1, turn.

Row 2: Sc in first sc and in each sc across: 14 sc; ch 1, turn.

Rows 3 through 13: Rep Row 2 eleven times more. At end of Row 13, do not ch 1. Finish off; weave in ends.

Back
Ch 15.

Rows 1 and 2: Rep Rows 1 and 2 on Front.

Rows 3 through 14: Rep Row 2 on Front 12 times more. Do not finish off.

Flap

Row 1 (right side): Sc dec in first 2 sc, sc in next sc and in each sc across to last 2 sc, sc dec in last 2 sc: 2 sc fewer than in previous row; ch 1, turn.

Rows 2 through 5: Rep Row 1 on Flap 4 times more. At end of Row 5: 4 sc.

Row 6: Sc dec in first 2 sc, sc dec in next 2 sc: 2 sc; ch 1, turn.

Row 7: Sc dec in first 2 sc: 1 sc. Finish off; weave in ends.

Joining

Place Front and Back with wrong sides together, matching rows and beg chain edge. Sl st bottom edges together. Sew side edges of Front and Back together with an overcast stitch.

Flap Edging

With right side facing, join with sl st in edge of last sc on Row 14 of Back, ch 1, sc in edge of same row, 2 sc in edge of Row 1 of Flap, sc in edge of each row of Flap to Row 7, 3 sc in sc dec on Row 7, sc in edge of each row of Flap to Row 1, 2 sc in edge of Row 1, sc in edge of Row 14 on Back. Finish off; weave in ends.

Braided Shoulder Strap

Cut three 48" long strands of yarn. With all 3 strands together, tie knot at one end. Braid entire length and tie knot at other end, adjusting to desired length of shoulder strap as necessary. Sew braid to side seams from bottom to top of Bag for shoulder strap as shown in photograph.

Tassel

Cut one 24" and one 54" long strand of yarn. Cut about 10 strands from remaining yarn twice desired length of Tassel and place these strands together on a flat surface. Fold 24" strand in half and place middle over middle of shorter strands. Fold shorter strands over 24" strand and tie 24" strand around shorter strands to form top of Tassel. Fold 54" strand in half, tie around Tassel about 1 1/2" down from top knot, wrap around Tassel and tie again, inserting ends in center of Tassel. Trim Tassel ends. Center and sew Tassel on bottom front of Flap as shown in photograph.

Finishing

Fold Flap over front of Bag. Sew one side of snap on back of Flap under Tassel. Sew other side of snap on front of Bag in corresponding position.

#97 EVENING BAG

SIZE
12" wide x 4" high

MATERIALS
Worsted weight yarn
  3 1/2 oz bronze

Note: *Photographed model made with Lion Brand® Glitterspun #135 Bronze*

Size G (4 mm) crochet hook
  (or size required for gauge)

Large-eyed, blunt needle

One 7/8" diameter snap

Decorative brooch (optional)

Stitch markers

GAUGE
16 sc = 4"

INSTRUCTIONS

Note: Bag is worked in one piece.

Bag

Starting at bottom of Flap, ch 4.

Row 1 (right side): Sc in 2nd ch from hook and in each ch across: 3 sc; ch 1, turn.

Row 2: 2 sc in first sc, sc in next sc, 2 sc in last sc: 5 sc; ch 1, turn.

Row 3: Sc in first sc and in each sc across; ch 1, turn.

Row 4: 2 sc in each of first 2 sc, sc in each sc across to last 2 sc, 2 sc in each of last 2 sc: 4 more sc than in previous row; ch 1, turn.

Rows 5 through 24: Rep Rows 3 and 4 ten times more. At end of Row 24: 49 sc. Place markers in first and last sc on Row 24.

Rep Row 3 until piece measures 13". At end of last row, do not ch 1. Finish off; weave in ends.

Finishing

Fold piece with wrong sides together so edges of last row match stitch markers. Sew right and left side seams together.

Shell Stitch Edging

With wrong side facing, join yarn with sl st in edge of last sc on Row 24 of Flap.

Row 1 (wrong side): Ch 1, sc in edge of each row on Flap from Row 24 to Row 2, sc in each of 3 sc on Row 1, sc in other edge of each row on Flap from Row 2 to Row 24: 49 sc; ch 1, turn.

Row 2 (right side): Sc in first sc; *shell in next sc, sc in next sc; rep from * across: 24 shells. Finish off; weave in ends.

Position one part of snap on back of Flap near point and sew in place. Sew remaining part of snap in place on front of bag. Pin brooch to front of Flap, if desired.

#98 DISCO

SIZE
6 1/2" wide x 6 3/4" high

MATERIALS
Worsted weight yarn
   3 1/2 oz black

Eyelash yarn
   1 3/4 oz black with rainbow
   accents

*Note: Photographed model made
with Lion Brand® Glitterspun
#153 Onyx and Lion Brand®
Fancy Fur #253 Bold Black*

Size G (4 mm) crochet hook
   (or size required for gauge)

Size J (6 mm) crochet hook

Sewing needle and thread to
   match

One 7/8" diameter snap

GAUGE
17 1/2 sc and 18 rows = 4" with
   worsted yarn and G hook

INSTRUCTIONS

Front

With worsted yarn and G hook, ch 29.

Row 1 (right side): Sc in 2nd ch from hook and in each ch across: 28 sc; ch 1, turn.

Rows 2 through 28: Sc in first sc and in each sc across: 28 sc; ch 1, turn. At end of Row 28, do not ch 1. Finish off; weave in ends.

Back

With worsted yarn and G hook, ch 29.

Row 1 (right side): Sc in 2nd ch from hook and in each ch across: 28 sc; ch 1, turn.

Rows 2 through 30: Sc in first sc and in each sc across: 28 sc; ch 1, turn. At end of Row 30, do not ch 1. Do not finish off.

Flap

Row 1: Sc dec in first 2 sc, sc in next sc and in each sc across to last 2 sc, sc dec in last 2 sc: 2 sc fewer than in previous row; ch 1, turn.

Rows 2 through 12: Rep Row 1 of Flap 11 times more. At end of Row 11: 4 sc.

Row 13: Sc dec in first 2 sc, sc dec in next 2 sc: 2 sc; ch 1, turn.

Row 14: Sc dec in first 2 sc: 1 sc. Finish off; weave in ends.

Trim

With eyelash yarn and J hook, ch 4.

Row 1: Sc in 2nd ch from hook and in each ch across: 3 sc; ch 1, turn.

Row 2: 2 sc in first sc, sc in next sc and in each sc across to last sc, 2 sc in last sc: 2 more sc than in previous row; ch 1, turn.

Rows 3 through 11: Rep Row 2 of Trim 9 times more. At end of Row 11: 23 sc.

Row 12: Sc in first sc and in each sc across: 23 sc. Finish off; weave in ends.

Finishing

Place Front and Back with right sides together. Sl st sides and bottom of Front and Back together, matching rows. Finish off; weave in ends. Turn right side out. Fold Flap over Bag. With sewing needle and thread, sew Trim to front of Flap. Sew snap closure on back of Flap and to corresponding spot on Front.

Strap

With worsted yarn and G hook, ch 4.

Row 1: Sc in 2nd ch from hook and in each ch across: 3 sc; ch 1, turn.

Row 2: Sc in first sc and in each sc across: 3 sc; ch 1, turn.

Rep Row 2 until Strap measures 31", or to desired length.

Fold Strap in half lengthwise and sl st long edges together, matching rows along length of Strap. Sew ends of Strap to inside seams at each side of Bag.

#99 FANCY FRINGE

SIZE
11 $\frac{1}{2}$" wide x 7" high

MATERIALS
Bulky weight bouclé yarn
  3 oz red

Super bulky bouclé yarn
  3 oz variegated

Note: Photographed model made with Lion Brand® Color Waves #313 Sunset Red and Lion Brand® Lion Bouclé #212 Popsicle

Size J (6 mm) crochet hook
  (or size required for gauge)

Sewing needle and thread to
  match

One $\frac{7}{8}$" diameter snap

2" piece of cardboard

GAUGE
9 $\frac{1}{2}$ sc and 10 sc rows = 4"

INSTRUCTIONS

Body

With red, ch 29.

Row 1: Sc in 2nd ch from hook and in each ch across: 28 sc; ch 1, turn.

Row 2: Sc in first sc and in each sc across: 28 sc; ch 1, turn.

Rep Row 2 until piece measures 14". Do not finish off.

Flap

Row 1 (right side): Sc dec in first 2 sc, sc in next sc and in each sc across to last 2 sc, sc dec in last 2 sc: 2 sc fewer than in previous row; ch 1, turn.

Rows 2 through 12: Rep Row 1 of Flap Shaping 11 times more. At end of Row 12: 4 sc.

Row 13: Sc dec in first 2 sc, sc dec in next 2 sc: 2 sc; ch 1, turn.

Row 14: Sc dec in first 2 sc: 1 sc; ch 1, turn. Do not finish off.

Finishing

Edging

With right side facing, work 3 sc in sc on Row 14 of Flap, sc evenly around entire piece, working 2 sc in edges of Row 1 of Flap and 3 sc in bottom corners; join with sl st in first sc. Finish off; weave in ends.

With wrong sides together, fold Row 1 of Body of bag up to last row of Body of bag. With sewing needle and thread, sew 2 sides of bag together. Fold Flap over front of bag. Sew snap to back of Flap and to corresponding spot on front of bag.

Strap

With variegated yarn, ch 4.

Row 1: Sc in 2nd ch from hook and in each ch across: 3 sc; ch 1, turn.

Row 2: Sc in first sc and in each sc across: 3 sc; ch 1, turn.

Rep Row 2 until strap measures 22" long, or to desired length.

Securely sew 1" of strap ends horizontally to top of Back of bag as shown in photograph, or as desired.

Fringe

Cut a piece of cardboard about 6" wide and 2 1/2" long. Wind variegated yarn loosely and evenly lengthwise around the cardboard. When the card is filled, cut the yarn across one end. Wind additional strands as you need them.

Fold one strand in half, and with the right side of the purse facing draw the folded ends from right to wrong side through each sc at bottom edge of bag and in each sc along edges of the flap. Pull the loose ends through the folded section and draw the knot up firmly. Space the knots evenly and trim the ends of the fringe.

#100 BASIC BLACK

SIZE
11" wide x 8 ¹/₂" high

MATERIALS
Super bulky yarn
  12 oz dark red

Note: Photographed model made with Lion Brand® Wool-Ease® Thick & Quick® #143 Claret

Size N (9 mm) crochet hook
  (or size required for gauge)

Rattan Purse Handles

Frog Closure

Sewing needle and thread to
  match

Large-eyed, blunt needle

GAUGE
8 sc and 9 ¹/₂ sc rows = 4"

STITCH GUIDE

Sc decrease (sc dec): (Insert hook in specified st and draw up a lp) 2 times, YO and draw through all 3 lps on hook: sc dec made.

INSTRUCTIONS

Note: Bag is worked in one piece.

Body

Ch 23.

Row 1 (wrong side): Sc in 2nd ch from hook and in each ch across: 22 sc; ch 1, turn.

Row 2 (right side): Sc in first sc and in each sc across: 22 sc; ch 1, turn.

Rows 3 through 42: Rep Row 2 forty times more. Do not finish off.

Flap

Row 1 (wrong side): Sc dec in first 2 sc, sc in next sc and in each sc across to last 2 sc, sc dec in last 2 sc: 2 sc fewer than in previous row; ch 1, turn.

Rows 2 through 9: Rep Row 1 on Flap 8 times more. At end of Row 9: 4 sc.

Row 10: Sc dec in first 2 sc, sc dec in next 2 sc: 2 sc; ch 1, turn.

Row 11: Sc dec in first 2 sc: 1 sc; ch 1, turn. Do not finish off.

Edging

With right side facing, work 3 sc in sc on Row 11 of Flap, sc evenly around entire piece, working 2 sc in edges of Row 1 of Flap and 3 sc in bottom corners; join with sl st in first sc. Finish off; weave in ends.

Finishing

With wrong sides together, fold Row 1 of Body of bag up to Row 40 of Body of bag. With sewing needle and thread, sew 2 sides of bag together. Fold Flap over front of bag. Sew frog closure to front of Flap and front of bag to correspond.

Using 1 strand of yarn and large-eyed, blunt needle sew 1 handle only to top of Bag as shown in photograph.

ABBREVIATIONS AND SYMBOLS

Knit and crochet patterns are written in a special shorthand, which is used so that instructions don't take up too much space. They sometimes seem confusing, but once you learn them, you'll have no trouble following them.

These are Standard Abbreviations

Beg	beginning
Blk st	block stitch
BL	back loop
BO	bind off
BPdc	Back post double crochet
BPsc	Back post single crochet
CL(s)	cluster(s)
CO	cast on
Cont	continue
Ch(s)	chain(s)
Dc	double crochet
Dec	decrease
Fig	figure
FPdc	front post double crochet
FPsc	front post single crochet
FPtr	front post triple crochet
g	gram(s)
Hdc	half double crochet
Inc	increase(ing)
K	knit
K1 b	knit one stitch through back loop
K2tog	knit two stitches together
K3tog	knit three stitches together
Long dc	long double crochet
Long sc	long single crochet
Mm	millimeter(s)
Oz	ounces
P	purl
Patt	pattern
Prev	previous
PSSO	pass the slipped stitch over
Rem	remain(ing)
Rep	repeat(ing)
Rev Sc	reverse single crochet
Rnd(s)	round(s)
Sc	single crochet
Sc dec	single crochet decrease
Sc2tog	single crochet 2 stitches together decrease
Sk	skip
Sl	slip
Sl 1K	slip 1 stitch as to knit
Sl 1P	slip 1 stitch as to purl
Sl st	slip stitch
Sp(s)	space(s)
SSK	slip, slip, knit
St(s)	stitch(es)
Stock st	stockinette stitch
Tbl	through back loop
Tog	together
Tr	triple crochet
Yib	yarn in back of needle or hook
Yif	yarn in front of needle or hook
YO	Yarn over the needle or hook
YRN	Yarn around needle

These are Standard Symbols

* An asterisk (or double asterisks**) in a pattern row, indicates a portion of instructions to be used more than once. For instance, "rep from * three times" means that after working the instructions once, you must work them again three times for a total of 4 times in all.

† A dagger (or double daggers ††) indicates that those instructions will be repeated again later in the same row or round.

: The number after a colon tells you the number of stitches you will have when you have completed the row or round.

( ) Parentheses enclose instructions which are to be worked the number of times following the parentheses. For instance, "(ch1, sc, ch1) 3 times" means that you will chain one, work one sc, and then chain again three times for a total of six chains and 3cs, or "(K1, P2) 3 times" means that you knit one stitch and then purl two stitches, three times.

Parentheses often set off or clarify a group of stitches to be worked into the same space or stitch. For instance, "(dc, ch2, dc) in corner sp."

[ ] Brackets and ( ) parentheses are also used to give you additional information.

KNITTING NEEDLES CONVERSION CHART

U.S.	0	1	2	3	4	5	6	7	8	9	10	10½	11	13	15	17
Metric	2	2.25	2.75	3.25	3.5	3.75	4	4.5	5	5.5	6	6.5	8	9	10	12.75

TERMS

Front Loop—This is the loop toward you at the top of the crochet stitch.

Back Loop—This is the loop away from you at the top of the crochet stitch.

Post—This is the vertical part of the crochet stitch

Join—This means to join with a sl st unless another stitch is specified.

Finish off—This means to end your piece by pulling the yarn through the last loop remaining on the hook or needle. This will prevent the work from unraveling.

Continue in Pattern as Established—This means to follow the pattern stitch as if has been set up, working any increases or decreases in such a way that the pattern remains the same as it was established.

Work even—This means that the work is continued in the pattern as established without increasing or decreasing.

Right Side—This means the side of the purse that will be seen.

Wrong Side—This means the side of the purse that is inside.

GAUGE

This is probably the most important aspect of knitting and crocheting!

GAUGE simply means the number of stitches per inch, and the numbers of rows per inch that result from a specified yarn worked with hooks or needles in a specified size. But since everyone knits or crochets differently—some loosely, some tightly, some in-between—the measurements of individual work can vary greatly, even when the crocheters or knitters use the same pattern and the same size yarn and hook or needle.

If you don't work to the gauge specified in the pattern, your purse will never be the correct size, and you may not have enough yarn to finish your project. Hook and needle sizes given in instructions are merely guides, and should never be used without a gauge swatch.

To make a gauge swatch, crochet or knit a swatch that is about 4" square, using the suggested hook or needle and the number of stitches given in the pattern. Measure your swatch. If the number of stitches is fewer than those listed in the pattern, try making another swatch with a smaller hook or needle. If the number of stitches is more than is called for in the pattern, try making another swatch with a larger hook or needle. It is your responsibility to make sure you achieve the gauge specified in the pattern.

The patterns in this book have been written using the knitting and crochet terminology that is used in the United States. Terms which may have different equivalents in other parts of the world are listed below.

United States	International
Double crochet (dc)	treble crochet (tr)
Gauge	tension
Half double crochet (hdc)	half treble crochet (htr)
Single crochet	double crochet
Skip	miss
Slip stitch	single crochet
Triple crochet (tr)	double treble crochet (dtr)
Yarn over (YO)	yarn forward (yfwd)
Yarn around needle (yrn)	yarn over hook (yoh)

Metric Equivalents					
inches	cm	inches	cm	inches	cm
1	2.54	11	27.94	21	53.34
2	5.08	12	30.48	22	55.88
3	7.62	13	33.02	23	58.42
4	10.16	14	35.56	24	60.96
5	12.70	15	38.10	30	76.20
6	15.24	16	40.64	36	91.44
7	17.78	17	43.18	42	106.68
8	20.32	18	45.72	48	121.92
9	22.86	19	48.26	54	137.16
10	25.40	20	50.8	60	152.40

CROCHET HOOKS CONVERSION CHART

U.S.	B-1	C-2	D-3	E-4	F-5	G-6	H-8	I-9	J-10	K-10 12	N	P	Q
Metric	2.25	2.75	3.25	3.5	3.75	4	5	5.5	6	6.5	0	10	15

STEEL CROCHET HOOKS CONVERSION CHART

U.S.	00	0	1	2	3	4	5	6	7	8	9	10	11	12	13	14
Metric	3.5	3.25	2.75	2.25	2.1	2	1.9	1.8	1.65	1.5	1.4	1.3	1.1	1.0	0.85	0.75

FELTING

If you have ever mistakenly put your favorite wool sweater in the washing machine and the dryer, you know what felting is. Not only has the sweater shrunk, but it is now a completely different texture.

Accidental felting is not a project to be desired, but when felting is done on purpose—as it is in many projects in this book—it produces a wonderful fabric that is softer, thicker and even warmer than the original.

History

Felting may actually be the oldest form of textile manufacturing, and it might even predate weaving and knitting. Felted fabric dating back to 6500 BC was actually discovered in Turkey. A tomb in Siberia revealed felted garments preserved in the permafrost dating back to 600 AD.

Many historians now feel that the concept of felting was probably spread by the hordes of Asian nomadic tribes that spread out across the continents. For a long time it has been assumed that the success of these conquerors—such as Genghis Khan—was due to their abilities to domesticate horses which allowed them to travel great distances with speed. Could the idea of felting have also been an important factor in their success?

Because a felted project is warmer for the same weight without becoming stiffer, it could be used not only for clothes but for tents as well. Felting makes a fabric that is almost completely wind and rain resistant. While the fabric could be stiff, it is not heavy so tents made of it were easy to transport. Fabrics made of a lighter felting served to keep the wearer protected from the harsh weather. Felted fabrics were a much better material than the animal hides that were used by other cultures. Wearing felted garments and sleeping in felted tents allowed the conquerors to survive the most horrible weather conditions.

Today nomadic tribes in Asia still make their clothes and their tents from the felted wool of their animals.

Materials

Only fibers from animals, such as sheep, goats, aplpacas, rabbits, can be used for felting. Natural fibers such as cotton or linen will not felt nor will man-made fibers such as acrylics.

Some animal fibers—such as superwash yarns—may have been treated to prevent them from felting. In addition, white yarns that have been bleached and off-white yarns may not felt well. If, therefore, you chose to use another yarn than the one listed in the instructions, make a felted swatch with this yarn to determine whether it will felt.

How to Felt

Felting occurs because the animal fiber is really the animal's hair. Just as in human hair, each strand is covered by scales. If the individual hairs are rubbed together, the scales will grab each other, and the whole material shrinks.

To make the scales catch, some form of abrasion is necessary. The quickest and easiest process is to use the washing machine where the agitation will provide the necessary abrasion. Ghenkis Kahn didn't have a washing machine. His tribal members used muscle to felt their projects. You can felt by hand!

Felting By Machine

Since you will be stopping and starting your machine during the process, it is important that you do your felting in a top loading machine.

Set your water setting to the lowest setting for the smallest load, choose the most powerful form of agitation, and elect the hottest water. While not absolutely necessary for the felting process, place your project in a zippered pillowcase or a mesh lingerie bag. This will keep any loose fuzz from clogging your machine. Add about a tablespoon of soap to the water. (Soap is preferred to detergent.) You will achieve the best results if you put some clean old jeans or tennis sneakers in the wash to provide more agitation.

After about five minutes, stop the washer and check the purse. It may have actually gotten larger as it relaxes in the water. Put the purse back in the water and continue the operation. Keep checking the process every 5 to 10 minutes until you feel that your felting is satisfactory.

It is advisable not to allow the purse to go through the entire rinse and spin cycles but to just rerun the wash cycle. Spinning could leave creases in your purse.

Finishing

Rinse the purse by hand in warm water and roll it in a large towel to remove the excess water.

If the felting has produced a flat piece of felted fabric, such as is required for a number of purses in this book, merely lay the felted piece onto a dry towel away from direct heat or sunlight. Shape the piece to the correct measurements given in the pattern. If the edge is rippling, baste a thread through the edge and gather it in. Remove the thread after the felting has dried.

If the project is a completed purse, take the time to block and shape your project while it is still wet. The wet wool will be extremely malleable, and you can form the purse into the desired shape. If necessary, put boxes inside your bag to achieve sharp corners. You may want to put plastic bags inside the purse while it dries to keep the required shape. Allow the purse to dry in a warm spot away from any direct heat or sunlight. Never put your felting in the dryer. Allow for as much time as necessary for the piece to dry; it could take several days depending upon the weather. After the project is completely dry, finish with a simple brushing to remove any excess fuzz.

All felting projects will shrink more in the length (the number of rows) than in the width (the number of stitches). Most felted projects will be about 85% of the width and 75% of the length of the project before felting

Felting by Hand

Since it is agitation which causes the scales to rub together and grab each other—thereby causing the fabric to shrink—you will now have to be the agitation force.

You can work in your kitchen sink or your bathtub or a separate large bowl. In order to eliminate getting water all over, don't fill the sink with too much water. Just a few inches is sufficient. Use the hottest tap water, add a little soap (no more than about one teaspoon) and start to knead (as if you were making bread) and rub, constantly changing direction.

Continue kneadng and rubbing the purse until it is the desired shape. Don't stop too soon. If the process seems to be taking too long, you might plunge the purse into a bowl of cold water. This will shock the fibers. You may want to work back and forth from hot to cold until you achieve the desired look. If you want to prevent "dishpan hands," you may want to use rubber gloves. If the purse is very large, you could put it in your bathtub and try stomping the project with your feet as if you were turning grapes into wine.

When you feel the purse is the correct size, remove it from the water and follow the instructions above on Finishing.

Care of Felted Purses

The felting process can start again if you re-create the necessary environment. So be careful about washing your felted purse. Treat it as you would any wool product. Washing the purse in the washing machine with hot water will continue the felting process.

TWISTED CORD

Cut 2 strands of yarn the required length. With both strands tog, hold one end and with someone holding the other end, twist strands to the right until they begin to curl. Fold the 2 ends tog and tie in a knot so that they will not unravel. The strands will now twist themselves tog. Adjust length if necessary.

I-CORD

Cord is worked from the right side only; do not turn. Stitches will fold toward the wrong side to form a double thickness cord.

CO 3 sts on one double-point knitting needle.

Row 1: With another double-point, K3; do not turn. Slide sts to opposite end of the needle.

Row 2: Take yarn around the back side of sts and with 2nd needle, K3; do not turn. Slide sts to opposite end of needle.

Rep Rows 1and 2.

TASSELS

Cut a piece of cardboard about 6" wide and the desired length of the finished tassel. Wind the yarn around the length of the cardboard the number of times necessary to make the desired tassel. Cut a piece of yarn about 20" long and thread a double strand into a tapestry needle. Insert the needle through all strands at the top of the cardboard, pull up tightly and knot securely, leaving ends for attaching to the purse. Cut the yarn at the opposite end of the cardboard, and remove the cardboard.

Cut another strand of yarn 12" long and wrap it tightly twice around the tassel approximately $1^{1}/2$" below the top knot. Knot securely and allow excess ends to fall in as part of the tassel.

ACKNOWLEDGEMENTS

The authors extend their thanks and appreciation to to the design departments at Coats & Clark, Lion Brand Yarn, Patons Yarns and Judi and Co for sharing many of their most creative designs with us.

Whenever we have used a special yarn we have given the brand name. If you are unable to find these yarns locally, write to the following manufacturers who will be able to tell you where to purchase their products, or consult their internet sites. We also wish to thank these companies for supplying yarn for this book.

Artyarns
39 Westmoreland Avenue
White Plains, New York 10606-1937
www.artyarns.com

Bernat Yarns
320 Livingston Avenue South
Listowel, Ontario
Canada N4W 3H3
www.bernat.com

Berroco, Inc.
14 Elmdale Road
Uxbridge, Massachusetts 01569
www.berroco.com

Brown Sheep
10062 Country Road 16
Mitchell, Nebraska 69357
www.brownsheep.com

Caron International
Customer Service
P. O. Box 222
Washington, North Carolina 27889
www.caron.com

Cascade Yarns
1224 Andover Park E
Tukwila, Washington
98188-3905

J&P Coats
Coats and Clark
Consumer Services
P.O. Box 12229
Greenville, South Carolina
29612-0229
www.coatsandclark.com

Crystal Palace Yarns
160 23rd St
Richmond, California
94804-1828

Dark House LLC
6996 Highway 2
Commerce City, Colorado
www.darkhorseyarn.com

DMC Corporation
South Hackensack Avenue
Port Kearny Building 10F
South Kearny, New Jersey
07032-4612
www.dmc-usa.com

Erdal Yarns Ltd.
2 Forest Avenue
Locust Valley, New York 11560-1713
www.erdal.com

Judi & Co.
18 Gallatin Drive
Dix Hills, New York
11746-7948
www.judiandco.com

Lily Yarn
320 Livingstone Avenue South
Listowel, Ontario
Canada N4W 3H3
www.sugarncream.com

Lion Brand Yarn
34 West 15th Street
New York, New York 10011
www.lionbrand.com

Noro Yarn Collection
315 Bayview Avenue
Amityville, New York
11701-2801
www.knittingfever.com

Patons Yarns
2700 Dufferin Street
Toronto, Ontario
Canada M6B 4J3
www.patonsyarns.com

Plymouth Yarn Co., Inc
500 Lafayette Street
P.O. Box 28
Bristol, Pennsylvania
19007-0028
www.plymouthyarn.com

Red Heart Yarns
Coats and Clark
Consumer Services
P. O. Box 12229
Greenville, South Carolina
29612-0229
www.coatsandclark.com

Tahki Stacy Charles
70-30 80th Street
Building 36
Glendale, New York
11385-7714
www.tahkistacycharles.com

TLC Yarns
Coats and Clark
Consumer Services
P. O. Box 12229
Greenville, South Carolina
29612-0229
www.coatsandclark.com

The authors thank the following contributing designers:

Shelby Allaho, Shamiah, Kuwait
Suzanne Atkinson, Orleans, Ontario, Canada
Joyce Bragg, Wilmington, North Carolina
Vashti Braha, Longboat Keys, Florida
Nancy Brown, Belfair, Washington
Donna Druchunas, Longmont, Colorado
Noreen Crone-Findlay, Ardrossan, Canada
Laura Gebhardt, Pickering, Canada
Barbara Goldhamer, Ansonia, Connecticut
Cynthia G. Grosch, Unionville, Connecticut
Tammy Hildebrand, Kernersville, North Carolina
Margaret Hubert, Pawling, New York
Jodi Lewanda, Farmington, Connecticut
Susan Lowman, Prescott Valley, Arizona
Susan McCreary, Erie, Pennsylvania
Melody MacDuffee, Mobile, Alabama
Marty Miller, Greensboro, North Carolina
Diane Moyer, Orange, Connecticut
Nancy Nehring, Sunnyvale, California
Jennifer Pace, Glen Allen, Virginia
Judith Solomon, Rolling Hills Estates, California
Kathleen Stuart, San Jose, California
Christine Walter, Orleans, Ontario, Canada
Mary Jane Wood, Glen Allen, Virginia

INDEX